Renaissance Discourses of Desire

Renaissance Discourses of Desire

Edited by
Claude J. Summers
and
Ted-Larry Pebworth

University of Missouri Press
Columbia and London

University of Missouri Press, Columbia, Missouri 65201
Printed and bound in the United States of America
5 4 3 2 1   97 96 95 94 93

Library of Congress Cataloging-in-Publication Data

Renaissance discourses of desire / edited by Claude J. Summers and Ted
   -Larry Pebworth.
        p.   cm.
    Includes index.
    ISBN 0–8262–0885–1 (alk. paper)
    1. English poetry—Early modern. 1500–1700—History and criticism.
2. Love poetry. English—History and criticism. 3. Psychoanalysis
and literature. 4. course analysis, Literary. 5. Desire in
literature. 6. Renaissance—England. 7. Sex in literature.
I. Summers. Claude J.   II. Pebworth. Ted-Larry.
PR535.L7R45   1993   92–44239
821'.309354—dc20   CIP

∞™ This paper meets the requirements of the American National Standard
for Permanence of Paper for Printed Library Materials, Z39.48, 1984.

Designer: Rhonda Miller
Typesetter: Connell-Zeko Type & Graphics
Printer and Binder: Thomson-Shore, Inc.
Typefaces: Belwe Light Italic and Sabon

For

Diana and Peter Benet
and in memory of John Mulder

Contents

Acknowledgments

This book and the scholarly meeting from which it originated have profited from the great effort, wide learning, and scholarly generosity of the conference steering committee. Achsah Guibbory, Judith Scherer Herz, Robert B. Hinman, John R. Roberts, Michael C. Schoenfeldt, and John T. Shawcross helped referee the submissions to the conference and offered valuable suggestions for revision. Their contributions have been extensive, and we join the authors of the essays in expressing gratitude for their insights and devotion. It is also our pleasant duty to acknowledge the support of the Horace H. Rackham Graduate School of the University of Michigan, and of the following administrators at the University of Michigan–Dearborn: Sheryl Pearson, chairman of the Department of Humanities; James C. Foster, dean of the College of Arts, Sciences, and Letters; and Eugene Arden, former vice-chancellor for Academic Affairs and provost.

Renaissance Discourses of Desire

Claude J. Summers and Ted-Larry Pebworth
Introduction

Love, either sacred or profane, is the preeminent subject of Renaissance literature. As William Kerrigan and Gordon Braden have observed, "In no subsequent period will love be the dominant preoccupation of lyric poetry, or would-be poets feel compelled, as a public demonstration of their seriousness, to animate the conventions of literary love."[1] It was surely this felt pressure of literary expectations that prompted a poet so concerned with his role and status as Ben Jonson to entitle the first poem of *The Forest* "Why I Write Not of Love." Such a title indicates the self-consciousness of his need to explain what must have seemed a serious limitation on his part. Despite his disclaimer, however, Jonson—like all the other major secular poets of the period—actually writes of erotic love fairly often and most movingly about failed love, as in the witty but poignant "My Picture Left in Scotland." More tellingly, "Why I Write Not of Love" is itself a love poem that expresses the human need for love in the face of time and deprivation. And as a meditation on the paradoxical mysteries of love, the work also neatly encapsulates the difficulties of the poet in approaching an elusive subject that persistently defies rationality and stubbornly refuses to be fettered even by art.

If love is a pervasive subject in Renaissance literature, attitudes toward it are hardly uniform. The discourses of desire of the period embrace works as dissimilar as the sonnets of frustrated love that

1. "Milton's Coy Eve: *Paradise Lost* and Renaissance Love Poetry," *ELH* 53 (1986): 27.

dominated the late Elizabethan era and the libertine invitations to lust that prevailed in Caroline court circles. They include both the obsessive (and resentful) devotion of Shakespeare's sonnets to a young man and Spenser's (uncharacteristically placid) celebrations of chaste married love. Among Renaissance discourses of desire are world-weary expressions of disgust with physicality as well as idealistic Neoplatonic love lyrics; and they incorporate traditions of erotic poetry ranging from the urgency of *carpe diem* to the philosophical bemusement of the *senex amans*. Representations of sexuality in the period range from the idyllic, prelapsarian naturalness of Adam and Eve in *Paradise Lost* to the greedy and lustful burning of the same couple after the Fall, from the tender union of lovers in "close united Extasie"[2] in Felltham's "The Reconcilement" to the cruel comedy of impotency in Behn's "The Disappointment." Writers throughout the seventeenth century variously idealize and demystify sex, alternately equating (or confusing) it with religious transcendence, as in Donne's "The Canonization," or exposing it as a mere bodily itch, as in numerous poems by Suckling and Rochester.

"Doing, a filthy pleasure is, and short: / And done, we straight repent us of the sport," Jonson writes of copulation,[3] echoing a post-coital depression expressed in other poems of the era, including Donne's "Farewell to Love" and Shakespeare's Sonnet 129, "Th' expense of spirit in a waste of shame." But ambivalence toward sexuality is hardly confined to the surprisingly large number of poems that express post-coital tristesse or other reactions against sexual satiety. Rather, it is the dominant impulse of most of the love poetry and nearly all the love theory of the period. At the very heart of Petrarchan and Platonic notions of love is the fear of sexuality. Indeed, the need to redirect sexuality's threatening energies into spirituality or to sublimate them into the contemplation of the divine animates most of the philosophical approaches to love in the seventeenth century. The pastoral tradition's emphasis on the innocence of love bespeaks both a nostalgic longing for an idyllic sexuality and a rueful recognition that such innocence is possible only in the timelessness of art. But perhaps

2. *The Poems of Owen Felltham,* ed. Ted-Larry Pebworth and Claude J. Summers (University Park, Pa.: *Seventeenth-Century News,* 1973), 17.

3. "Underwood 88," in *Ben Jonson,* ed. C. H. Herford, Percy Simpson, and Evelyn Simpson, 11 vols. (Oxford: Clarendon Press, 1925–1952), 8:294.

more surprisingly, at the very heart of the anti-Petrarchan, anti-Platonic libertine tradition is disillusionment with the very sexual fulfillment it advocates. The great irony of libertinism's successful insurgency against Petrarchism during the seventeenth century is that it led to a sexual despair that mocks its success. Even as the ideal of unrequited love is replaced by ideals of mutuality and union—as "pure lovers soules descend / T'affections, and to faculties, / Which sense may reach and apprehend"[4]—the result is not the sexual and spiritual contentment that Donne's "Extasie" promises, but a different kind of frustration, one that disappointedly devalues the consummation that has been so devoutly wished.

Notwithstanding the presence of an abundance of individual poems singing the bliss (or fantasy) of shared sexual happiness and celebrating an ideal of "cleanly-*Wantonnesse*,"[5] most love poetry in the Renaissance is a poetry of complaint and depletion, oscillating between the poles of frustration, on the one hand, and of carnal disgust attendant upon the satisfaction of sexual desire, on the other. The history of the seventeenth-century love lyric is more complicated than simply the displacement of Petrarchan ideals by Ovidian ones, but this development says a great deal about changing sexual as well as literary attitudes during the century. The unhappiness implicit—and often startlingly explicit—in both Petrarchism and libertinism may be a direct result of the Christian tradition's tragic failure to reconcile *eros* and *caritas,* or it may be, as Kerrigan and Braden suggest, a validation of Freud's insight about the peculiarity of human sexuality, that "complete and unequivocal satisfaction of sexual desire is an impossible attainment."[6] In any case, this record of love's failure is both a product and a process of the sexual anxieties that pervade seventeenth-century literature generally.

Those sexual anxieties are not dissimilar from our own, which may explain why seventeenth-century literature continues to speak so directly to late twentieth-century readers, yet they are also peculiarly expressive of their own era as well. As recent historians of

---

4. *The Complete English Poems of John Donne,* ed. C. A. Patrides (London: Dent, 1985), 101.

5. Robert Herrick, "The Argument of his Book," *The Complete Poetry of Robert Herrick,* ed. J. Max Patrick (New York: New York University Press, 1963), 11.

6. "Milton's Coy Eve," 38.

sexuality have stressed, attitudes toward love, marriage, and sexuality are culturally specific rather than universal. To some degree, each society, by means not fully understood, constructs its own sexualities. But this is not to say that there is no continuity between different historical constructions of sexuality or that love and sex are not universal human emotions and needs. As the historian John Boswell has observed: "The literature of falling in love in all Western societies . . . is so similar that . . . *poets* are struck that it's the same phenomenon and they constantly repeat the love literature of previous ages and apply it to their own experience."[7] Poets of the English Renaissance certainly recognized a continuity between their experiences of love and, say, those of the poets of classical Greece and Rome and of fourteenth-century Italy. Nevertheless, their depictions of sex and love do not merely echo universal attitudes and recapitulate transhistorical experiences. Rather, they reflect, express, embody, and help shape the social attitudes of their own time and place, even when they oppose the dominant sexual ideologies of their society.

The cultural specificity of sexual attitudes demands a historical approach to discourses of desire. Insofar as literature documents (or challenges) its period's sexual beliefs and prohibitions, it is an extraordinarily valuable resource for setting and charting the outlines of sexual ideology at any particular time. More than any other form of discourse, literature most fully articulates desire, presenting it from the inside rather than from the outside, expressing emotion and subjectivity as well as reason and logic. Conversely, the interpretive constructs of reality that constitute our notion of history provide indispensable contexts in which to locate and probe texts, as well as important lenses through which to view and anatomize both neglected and overly familiar works. Hence, the relationship of literature and history is always reciprocal and reflexive, and crucially so in the case of literary representations of sexuality, which focus on issues—such as erotic desire, courtship rituals, gender definitions, and sexual and cultural anxieties—that are simultaneously highly localized yet universally, and therefore sometimes misleadingly, familiar.

The historically sensitive essays collected in this volume explore the

7. Lawrence Mass, "Sexual Categories, Sexual Universals: An Interview with John Boswell," *Christopher Street* 13, no. 6 (1990): 34.

discursive representations of sexuality in the non-dramatic literature of the late Renaissance, clarifying Renaissance ideas and ideals about love and sexuality and examining the manifestations of those ideas and ideals in literature. Utilizing a variety of critical methods and ideological presuppositions, these essays confront important questions about the relationship of sexuality and textuality in the period, about the intertwining of political and sexual discourse, about attitudes toward gender and the differences between men and women as desiring subjects, about the representation of homoerotics and the discourses of homosexuality (and homophobia), about the impact of economic and social ideologies on love poetry and sexual expression, and about the erotics of criticism. For all their diversity of subject matter and approach, however, these essays are unified in their regard of sexuality and its representations in literature as key elements in the cultural semiotics of the Renaissance. That is, the concern of the contributors is less in documenting particular sexual attitudes and practices than in exploring how sexuality is accorded meaning in the period. From this perspective, sexuality is not a cordoned-off area of privacy, but a complex human impulse subject to social management, interpretation, and (re)construction. The discourses of desire that textualize early modern sexuality also necessarily inscribe a wide spectrum of Renaissance cultural concerns, from spirituality to economics and from the construction of individual identity to the yearning for a new social order.

The original, abbreviated versions of all of the essays included here were presented at the ninth biennial Renaissance conference at the University of Michigan–Dearborn, October 19–20, 1990.[8] The final

8. Selected papers from the first eight Dearborn conferences have been published: those from the 1974 conference as *"Trust to Good Verses": Herrick Tercentenary Essays*, ed. Roger B. Rollin and J. Max Patrick (Pittsburgh: University of Pittsburgh Press, 1978); those from the 1976 conference on seventeenth-century prose as a special issue of *Studies in the Literary Imagination* 10, no. 2 (1977), ed. William A. Sessions and James S. Tillman; those from the 1978 to the 1988 conferences were edited by Claude J. Summers and Ted-Larry Pebworth and were published as *"Too Rich to Clothe the Sunne": Essays on George Herbert* (Pittsburgh: University of Pittsburgh Press, 1980); *Classic and Cavalier: Essays on Jonson and the Sons of Ben* (Pittsburgh: University of Pittsburgh Press, 1982); *The Eagle and the Dove: Reassessing John Donne* (Columbia: University of Missouri Press, 1986); *"Bright Shootes of Everlastingnesse": The Seventeenth-Century Religious Lyric* (Columbia: University of Missouri Press, 1987); *"The Muses Common-Weale": Poetry and Politics in the Seventeenth Century* (Columbia: University of Mis-

versions printed here have benefited from the stimulating exchanges and responses afforded by the conference, and they intersect, reinforce, and challenge each other in significant and interesting ways. But the essays were written independently and without consultation among the authors. No topics or approaches were suggested or assigned, and none were proscribed. All the essays are historically grounded and critically based, but they vary widely in their historical perspectives and critical techniques and in their scope and focus. The only criterion for selection has been that each essay contribute to the understanding and informed appreciation of the representation of sexuality in the non-dramatic literature of the late Renaissance in England.

In the opening essay, Raymond B. Waddington places Shakespeare's fascinatingly problematic Sonnet 20 within the rich social and literary contexts that inform it, especially sixteenth-century attitudes toward sex transformation and bisexuality and interpretations of bisexual myths. Knowledge of these contexts helps illuminate the poetic strategies by which Shakespeare constructs his startling creation myth of the "master mistress" and projects his enigmatic meaning. Describing Sonnet 20 as a milestone in the "familiar descending journey by which the idealizations of Platonism and of mythology are accommodated to the realities of the human condition," Waddington also sees the poem as part of a larger movement in which the privatization of erotic desire engenders a complex self-awareness of the constraints and conflicts imposed by biological and socially defined sexual identity.

In the first of several essays in the volume that consider the mingling of the sexual and the political in Renaissance literature, Mary Villeponteaux exposes the paradoxes inherent in the language of Petrarchan desire that characterizes Elizabethan political discourse by exploring Spenser's portrait of Belphoebe in Book III of *The Faerie Queene*. Like Elizabeth's, Belphoebe's presence both demands desire and forbids it with disturbing political and psychosexual implications. In Villeponteaux's revisionary reading, Belphoebe is a negative figure, embodying not just Spenser's warning to the queen, but his outright censure of her obdurate virginity. In his portrait of Belphoebe,

souri Press, 1988); *On the Celebrated and Neglected Poems of Andrew Marvell* (Columbia: University of Missouri Press, 1992).

the poet characterizes Elizabeth's position as beyond the realm of ordinary human desires and, hence, a rebuke to masculine power. Insofar as it fails to accommodate male desire, Elizabeth's transformation of her natural body into an immutable public presence—as exemplified in her motto, *semper eadem*—implicitly threatens the very "political Petrarchism" that it simultaneously encourages.

William Shullenberger takes as his subject the specific and characteristic ways in which Donne creates a visual field in his amatory poetry and stations an observing third party in relation to it. Shullenberger examines this voyeuristic incursion of a third party as a social, psychological, and aesthetic phenomenon: "Socially, as an index of the conditions under which love could be made in the late Elizabethan and early Jacobean household; psychologically, as an expression of Donne's anxiety about being watched and longing to be watched; and aesthetically, as a way of implicating the reader and the act of reading in the poem." In introducing the third party in his love lyrics, Donne also introjects the public discourse of the poem into the apparently private discourse of the poem's love making. The presence of the erotic spectator in Donne's poetry, Shullenberger notes, reminds the reader that the pleasure of the text is itself voyeuristic.

Donne's extraordinary dramatic monologue "Sapho to Philaenis" is the subject of Stella Revard's essay, in which she argues that Donne's aim in the poem is to adopt the voice of the original Sappho rather than that of the Sappho of Roman tradition. Through the Sapphic voice, he attempts to define homoerotic love, in the process envisioning the return of a lost golden age of sexual freedom and equity in love. Revard finds that Donne largely succeeds in exploiting the Sapphic voice and attitudes toward love, but that he fails to capture Sappho's passionate abandon and lyric simplicity. Ultimately, "Sapho to Philaenis" is more Donnean than Sapphic: "Donne began his elegy with the serious motive of looking through Sappho's eyes. We must not blame him that he only succeeded in looking over her shoulder."

Theresa DiPasquale traces the repeated linkages in Donne's love poetry of Roman Catholicism and Petrarchism. The utterances of Donne's unrequited lovers are often reminiscent of specifically Roman piety. Faced with the rejection of their faith and devotion to a creed of nonfulfillment—an "orthodoxy of frustration"—the Petrarchan personae of poems like "Loves Deitie," "The Funerall," and "Twicknam

Garden" speak in defensive counter-Reformation accents. They redefine love and desire in order to uphold their traditional faith. For
Donne, DiPasquale argues, "Petrarchism is love's papistry, the Babylonian captivity of desire."

Anthony Low identifies the absence of the Petrarchan tradition as
perhaps the most radical quality in Thomas Carew's love poetry. He
traces the roots of this absence to Carew's family situation and his
experience within a changing economic system. Carew's development of a "new-model" love poetry in England—libertine, antiau-
thoritarian, non-Petrarchan—is seen as closely related to his break
with his family, which forced him to find other forms of love and
patronage outside the traditional kinship system: "From a position in
the patronage network that was filial and duteous, Carew moved to a
position of mutual advantage, as the hired wit to a King's favorite." If
Carew's reinvention of himself led to a new kind of poetry that emphasizes opportunism and self-interest in love, that poetry also recognizes love as a mutual transaction between lovers who are equals.
Thus, Carew's redefinition of love parallels significant economic changes
in seventeenth-century England, as a free-market economy displaced
a feudal one.

M. L. Donnelly explores the conventions of *précieux* and *libertin*
in the amatory lyrics of Suckling and Carew. Although the libertinism of the taverns and the *préciosité* associated with Queen Henrietta Maria seem polar opposites, yet the two positions regarding love
evoke and demand the other, as is clear in the works of the two most
successful Caroline court poets, Suckling and Carew. Suckling's typical stance in his amorous lyrics is to take life on its simplest terms,
ostensibly sweeping away all social constructs to appeal to nature,
usually defined simply as self-gratification. But in poems like "Loves
Feast," he reveals genuine ambivalence about the libertinism that he
ostentatiously embraces. Although working within different conventions and with a different level of self-consciousness from Suckling,
Carew in "The Rapture" also reveals a dissatisfaction with the received
order of things, as he forces a direct confrontation between the conflicting and competing values of his age's conceptualization of eros.

In a spirited discussion of "the erotics of criticism," Roger B. Rollin
questions the tactics and criteria of those critics who—in their discomfort with the eroticism of Robert Herrick's *Hesperides*—have

attributed to the poet an infantile or deviant sexuality. Because critics' evaluations of erotic themes, tones, and moods are likely to reflect their own unconscious wishes, anxieties, conflicts, and frustrations, the responses to Herrick's amatory verse may be more revealing of the critics than of the poetry. When critics insist upon evaluating not merely the literary quality of erotic poetry but also the quality of the eroticism displayed in the poetry, then, Rollin contends, the hermeneutics of erotica inevitably becomes erotic hermeneutics. In a careful reading of Herrick's witty dream-poem "The Vine," Rollin vindicates it as "psychologically authentic and adult," the work of a self-conscious artist quite aware of what he is revealing about the human sexual imagination.

Joseph Cady challenges the social constructionist (or "new-inventionist") idea that homosexuality and heterosexuality were not recognized as distinct, categorical orientations in the Renaissance. He argues that the Renaissance not only had a definite comprehension of distinct sexual orientations, but it held so strongly to other-sex attraction as the norm for human sexuality that the general language of desire was sufficient to denote it. Same-sex attraction was presumed to be so secondary and eccentric that an identifying language for it was derived from the language for heterosexuality, as in the terms "masculine love" and "male whore." Among the implications of Cady's examination of the Renaissance language for sexuality are that there is a greater continuity between Renaissance and modern conceptions of homosexuality than social constructionists typically grant, that heterosexuality is as crucial and problematic a topic for the historical study of sexuality as is homosexuality, and that Renaissance writers wrote of desire "in an atmosphere of marked cultural constraint and jeopardy, knowing, on some level of their beings, that their society sanctioned only one discourse about the gender direction of desire, a discourse that those who were inclined to depart from did so only at their own risk."

The forbidden nature of the discourse of same-sex desire is also at the heart of Winfried Schleiner's essay on Burton's use of *praeteritio* in discussing homosexuality in the *Anatomy of Melancholy*. Burton's disquisition on same-sex relationships is clearly circumscribed by being written in Latin and by being presented in a way that calls attention to itself: Burton's own sentences are printed in italics, while his quotations are printed in roman type, reversing the normal format of the rest of his book. Although the passage on homosexuality is brief, it incorporates an enormous amount of curious information (and misinformation) about the subject, in effect providing an illuminating guide to orthodox Protestant thinking about same-sex relationships in the Renaissance. Schleiner clarifies Burton's tactics of highlighting and omitting (or highlighting by omitting) in his use of numerous and varied sources, and suggests that the discussion of same-sex relationships—for all its well-documented derivativeness—is also revealing of Burton's personal ambivalence about homosexuality.

In his essay, Eugene R. Cunnar traces the classical sources and Renaissance manifestations of the myth of a sexual golden age in which male desire and sexuality were free of laws and inhibitions. Examining works by Donne, Carew, Herrick, Cowley, and Lovelace, among others, Cunnar documents the popularity of this myth during the seventeenth century and argues that it provided male poets a means to construct fantasies designed to secure their domination of women even as it also alleviated their sexual anxieties. Although the male speakers of these poems promise mutuality to the women they address, they actually express very little concern about women's desire, a deficiency responded to by Aphra Behn in her own projection of a sexual golden age from a feminine viewpoint.

In an essay also concerned with the fantasy of the golden age of uninhibited sexuality, Achsah Guibbory argues that the intimacies of the private world and the social orders of the public are complexly intertwined in seventeenth-century love poetry. Focusing on Carew's "Rapture," Lovelace's "Love made in the first Age: To *Chloris,*" and Aphra Behn's "Golden Age," Guibbory notes that all three poems construct models of human sexuality and sexual relationships that are analogous to models of political order and that they all define their ideals in opposition to existing social and political structures and assumptions. But whereas the libertinism of Carew and Lovelace is essentially conservative, constructing gender, sexuality, and desire in ways that reinforce female obedience and submission and that reflect royalist political sentiment, the vision of Aphra Behn is quite different. Her "feminist libertinism" subverts the sexual and political ideals celebrated by the male poets; it explodes cultural notions of female passivity and privileges the private sphere over the public.

Protesting against a tradition that denies the sexual content of lesbian literature, Arlene Stiebel examines masking techniques in the poetry of Katherine Philips and Aphra Behn. Both poets employ traditional literary conventions—including the courtly love address to the beloved and her response, the idealized pattern of Platonic same-sex friendship, and the hermaphroditic perfection of the beloved who incorporates the best qualities of both sexes—but the voice of the lover is not disguised as male. The conventions help make the representations of a woman's desire for a female lover seem conventional enough, but even as the poems mask the reality of sexual desire, they simultaneously reveal it as well. As Stiebel demonstrates, the apparent "innocence" of lesbian love in seventeenth-century poetry is itself an ironic mask.

In "Demystifying Disguises: Adam, Eve, and the Subject of Desire," Catherine Gimelli Martin turns to the thorny question of gender relationships in *Paradise Lost*. Challenging feminist readings of the poem that stress the inequality of Adam and Eve, Martin argues that in the course of the epic the characters alter and develop both in their capacities as human subjects and as male and female prototypes. The poem's characteristic mode of emblematic outline and qualification, of statement and revision, ultimately reveals that Eve's subjection to Adam's authority is more apparent than real. Hierarchy is subject to temporal interpretation and initiative, not to innate natural dispositions. Moreover, the gender distinctions in *Paradise Lost*—particularly the attribution to Eve of an intuitive, responsive ear as opposed to Adam's rational, active eye—actually grant her a source of authority equivalent (and potentially superior) to Adam's. The poem establishes self-knowledge and recognition of difference as the proper and only channels of true union and communion. Thus, Martin concludes, "Autonomy becomes the metonymy of male and female gifts and desires which, in perfect balance, generates the synecdoche of divine intercourse and human marriage alike."

The volume concludes with excerpts from a panel discussion in which Paul G. Stanwood, Diana Treviño Benet, Judith Scherer Herz, and Debora Shuger discuss varied aspects of the seventeenth-century discourses of desire, ranging from the link between religious faith and profane desire, the emergence of women writers, and the new prominence of gay and lesbian topics in Renaissance literature to the question of subjectivity in the seventeenth century and the distinction between erotic desire (the longing for union with the beloved) and sexual desire (genital arousal). The lively discussion helps focus some issues raised in the essays and in other recent scholarship on Renaissance sexuality, while also pointing to aspects of desire that have been neglected or inadequately treated.

In their varied approaches, these essays illustrate the richness of the topic and of its susceptibility to a number of critical techniques and vantage points. Illuminating important authors and significant texts, the essays collected here contribute to a fuller understanding of the complexities and range of seventeenth-century discourses of desire, while also helping chart the outlines of the period's sexual ideologies and anxieties.

Raymond B. Waddington

The Poetics of Eroticism
Shakespeare's "Master Mistress"

"A woman's face with nature's own hand painted / Hast thou, the master mistress of my passion." As Joseph Pequigney recently observed, "The figure depicted in Sonnet 20 is, in its simplest outlines, that of a woman with a penis." What kind of thing is that to say about a friend, lover, nobleman, patron? Critical responses to Sonnet 20 too frequently allow their energy to be diverted into wholly unprofitable speculation on the nature of the poet's own sexuality or, more simply, short-circuited by the enormity of what the poem seems to be saying. George Steevens found it "impossible to read . . . without an equal mixture of disgust and indignation"; Hyder Rollins described it as "about the most indecent sonnet of the lot"; and Gerald Hammond has labeled it "a piece of grotesquery."[1] Perhaps our contemporary

---

1. The *Sonnets* are quoted from Stephen Booth, ed., *Shakespeare's Sonnets* (New Haven: Yale University Press, 1977). The present essay is an abstract and brief chronicle of a monograph-in-progress that seeks to understand Sonnet 20 in its sixteenth-century contexts. For full development of those contexts, I must refer the reader to the longer study. I also draw some paragraphs from a related essay, "'All in All': Shakespeare, Milton, Donne and the Soul-in-Body *Topos*," *English Literary Renaissance* 20 (1990): 40–68. I am grateful to Massimo Ciavolella and Donald Beecher for the first opportunity to try out these ideas at the "Eros and Anteros" colloquium (Toronto 1987). In sequence, the quotations are from: Joseph Pequigney, *Such Is My Love: A Study of Shakespeare's Sonnets* (Chicago: University of Chicago Press, 1985), 37; for Steevens, *The Sonnets of Shakespeare*, ed. Raymond Macdonald Alden (Boston: Houghton Mifflin, 1916), 56; *A New Variorum Edition of Shakespeare, The Sonnets*, ed. Hyder E. Rollins, 2 vols. (Philadelphia: Lippincott, 1944), 2:239; and Gerald Hammond, *The Reader and Shakespeare's Young Man Sonnets* (Totowa, N.J.: Barnes & Noble, 1981), 109.

taste for confessional poetry leads us astray, despite what we have been taught about reading Renaissance poems as rhetorical addresses.[2] Yet the question of what the poet tells the young man, and the related one of how he says it, should take precedence over the question of what it reveals about himself.

The commentators who have managed to keep this in mind raise some basic issues. James Winney muses: "Only an oddly imperceptive reader could mistake this sonnet for a complimentary address. Few men, however good-looking, would enjoy being told that they were designed to be women; and one who had just reached manhood would be still less amused if his sex were called into question, however wittily." And E. B. Reed remarks, "This sonnet has hardly the tone in which Shakespeare, the actor, could address a nobleman of high rank." These objections confess a concomitant bewilderment: the sonnet self-evidently does what common sense decrees it cannot do. To explain how the poem succeeds in doing just that requires a more extensive look at sixteenth-century sexual attitudes and their literary and cultural manifestations than is possible here. Instead, I shall touch on several relevant areas that, however briefly explored, should inform our responses to the sonnet. The first of these is medical attitudes toward sex transformation and bisexuality; the second, sixteenth-century interpretations of bisexual myths; and, finally, some of the formal and generic strategies by which Shakespeare projects the meaning of the poem.[3]

In narrative content, Sonnet 20 is a creation myth, an invented fable of origins to explain the existence of a particular phenomenon, with a description of the latter comprising the octave and the fable the sestet. Nature first created this extraordinary young man as woman, but then "fell a-doting" and converted her to a man. Behind this deceptively artless piece of flattery resonate several pseudo-scientific

---

2. To cite just one example, see Marion Trousdale, "A Possible Renaissance View of Form," *ELH* 40 (1973): 179–204. Kenneth Muir, *Shakespeare's Sonnets* (London: George Allen & Unwin, 1979), sensibly reiterates warnings against reading the *Sonnets* as confessional.

3. Winney, *The Master-Mistress: A Study of Shakespeare's Sonnets* (New York: Barnes & Noble, 1968), 152–53; and Reed, ed., *Shakespeare's Sonnets* (New Haven: Yale University Press, 1948), 81. Winney attempts to resolve the impasse by eliminating the young nobleman: "Shakespeare is not analyzing the character of an actual person but exploring a complex of ideas which his creative consciousness holds together" (154).

controversies to which we should be responsive. In book 3 of *Il Cortegiano,* Gasparo Pallavicino recites some misogynist commonplaces:

> Very learned men have written that, since nature always intends and plans to make things most perfect, she would constantly bring forth men if she could; and that when a woman is born, it is a defect or mistake of nature, and contrary to what she would wish to do: as is seen too in the case of one who is born blind, or lame, or with some other defect; and, in trees, the many fruits that never ripen. Thus, a woman can be said to be a creature produced by chance and accident.[4]

Foremost among these learned men would be Galen and Aristotle, who regard a woman as an imperfectly developed version of man: "Because of lack of heat in generation, her sexual organs have remained internal, she is incomplete, colder and moister in dominant humours, and unable to 'concoct' perfect semen from blood." In his *Generation of Animals,* Aristotle notoriously compares woman to a eunuch, an impotent male, and a deformed male. Of the difficult word [πεπηρωμένων] he translates as 'deformed,' A. L. Peck comments, "Other attempts to bring out the meaning . . . would include 'imperfectly developed,' 'underdeveloped,' 'malformed,' 'mutilated,' 'congenitally disabled.'" Two presumptions underlie the "deformed male" theory: "That the hottest created thing is the most perfect, and that a direct comparison can be made between the genitalia of man and woman in function, number and form."[5]

Retrospectively, it is evident that Shakespeare's Mother Nature is an Aristotelian-Galenic creationist who has effected the sexual metamorphosis by remedying the deficiency of heat in female physiology. Lines 5 and 6, "An eye more bright than theirs, . . . / Gilding the object whereupon it gazeth," implicitly cast the young man's roving eye as the sun, eye of the world and natural alchemist, a comparison that also occupies a quatrain of Sonnet 33:

4. Baldesar Castiglione, *The Book of the Courtier,* trans. Charles S. Singleton (Garden City, N.Y.: Anchor Books, 1959), 311, 213.

5. Ian Maclean, *The Renaissance Notion of Woman* (Cambridge: Cambridge University Press, 1980), 31; Aristotle, *Generation of Animals,* trans. A. L. Peck, Loeb Classical Library (Cambridge: Harvard University Press, 1963), 2.3.737a 26, 28. On the gender implications of Aristotle's theory, see the ground-breaking essay by Maryanne Cline Horowitz, "Aristotle and Woman," *Journal of the History of Biology* 9 (1976): 183–213.

> Full many a glorious morning have I seen
> Flatter the mountain tops with sovereign eye,
> Kissing with golden face the meadows green,
> Gilding pale streams with heav'nly alchemy.
>
> (1–4)

Since the masculine sun is the source of heat as well as light, Nature has corrected the deficiency in humor that first arrested this creature's development. It would be wrong to imagine the sex change as a grafting operation, the simple supplying of a penis, however immediately the furiously punning sestet tempts us to do so: "And by addition me of thee defeated, / By adding one thing to my purpose nothing" (11–12). "Add" and "addition" do have a mathematical sense here, since the poet is playing on the ancient symbolism of the first even and odd numbers, two and three, as symbols for the feminine and masculine principles: "By adding one thing," a penis, "to my purpose nothing," both *no thing* or vagina and no longer a feminine number, so *nothing*. But the primary meaning of "addition" is "augmentation" rather than "attachment," as the next line makes clear: "prick'd thee out" (13) punningly means "selected you from a list," but, literally and precisely, it means that the inverted and internal female genitalia have been drawn out to proper, external male form by the function of heat, a process that the physician Ambroise Paré describes in his case histories of women who become men.[6]

If Shakespeare expects us to respond to staples of physiological and anatomical discourse, he yet alludes to them selectively, elusively, and perhaps not consistently. A perfect woman should be a logical impossibility in the views of Aristotle and Galen, but this woman is not "a defect or mistake of nature." Nature, instead, seems to have set out to create a superior woman, "more bright" and "less false" than others of the species, succeeding so well that, Pygmalion-like, she becomes infatuated with her own handiwork and falls "a-doting"

---

6. On the number symbolism, see Plutarch, *Moralia*, 263f–64a; and R. B. Waddington, *The Mind's Empire: Myth and Form in George Chapman's Narrative Poems* (Baltimore: Johns Hopkins University Press, 1974), 162–64. For the sexual implications of *thing* and *nothing*, see Booth's note on line 12. Ambroise Paré, *Des Monstres et Prodiges*, ed. Jean Céard, Travaux d'Humanisme et Renaissance 115 (Geneva: Librairie Droz, 1971), chap. 7, "Histoires Memorables de Certaines Femmes qui sont Degenerees en Hommes," 29–30. See also Maclean, *Renaissance Notion*, 33, 38–39.

over what "she wrought." Classical physiology, with its bias toward male superiority, should insist on a complete sexual conversion for perfection. Here, however, both external and internal qualities, face and heart, remain female; the dominant impression is of male genitalia on a female body, thus "addition" as "attachment" after all, even if effected naturally. This "master mistress" may steal "men's eyes and women's souls amazeth," but the colder context of medical examination might remind us that in the sixteenth century such combinations almost invariably were categorized as monsters.[7]

Sonnet 20 is a blazon, an anatomy of the young man's beauty in terms that can only be described as "bisexual." Readers have responded by identifying the character of his beauty as "androgynous" or "hermaphroditic," the interchangeability of adjectives accurately reflecting dictionary definitions, which treat the words as synonyms. It is important to remember, however, that the myths underlying the adjectives have very different implications. Aristophanes' fable of the Androgyne, the double beings who—split in two by an angry Zeus—perpetually seek to reunite themselves, is wholly positive in thrust. It presents love as a quest for fulfillment, wholeness, harmony, reintegration, and health. Ovid's story of how Salmacis and Hermaphroditus were fused into one body is, in contrast, a punishment for the avoidance of love. Both myths are pertinent to understanding Sonnet 20, but they need to be considered separately.

Tracing the Androgyne myth from Ficino through Pico della Mirandola, Leone Ebreo, Erasmus, Rabelais, and Etienne Pasquier, one finds a rich variety of commentaries and interpretations; however, as the myth progresses through philosophic discourse to love treatises and emblem books, a dominant interpretation is established. Although the Androgyne could symbolize an Adamic state of spiritual perfection, the harmoniously tempered and virtuous mind, or the union of the individual soul with God, the most common meaning was simply marriage. The marital Androgyne was used variously to imply the amelioration of carnal lust to lawful propagation, a platonic union of spirits, a Pauline apprehension of Christian charity, or a combination

7. Maclean comments, "It is generally agreed that hermaphrodites belong not at a mid point on the sexual spectrum between (normal) female and (normal) male births, but rather to the category of monster" (*Renaissance Notion,* 39). The medical attitude is exemplified by Paré's dichotomous title.

of these connotations; as myth and image evolved in general usage, however, the idea of marriage remained foremost. It has long been recognized that the first seventeen of Shakespeare's *Sonnets,* the "marriage" sonnets, are a closely linked group urging the young man to perpetuate himself by begetting a son. The androgynous blazon of Sonnet 20 allusively reprises the theme of the first group, even while ambiguously recognizing the greater likelihood of a possibility acknowledged in the opening sonnet: "But thou, contracted to thine own bright eyes, / Feed'st thy light's flame with self-substantial fuel" (Sonnet 1.5–6). If he is indeed already married to himself in narcissistic sterility, the symbol of an anticipated completion and fulfillment in heterosexual marriage dissolves and redefines in the negative image of the hermaphrodite. Not prodigy, but monster.[8]

When Plato apparently invented the fable of the Androgyne, he transformed a concept into a myth, thus converting the adjective, *androgynos,* into a proper name. Nonetheless, the reality, or at least the fear, of bisexual individuals in Greek culture preceded Plato's literary invention, which—even in Aristophanes' narration—has the effect of a quixotic rehabilitation, as he remarks, "For though [*androgynos*] is only used nowadays as a term of contempt, there really was a man-woman in those days, a being which was half male and half female" (*Symposium,* 189E). Conversely, *Hermaphroditos* was first a proper name and only later became a synonym of *androgynos* in popular usage. A cult of the minor god Hermaphroditus seems to have emerged in the fourth century B.C., although Hellenists are divided on whether the cult had native or foreign origins.[9]

The earliest sculptural representations of Hermaphroditus project him as, like Eros and Dionysos, an adolescent god, a physical type realizing a synthesis of masculine and feminine beauty. Later the standing figure of the ephebe came to be supplanted by the purely feminine beauty of the reclining or sleeping Hermaphroditus whose identity is

8. For full discussion with documentation of the Androgyne in the sixteenth century, see my forthcoming monograph on Sonnet 20. On the "marriage group," see, Muir *Shakespeare's Sonnets,* 35–41, 45–52.

9. Quotation translated by Michael Joyce, in *The Collected Dialogues of Plato,* ed. Edith Hamilton and Huntington Cairns, Bollingen Series, no. 81 (Princeton: Princeton University Press, 1961), 542. For the evolution of *Hermaphroditos* into its synonym, see Marie Delcourt, *Hermaphrodite: Myths and Rites of the Bisexual Figure in Classical Antiquity,* trans. Jennifer Nicholson (London: Studio Books, 1961), 48.

revealed only by the male genitalia.[10] Along with the shifting of physical types of representation, we can mark a concomitant shifting of attitudes toward the god as the ambivalence of response that, according to Marie Delcourt, is always present, hardens in the negative. The threat of the abnormal may be exorcised by contempt and ridicule. This is the cultural situation reported by two first century B.C. writers. Diodorus Siculus, although looking back to an earlier time, reports pro and con:

> Hermaphroditus . . . was born of Hermes and Aphrodite and received a name which is a combination of those of both his parents. Some say that this Hermaphroditus is a god and appears at certain times among men, and that he is born with a physical body which is a combination of that of a man and that of a woman, in that he has a body which is beautiful and delicate like that of a woman, but has the masculine quality and vigour of a man. But there are some who declare that such creatures of two sexes are monstrosities, and coming rarely into the world as they do they have the quality of presaging the future, sometimes for evil and sometimes for good.[11]

Pliny puts it more succinctly, stating, "Formerly hermaphrodites were considered as terrifying apparitions, but today only as objects for jest."[12]

Ovid's *Metamorphoses,* 4.285–388, the canonical literary text, concentrates the evolution of the myth. In his account, when the lovely boy spurns the advances of the water nymph Salmacis, she prays to the gods that she and Hermaphroditus might forever become one being, one body. The gods grant her request, as they also grant Hermaphroditus's bitter prayer that anyone thereafter entering the water of Salmacis's fountain become, like himself, effeminate. An equation of bisexuality with asexuality underlies Ovid's narrative: "Neutrumque et utrunque videntur."[13] The invented story of metamorphosis

10. See Delcourt, *Hermaphrodite,* 43–67; and, for a fuller consideration of the typology of hermaphroditic presentations, see her later study, *Hermaphroditea: Recherches sur l'etre double promoteur de la fertilite dans le monde classique,* Collection Latomus, no. 86 (Brussels: Latomus, 1966).

11. Diodorus Siculus, *Historical Library,* trans. C. H. Oldfather, Loeb Classical Library, vol. 2 (London: Heinemann, 1967), 6.5.361.

12. Pliny, *Natural History* 7.34, quoted by Delcourt, *Hermaphrodite,* 45.

13. See Delcourt, *Hermaphrodite,* 53–55. "But neither, and yet both" (Rolfe Humphries translates the phrase); and *Ovid's Metamorphoses* (Bloomington: Indiana University Press, 1955).

only retraces the historical transformation of Hermaphroditus. In unmanning Hermaphroditus, Ovid does present him as a monstrosity even while allowing him Diodorus's "quality of presaging the future . . . for evil" in cursing the fountain with his impotence. At the same time, the elements of literary parody in Ovid's story suggest that for him, as for Pliny, Hermaphroditus is simultaneously an object for jest.[14]

Renaissance artists, commencing at least with Giorgione, responded directly to surviving examples of the classical Hermaphroditus in sculpture and gem carvings and, consequently, invested their recreations with something of the mysterious power of bisexuality. For poets, however, the *locus classicus* was the *Metamorphoses,* and the potent example of Ovid—reinforced by the tradition of moralized commentary, by the illustrated editions of Ovid, and by the emblem books—kept the literary depictions of Hermaphroditus impotent.[15] An emblem in Barthelemy Aneau's *Picta Poesis* (1552) shows an aggressive Salmacis wrestling a worried Hermaphroditus down into the fountain; in the left background, an hermaphroditic figure foretells the outcome; and the title bluntly interprets the action: "Fons Salmacidos, Libido Effoeminans." During the 1590s, Ovid's Hermaphroditus achieved the status of an archetype in the fashionable erotic, mythological poetry, for most of which Aneau's moralistic comment remains an apt description. When Spenser and Donne attempt to accentuate the positive with a "faire" or "blest" hermaphrodite, they are working against the grain of poetic convention.[16]

In the response to sexual abnormality, however, it is impossible to eliminate the negative, as we see when we examine the history of Hermaphroditus's mythic twin and opposite, Priapus. Emerging in

14. On the parodic elements, see G. K. Galinsky, *Ovid's Metamorphoses: An Introduction to the Basic Aspects* (Berkeley: University of California Press, 1975), 186–90.

15. See, particularly, Seymour Howard, "The Dresden *Venus* and Its Kin: Mutation and Retrieval of Types," *Art Quarterly* 2 (1979): 90–111, who relates Giorgione's *Sleeping Venus* to the Sleeping Hermaphrodite type. On the allegorized Ovid, see Don Cameron Allen, *Mysteriously Meant: The Rediscovery of Pagan Symbolism and Allegorical Interpretation in the Renaissance* (Baltimore: Johns Hopkins University Press, 1970), 163–99; and, for illustrated editions, M. D. Henkel, "Illustriete Ausgaben von Ovids Metamorphosen in XV., XVI. und XVII. Jahrhundert," *Vorträge der Bibliothek Warburg, 1926–27,* 6 (1960): 58–144.

16. See the 1590 ending to book 3 of *The Faerie Queene;* and Donne, "To Mr. *Tilman* after he had taken orders," l. 54.

the mythological pantheon slightly later than Hermaphroditus, Priapus evinces their kinship in two obvious ways, parentage and function. They are half-brothers—Priapus is reported to be the son of Dionysos and Aphrodite (leading to, or possibly stemming from, an easy moralization: wine and beauty create lust)—and, as Hermaphroditus originally was the god of sexual union, so Priapus is always the deity of fertility, abundance, and potency.[17] Originally, according to Diodorus Siculus (4.6.2), he was simply the phallus personified. The naked potency of Priapus, universal principle of generation, quickly extended his function from simple embodiment of sexual fertility to his full-fledged role as god and guardian of orchards, gardens, and harvests—scarecrow and protector against thieves. It is this greater range of influence over human activity, Delcourt speculates, that caused Priapus to assume many of the attributes and offices of Hermaphroditus, even some aspects of his bisexuality.[18] She traces the process, parallel to that in the sculptural representations of Hermaphroditus, by which the initially grotesque and monstrous images of Priapus are beautified and even feminized. But writers always remembered the deformity of Priapus.

The 1552 Prologue to Rabelais's *Quart Livre* is an exuberant celebration of the Priapus myth, presenting it through a descending sequence of types—Priapus himself, Mercury, Couillatris, and Rabelais—as a parable of the inspired poet-writer's creative potency. Rabelais balances an inherently unstable combination. On the one hand, he uses Priapus as a symbol, and, on the other, he makes his physical presence grotesquely human. The two do not lie easily in one bed. As Delcourt observes: "Priapus brings fertility to gardens and cowsheds, yet parents would be horrified at a newborn child who resembles him. An idea may be translated into symbols, so long as they do not become so exact that they coincide with concrete reality." Poussin's drawing of *The Birth of Priapus,* one of a set intended for a new illustrated edition of Ovid, makes Delcourt's point exactly. A per-

17. See Delcourt, *Hermaphrodite,* 50–52; also Hans Herter, *De Priapo,* Religionsgeschichtliche Versuche und Vorasbeiten 32 (Giessen: Verbeg von Alfred Topelmann, 1932), especially 138–70 for the confusion of Priapus and Hermaphroditus. H. J. Rose, *A Handbook of Greek Mythology* (New York: Dutton, 1959), 149, notes, "According to some genealogies, Priapos also was a child of Hermes and Aphrodite," which draws the twinning with Hermaphroditus even closer.

18. See Delcourt, *Hermaphrodite,* 52; and Herter, *De Priapo,* 138–70.

Poussin's *The Birth of Priapus*. Windsor Castle, Royal Library. © 1992 Her Majesty Queen Elizabeth II.

verse epiphany, the scene centers on the revelation of the infant's physical deformity to a group of nymphs who turn away in pretended horror and revulsion, although their expressions disclose delight at the scandal. Anthony Blunt comments, "As far as possible, Poussin eliminates the supernatural [and] introduces a sense of drama into the drawings." His Priapus, therefore, is no god, but a deformed infant. A human baby with a monstrous *membrum virilis*.[19]

The disproportion of Priapus illuminates the more oblique strategy and tone of Shakespeare's Sonnet 20, a celebration of the young man's androgynous beauty and an analysis of its effects on others. The praise is conceived as an anatomical blazon, with each odd line of the octave specifying a single feature: "A woman's face" (1), "A woman's gentle heart" (3), "An eye more bright than theirs" (5), "A man in hue all hues" (7). *Hue* carries the primary sense of form, shape, or appearance with secondary implications of complexion and color and, possibly, of an apparition. Thus, a man in appearance, the "master mistress" epitomizes all physical beauty, is an archetype of

19. Delcourt, *Hermaphrodite,* 51; Blunt, *Nicolas Poussin,* Bollingen Series, no. 35.7 (New York: Pantheon, 1967), 45.

sexual attractiveness, as his hue "steals men's eyes and women's souls amazeth."[20] The implied subtext, "all in all and all in every part," means that his own "soul" is the aura of sexual attractiveness that is completely and perfectly manifested in every part of his body.[21] The blazon is completed, however, with the part that stands for the whole:

> And for a woman wert thou first created,
> Till nature as she wrought thee fell a-doting,
> And by addition me of thee defeated,
> By adding one thing to my purpose nothing.
> But since she prick'd thee out for women's pleasure,
> Mine be thy love, and thy love's use their treasure.
>   (9–14)

The rhetorical exaggeration here—four lines as opposed to the two for each of the other anatomical features enumerated—assigns dominance to the phallus in the physical portrait. The effect is similar to the anatomical exaggeration employed by Renaissance artists in the representations of ithyphallic satyrs and gods; for instance, the *Garden of Vertumuus* engraving from Fontainebleau or the ithyphallic herm of the *Sacrifice to Priapus* woodcut from the *Hypnerotomachia Poliphili*. As in the scene of the Priapic worshippers, Shakespeare's young man has "all hues in his controlling, / Which steals men's eyes and women's souls amazeth" (7–8). Himself an "unmoved mover" (Sonnet 94.3–4), the young man becomes, in Northrop Frye's apt phrase, "an erotic messiah."[22]

Because he is a human and not a god, however, here the exaggeration differs from the woodcut in its flirtation with the ridiculous. One might note in passing the sonnet's exploitation of conventions from Latin Priapic verse. These include: plays upon obscene words ("prick"

20. See T. W. Baldwin, *On the Literary Genetics of Shakespeare's Poems and Sonnets* (Urbana: University of Illinois Press, 1950), 165–56; and the notes to line 7 by Booth and by John Kerrigan, in *The Sonnets and A Lover's Complaint* (Harmondsworth: Penguin, 1986). A particularly convoluted sexual innuendo is perceived in line 8 by Martin Green, *The Labyrinth of Shakespeare's Sonnets* (London: Charles Skilton Ltd., 1974), 59–81.

21. On the use of this philosophical topos in the sonnet, see Waddington, "'All in All,'" 48–53.

22. "How True a Twain," in *The Riddle of Shakespeare's Sonnets* (New York: Basic Books, 1962), 42.

Francesco Colonna's *Sacrifice to Priapus* from his book *Hypnerotomachia Poliphii* (1499). The Huntington Library, San Marino, California.

and "nothing"); the personification of the phallus (here, by synecdoche, the part becomes the whole); and the fiction of the poem as
both an offering to the god and a threat by the god. The sonnet pays
tribute to the young man's unequalled beauty and sexuality, while
hinting that too much sexuality is as unnatural as too little. Priapus
and Hermaphroditus are true brothers in this essential respect. As
Marie Delcourt has commented, "An abnormal formation of the generative organs seemed to the Ancients the extreme of monstrosity."[23]

With dazzling technical facility, Shakespeare uses formal, pro-
sodic, and generic cross-blendings to symbolize the ambivalent sexuality that is the essence of this beautiful young man's character. The
poet's handling of the blazon evokes both English and French generic
strategies. The progressive anatomical catalogue is more usual in the
English blazon, whereas the *Blasons anatomiques du corps feminin*
more frequently celebrate a single part of the body. The rhetorical
manipulation of the catalogue in Sonnet 20 results in a poem that
nicely conforms to Schmidt's definition of the French *blason* as "a
series of repetitive verbal convergings on the given central object."[24]
Further, the tonal and attitudinal ambivalence of the sonnet suggests
an internal cooptation of the *contre blason,* a dispraise designed to
disgust or to provoke a moralistic attitude toward the body. The undercurrent of mockery set against the effusive, exaggerated praise
gives Sonnet 20 a tonality not unlike that in Niccolo Bellin da Mode-
na's celebrated bisexual portrait of Francis I. Despite the verses ex-
tolling the monarch as a god, the artist has grafted Francis's head on a
woman's body. This is not the transcendent Androgyne, but the effeminate Hermaphroditus—a comic monstrosity.[25]

Georgio Melchiori has analyzed the formal structure of Sonnet 20
in which the central lines 7 and 8 make the only references to *man*
while the surrounding lines describe *woman:* feminine without, mas-

---

23. On these conventions, see Amy Richlin, *The Garden of Priapus: Sexuality and
Aggression in Roman Humor* (New Haven: Yale University Press, 1983), 116–27; Delcourt, *Hermaphrodite,* 43.

24. D. B. Wilson, *Descriptive Poetry in France from Blason to Baroque* (Manchester:
Manchester University Press, 1967), 8.

25. As I argue in "The Bisexual Portrait of Francis I: Fontainebleau, Castiglione, and
the Tone of Courtly Mythology," *Playing with Gender: A Renaissance Pursuit,* ed. J. R.
Brink, M. C. Horowitz, and A. P. Coudert (Urbana: University of Illinois Press, 1991),
99–132.

culine within.[26] Similarly, the English "masculine lines" of the sonnet
are feminized by the use of feminine rime throughout, the only such
occurrence in the entire sequence. A fusion of identities occurs with
the hybridization of the sonnet itself. Because the sequence of argument so emphatically follows an octave-sestet pattern, the poem requires us at once to apprehend English and Italian sonnet modes.
Rosalie Colie's accounts of generic encoding might allow us to perceive that the Italian sonnet itself had come to symbolize the unattainable ideal beauty to whom it was so frequently addressed; that is,
the body of the sonnet represents the body of the beloved. The metaphor of text as human body, pervasive in the language of rhetorical
theory, extends easily from the notion of literary creativity as procreation and perpetuation: "Nor shall Death brag thou wand'rest in
his shade, / When in eternal lines to time thou grow'st" (Sonnet 18.
11–12).[27] More particularly, sixteenth-century critics were given
to contrasting the "masculine" and "feminine" genres of epic and
lyric.[28] For Petrarchists the identification between the body of the
poem and the body of the beloved would be something more than a
psychologically necessary substitution for the distant and disdainful
beauty. Since in a very direct sense she is the poet's creation, the sonnet has a greater reality and apprehensibility than its subject.[29]

Sonnet 20's disturbing juxtaposition of English and Italian, Latin
and French, masculine and feminine codes culminates with the closing couplet that delivers the "prick" of the epigram from which it
derives formally. At the same time, however, it is figuratively both the

26. *Shakespeare's Dramatic Meditations* (Oxford: Clarendon, 1976), 111–12.
27. For generic encoding, see especially Colie, *The Resources of Kind: Genre-Theory in the Renaissance* (Berkeley: University of California Press, 1973). The metaphor of text as body especially is pervasive in Montaigne. See Robert D. Cottrell, *Sexuality/Textuality: A Study of the Fabric of Montaigne's Essais* (Columbus: Ohio State University Press, 1981), especially 109, 127–28; and Lawrence D. Kritzman, *The Rhetoric of Sexuality and the Literature of the French Renaissance* (Cambridge: Cambridge University Press, 1991), 133–47.
28. See Paul Julian Smith, "Barthes, Gongora, and Non-Sense," *PMLA* 101 (1986): 84–86, for citations from Quintilian, Scaliger, Tasso, and others. Smith also quotes Fernando de Herrera (1580), contrasting the feminine vices of Italian style with the masculine virtues of Spanish style (85–86).
29. For a late, and therefore particularly clear, example, see Giambattista Marino's sonnet, "Seno," in *Amori*, introduction and notes by Alexandro Merlini, Biblioteca Universale Rizzoli (Milan: Rizzoli, 1982), 71; and Merlini's instructive commentary, 135–39. I owe this reference to Paolo Cherchi.

anatomical "prick" that it describes and the "tail" of the *sonetto cau-dato*.[30] In sixteenth-century usage, *coda, cauda,* and *tail* all had possible sexual meanings as either the male or female genitals; and in poetic usage of the "tailed" sonnet there was an obvious and frequent play on this correspondence—among others, by Aretino in his *Sonetti lussuriosi*—referring to the anatomical "tail" in the tail of the sonnet. The form of Sonnet 20 itself, thus, inscribes the figure of a woman with a penis.

In his magisterial study of *Cellini,* John Pope-Hennessy reflects on the difficulty of reconstructing sexual attitudes in a distant culture but risks a formulation: "Cinquecento life seems generally to have conformed to a bisexual norm." This obviously needs considerable qualification. But it does seem true that gender attitudes in sixteenth-century humanist, literary, and courtly circles largely were an adaptation of the Roman values projected to them through Latin literature, of which Paul Veyne offers this summary: "To be active was to be male, whatever the sex of the compliant partner. To take one's pleasure was virile, to accept it servile—that was the whole story." Looking at the couplet from the perspective of this active-passive/masculine-feminine paradigm, we find a passive young man "used," sexually exploited, by aggressively unfeminine women, yet himself potentially exploiting, actively "using" the love of the poet, who—like the creator, Mother Nature—"wrought thee" and "fell a-doting," thus switching from an active to a passive role, inverting the young man's pattern. "Mine be thy love, and thy love's use their treasure."[31]

The bisexuality of the beautiful young man itself may be a consequence of Nature creating in her own image. The poet's choice of pronoun designates Nature female, but he might expect us to know what we learn from sixteenth-century dictionaries: the word *nature*

30. For discussions of the interplay of sonnet and epigram, see Colie, *The Resources of Kind,* 67–75; and *Shakespeare's Living Art* (Princeton: Princeton University Press, 1974), 68–134. She is concerned with tones, however, rather than forms. On the *sonetto caudato,* see Leandro Biadane, *Morfologia del sonetto nei secoli XIII-XIV* (Florence: Casa editrice le lettere, 1977), 65–78; and Jean Dubu, "Le *sonetto caudato* de Michel-Ange à Milton," in *Le sonnet a la Renaissance,* ed. Yvonne Bellenger (Paris: Aux Amateurs de Livres, 1988), 111–18.
31. Pope-Henessy, *Cellini* (New York: Abbeville Press, 1985), 254. Veyne, "Homosexuality in Ancient Rome," in Philippe Ariès and Andre Bejin, eds., *Western Sexuality: Practice and Precept in Past and Present Times,* trans. Anthony Forster (Oxford: Basil Blackwell, 1985), 26–35; quotation, 29–30.

means the "membres of generacyon" (1538); "the privie members of man or beast" (1587); "the quaint of a woman, or privie parts of any man or beast" (1611). If I am correct in believing his myth is a subtext of the sonnet, it may be pertinent that Priapus is described as "Dio della Natura."[32] Nature's sexuality, therefore, may be as indeterminate as the young man's, and behind her, of course, lurks the poet whose own art outdoes nature. Charged with profoundly ambivalent eroticism to the end, the sonnet makes its provocative statement through the encoded sexual myths and amatory poetic genres, both high and low, of the culture from whence it comes.

As with another biform deity, Janus, Sonnet 20 looks to the future while looking to the past. Or, to stay within the pantheon already established in this essay, like Hermaphroditus, it has the power of presaging the future. Formally, it displays all the tendencies toward generic mixture and hybridization that Rosalie Colie found characteristic of seventeenth-century poetry. Conceptually, the sonnet is one milestone in the familiar descending journey by which the idealizations of Platonism and of mythology are accommodated to the realities of the human condition.[33] In its concern with deviant sexuality and its projection through literary kinds, Sonnet 20 holds its place in a larger movement in which the development of privacy inculcates development of erotic arts and literature.[34] The privatization of erotic desire in itself engenders a complex self-awareness of the constraints, and frequent conflicts, imposed by biological and socially defined sexual identity. Inevitably, this privatization and self-awareness help shape the discourses of desire throughout the following century.

32. See, s.v., Sir Thomas Elyot, *Dictionary* (1538); Thomas Thomas, *Dictionarium Linguae Latinae et Anglicanae* (1587); and John Florio, *Queen Anna's New World of Words* (1611). All conveniently have been reprinted in facsimile by Scolar Press (English Linguistics Series, nos. 221, 330, 105). See the descriptions of statues identified as Priapus by Clifford M. Brown, *Cesare Gonzaga and Gerolamo Garimberto: Two Renaissance Collectors of Greco-Roman Antiquities,* Garland Studies in the Renaissance (forthcoming).

33. For Hermaphroditus, Lauren Silberman complicates the choices, but does not alter the general pattern of development. See "Mythographic Transformations of Ovid's Hermaphrodite," *Sixteenth Century Journal* 19 (1988): 643–52.

34. See *A History of Private Life. Vol. 3: Passions of the Renaissance,* ed. Roger Chartier and trans. Arthur Goldhammer (Cambridge: Harvard University Press, 1989), especially 327–61, 363–93.

Mary Villeponteaux

Semper Eadem
Belphoebe's Denial of Desire

In July of 1596 Queen Elizabeth's Privy Council ordered all public officers to assist the Serjeant Painter in seeking out and destroying those portraits of the queen that were "to her great offense." The "vile copies" of one "ill Painting" that was confiscated provided the cooks at Essex "with Peels for the use of their Ovens" for several years. This act culminated more than thirty years of sporadic attempts on the part of the crown to control the production of images of the queen, attempts whose urgency increased as the great queen aged. By the 1590s the crown was actively promoting the simplified and formalized "Mask of Youth" developed by Nicholas Hilliard in which the queen's features, rather than being presented realistically, were "reduced to only a few schematic lines." But if Elizabeth desired such simplistic depiction of her person, obviously she did not demand equally spare settings, for royal portraits featured increasingly complex symbolism in the queen's dress and surroundings as Elizabeth's reign progressed. An obvious example is the Armada portrait, which shows Elizabeth holding the globe with an imperial crown above it. The attack of the English ships and the subsequent wreck of the Armada appear simultaneously behind her. Her fantastic costume, covered with pearls and ribbons, reflects her status as queen of beauty and exemplar of chastity. Roy Strong has identified the point in Elizabeth's reign when her portraits became elaborately allegorical: the first appeared in 1579.[1] Interestingly enough, this

1. *Gloriana: The Portraits of Queen Elizabeth* (London: Thames and Hudson, 1987),

was the year it became virtually certain that Elizabeth would never marry. Elizabeth was forty-six, so the hope that she might produce an heir was fading, but when she and the Duke of Alençon renewed their courtship in 1578, some people optimistically commented that the queen's good health and strong body might allow her still to bear children. The possibility of such a marriage had died by the end of 1579, however, killed by Parliamentary hesitation over approving a match (which was, realistically speaking, unlikely to produce children) between their queen and a Catholic. And it was during this time of fading hope for an appropriate match, the years immediately before and after 1580, when the ingredients of "the cult of the Virgin Queen" were very rapidly put together, even deliberately orchestrated, according to Strong.[2]

Thus we might connect some distinguishing features of Elizabeth's portraits painted after this period—simplistic, stylized facial representation and elaborate allegorical settings—with *the* distinguishing feature of her monarchy: she was an unmarried female ruler of a patriarchal society. By effacing her person and elaborating the symbolic setting in which she is placed, her portraits indicate a split between her natural body and political body: her person (natural body) recedes while her role as prince (her political body) emerges.[3]

In her rhetoric Elizabeth sometimes called attention to that division between her body natural and body politic: in speeches and proclamations she often represented her power in terms of masculine images and epithets. She called herself "prince" and, as she grew older and physically frailer, referred to herself with increasing frequency as "king."[4] She used androgynous language to palliate her subjects' dis-

---

147; quotation, 41. For the discussion of the destruction of the offensive portraits, see pp. 14–16.

2. J. E. Neale, *Queen Elizabeth I* (1934; reprint, Garden City: Doubleday, 1957), 243–53; Strong, *Gloriana,* 42; Allison Heisch identifies the eighties as the period during which the circulation of some of the queen's speeches also began to be carefully orchestrated. See "Queen Elizabeth I: Parliamentary Rhetoric and the Exercise of Power," *Signs: Journal of Women in Culture and Society* 1 (1975): 45.

3. See Ernst H. Kantorowicz for a detailed account of the complex philosophy of "the king's two bodies," the body natural and the body politic (*The King's Two Bodies: A Study in Mediaeval Political Theology* [Princeton: Princeton University Press, 1957]).

4. Leah S. Marcus, "Shakespeare's Comic Heroines, Elizabeth I, and the Political Uses of Androgyny," in *Women in the Middle Ages and the Renaissance: Literary and Historical Perspectives,* ed. Mary Beth Rose (Syracuse: Syracuse University Press, 1986), 140.

comfort with her femininity, as for example in the famous Tilbury speech on the occasion of the defeat of the Spanish Armada, when she declared, "I have the body of a weak and feeble woman, but I have the heart and stomach of a king."[5] However, even more pervasive than the masculine imagery she used to represent her power was the language of desire she and her courtiers used to represent their relationship. The language of courtly love and Petrarchism in particular prevailed in Elizabeth's court, as many scholars have observed: "she only" was the "queen of love and beauty," in the terms of a song by John Dowland; she was tantalizing object of desire; her courtiers frequently expressed their desire for political favor in terms of the Petrarchan lover's desire for sexual favor. The "political Petrarchism" of Elizabeth's court eroticized the terms of power, making Elizabethan political discourse a discourse of desire.

We might read *The Faerie Queene* as a portrait of Elizabeth that attempts to present, in the figure of Belphoebe, a "Mask of Youth" placed in a complex allegorical setting, thus enacting the same division between the queen's two bodies that Elizabeth's portraits seem to decree, and attempting to separate the discourses of erotic and political desire. Spenser articulates just such a split when he says,

> Ne let his fairest *Cynthia* refuse,
> In mirrours more then one her selfe to see,
> But either *Gloriana* let her chuse,
> Or in *Belphoebe* fashioned to bee:
> In th'one her rule, in th'other her rare chastitee.
> (3.proem.5.5–9)[6]

But this attempt deconstructs: Although Belphoebe is placed in opposition to Gloriana and thus Elizabeth's "rule," and although she supposedly represents Elizabeth's "chastity," a component of her body natural embodies also, quite clearly, Elizabeth's political power. The

5. Katharina M. Wilson, ed., *Women Writers of the Renaissance and Reformation* (Athens: University of Georgia Press, 1987), 542.

6. This and all further quotations from *The Faerie Queene* refer to A. C. Hamilton's edition (London: Longman, 1977).

idea of the king's two bodies must deconstruct in the case of the queen because her power is inseparable from her body. The doctrine of the king's two bodies asserts that the king's body politic, unlike his body natural, is "void of Infancy and old Age, and other natural Defects and Imbecilities." However, in Elizabeth's case, her body natural and its "defect" of femaleness became a potent symbol of her reign. Her virginity signifies the power she will not relinquish to a husband, and as Louis A. Montrose has also suggested, her inviolable "virgin knot" came to signify the inviolable security of the realm.[7] Furthermore, the unmarried queen's role of "cruel fair," the beloved object of her courtiers' desire, inscribes her body in the place of political favor and preferment. As various scholars have recently shown, Elizabeth's courtiers frequently represented their literal desire for any number of favors (audience, payment, preferment, and so on) in terms of a lover's desire for his beloved, thus posing the reverse possibility: that we might read texts that appear to describe dramas of erotic desire as texts about political desire.[8] That the "forms are doubled" has become a familiar idea, but the doubling of the erotic and political engenders certain problems and paradoxes that need further scrutiny. One casualty of the doubling I've already mentioned—the deconstruction of the queen's two bodies. Reading Spenser's Belphoebe, we can identify other problems caused by the merging of the political and the erotic. Belphoebe's role seems to suggest a specific and powerful paradox that underlies Elizabeth's eroticization of political power—a contradiction in the terms of desire. Belphoebe's pres-

7. Edmund Plowden's *Commentaries or Reports,* collected and written under Queen Elizabeth (London, 1816), quoted in Kantorowicz, *The King's Two Bodies,* 7; Montrose, "The Elizabethan Subject and the Spenserian Text," in *Literary Theory/Renaissance Texts,* ed. Patricia Parker and David Quint (Baltimore: Johns Hopkins University Press, 1986), 315. The political Petrarchism of Elizabeth's court has been the subject of much recent critical discussion, some of it centered on the question of who controlled the queen's representation. Montrose sees Elizabeth as "more the creature of the Elizabethan image than she was its creator" (310). He also discusses the male subject's anxiety about the fact that the female/other is in the place of authority. I want to elaborate on this insight and examine specifically some paradoxical elements in Elizabeth's (and Belphoebe's) stance that produce male anxiety.

8. See, for instance, Arthur Marotti's "'Love Is Not Love': Elizabethan Sonnet Sequences and the Social Order," *English Literary History* 49 (1982): 396–428.

ence both demands desire and forbids it, as does Elizabeth's, and in both political and psychosexual terms, this denial of desire has disturbing implications for Elizabeth's male subjects, just as it does for Belphoebe's devoted squire, Timias.

Like Elizabeth's, Belphoebe's is the body natural made public icon: her beauty is an object of regard for the male characters and the male poet as well. At her first appearance in the poem the poet describes her in superhuman terms and in closer detail than he does any other woman in *The Faerie Queene:*

> Her face so faire as flesh it seemed not,
> But heauenly pourtraict of bright Angels hew,
> Cleare as the skie, withouten blame or blot,
> Through goodly mixture of complexions dew;
> And in her cheekes the vermeill red did shew
> Like roses in a bed of lillies shed,
> The which ambrosiall odours from them threw,
> And gazers sense with double pleasure fed,
> Hable to heale the sick, and to reuiue the ded.
> (2.3.22)

The poet flatters the queen with this Petrarchan depiction of Belphoebe's face as both flower bed and holy angel's visage. The elaborate blazon that follows—nine stanzas of physical description—befits this Diana figure. But as Judith H. Anderson and more recently Maureen Quilligan have suggested, there is more to Spenser's portrayal of Belphoebe than this surface flattery. Anderson finds a warning in this portrayal—a warning about the dangers and costs of queenly power. Quilligan has suggested that Spenser accommodates that power by using comedy to distance (and even dismantle) the implicit threat Belphoebe, as a shadow of the queen, imposes. I find their respective accounts of Belphoebe convincing but incomplete, since Spenser's portrayal of the virgin huntress seems to me significantly more negative than either of these critics suggests. According to my reading, Belphoebe embodies not just a warning but outright censure, nor is she successfully distanced through comedy, but rather she permanently looms as a threatening and emasculating force.[9]

When Belphoebe confronts the surprised Braggadocchio, her relationship to Diana becomes apparent, and at the same time the implicitly threatening quality of her presence begins to surface, for the episode contains allusions to the myth of Actaeon. Trompart and Braggadocchio are a broadly comic parody of Actaeon and his companion hunters: the two "knights," far from boldly hunting in the forest, are in fact creeping along in terror at every rustle of a leaf or whistle of the wind. But when they encounter Belphoebe, she is hunting, searching for a wounded hind she has shot. Trompart speaks to her first because Braggadocchio, the coward, hearing her approach, hides in the bushes. When Belphoebe sees the bush in which he is hiding move, she assumes she has found her hind and aims an arrow into its leaves. The case of mistaken identity suggests a relationship between Braggadocchio and a hunted stag, a relationship that recalls Actaeon, particularly since both have chanced upon Belphoebe in the woods. And although Belphoebe is not bathing as was Diana when Actaeon saw her, Braggadocchio's subsequent clumsy, lustful lunge at Belphoebe puts him in the same category as Actaeon, who is usually understood to have had a licentious motive for spying on Diana.[10]

Nancy J. Vickers in her famous essay "Diana Described" analyzes the connection between the Actaeon myth and the Petrarchan blazon that is suggested in the *Rime sparse:* she reads the blazon, the enumeration and description of the woman's body parts, as a dismemberment of the woman in response to her perceived power to dismember the man who views her (just as Actaeon is torn apart after he watches Diana bathing). The threat inherent in a feminine totality that is different, essentially other to the male, is neutralized through this "descriptive dismemberment." That such an implicit threat exists in Belphoebe is believable for many reasons, including her allegorical dimension as

9. Anderson, "'In liuing colours and right hew': The Queen of Spenser's Central Books," in *Poetic Traditions of the English Renaissance,* ed. Maynard Mack and George deForest Lord (New Haven: Yale University Press, 1982), 47–66; Quilligan, "The Comedy of Female Authority in *The Faerie Queene," English Literary Renaissance* 17 (1987): 156–71.

10. According to Leonard Barkan in "Diana and Actaeon: The Myth as Synthesis," the most widespread version of this myth explains Actaeon's motive for watching Diana as "intentional voyeurism" (*English Literary Renaissance* 10 [1980]: 317–59).

Elizabeth's avatar, since the queen has actual power of dismemberment over her subjects.[11]

Thus Belphoebe may be a more menacing figure than she first appears, embodying as she does a feminine power with a threatening
analogue in real life. Indeed, Spenser specifically paints Belphoebe's
power as Amazonian. Belphoebe is a warrior-huntress who is clearly
(though never overtly) linked to the cruel and emasculating Amazon
Radigund. Both wear traditional Amazonian attire of buskins and
camus, and Spenser also compares Belphoebe to Penthesilia in the
simile that Harry Berger, Jr., finds conspicuously irrelevant. The Amazon of legend was sometimes used in popular writing to represent
Queen Elizabeth, although she herself never drew this comparison.
In book 3 when Spenser praises the women of antiquity he avoids the
comparison as well, setting Britomart and Elizabeth apart from Penthesilia, mentioning them in the same stanza but clearly distancing
his knight and his queen from the Amazon who helped to defend
Troy in battle (3.4.2–3). Yet he does not hesitate to describe Belphoebe in these terms; even more interesting, he focuses on Penthesilia's death rather than her triumph in his simile:

> Or as that famous Queene
> Of *Amazons,* whom *Pyrrhus* did destroy,
> The day that first of *Priame* she was seene,
> Did shew her selfe in great triumphant ioy,
> To succour the weake state of sad afflicted *Troy.*
> (2.3.31.5–9)

The story of Penthesilia's death has several versions, but in one she is
killed by Pyrrhus, the cruel son of Achilles, while in most other stories
she is reported to have been killed by Achilles himself, who then un-
laced her helmet, saw her beauty revealed, and wept with regret that
he had killed her. In still other versions Achilles cannot bring himself
to kill her after he sees her beauty revealed. I suggest that this allusion to Penthesilia's death here at Belphoebe's introduction is not

11. "Diana Described: Scattered Woman and Scattered Rhyme," in *Writing and Sexual Difference,* ed. Elizabeth Abel (Chicago: University of Chicago Press, 1982), 95–
109.

irrelevant but foreshadows the moments in books 4 and 5 when Arthegall will be defeated by the beauty of an Amazon: first by Britomart, whom Spenser hesitates to link directly to the Amazons and who in fact does not defeat Arthegall per se when he is stunned by her beauty. Rather, theirs is a mutual inability to continue the fight, and if anything it is she who is captive to him after he "brings her to bay" at the end of their courtship. It is Radigund's story that most clearly echoes Penthesilia's: Arthegall knocks her down in battle and is prepared to administer the final blow when, removing her helmet, he sees her face. Her beauty unmans him and he becomes her captive. The same story, or some version of it, is suggested in Spenser's initial description of Belphoebe, thus linking her to Radigund, who represents the "monstrous regiment" of women who have "shaken off the shamefast band, / With which wise Nature did them strongly bynd" (5.5.25.2–3).[12]

Along with Belphoebe's connection to Radigund, there is also a certain obduracy that Spenser depicts and sometimes seems to condemn in Belphoebe. As Amoret's twin, she exemplifies the opposite of Amoret's vulnerability: Belphoebe's impermeable body is a fortress; the counterpart of Amoret's gaping wound in Belphoebe's history is the ruby cut in the shape of a bleeding heart.[13] Even at the moment when Belphoebe first discovers and pities the wounded Timias, Spenser hints that despite this momentary experience of tenderness, Belphoebe's heart is normally hard. After describing Timias's pathetic condition in detail, the poet comments, "Saw neuer liuing eye more heauy sight, / That could haue made a rocke of stone to rew," and then a moment later he reports that on seeing the dying Timias Belphoebe grew "full of soft passion and vnwonted smart: / The point of pitty perced through her tender hart" (3.4.30.1–2 and 8–9).

---

12. Berger, *The Allegorical Temper: Vision and Reality in Book II of Spenser's Faerie Queene* (New Haven: Yale University Press, 1957), 123–32. Berger concludes that the apparently irrelevant reference to Penthesilia brings the death and war of human history into an otherwise completely mythological picture, enriching the texture of Belphoebe's description and refracting the poem's central issues onto her image. James Nohrnberg, *The Analogy of* The Faerie Queene (Princeton: Princeton University Press, 1976), 451. The story that *Pyrrhus* killed Penthesilia Hamilton ascribes to "popular legend," and Berger ascribes to Caxton's translation, *The Recuyell of the Historyes of Troye*.

13. Judith Anderson describes the ruby that leads Belphoebe to Timias as "a jeweler's replica of Amoret's heart in the Masque of Cupid" ("The Queen of Spenser's Central Books," 59).

Not only is the pain she feels "unwonted," that is, both unusual and unwanted, but there is also a submerged comparison between her heart and "a rocke of stone" along with the overt description of her heart as "tender."

Nancy Vickers discusses the Actaeon myth as a parable of the male's fear of the female's exposed body and its vulnerability, but in Belphoebe such exposed vulnerability never occurs. Vickers reads in the story of Actaeon a reference to incest and transgression: the myth evokes the powerless male child's fear at the sight of the powerful and forbidden woman—the mother—who also, when viewed, appears to lack body parts he has and so suggests the possibility of castration. The difference between that primal mother-figure and Belphoebe is that the actual body of the mother and Diana's body in the Actaeon myth are exposed; the body of Belphoebe remains a secret "enviously" guarded. The resonant image connected with Belphoebe is the rose carefully closing up its "silken leaves" in self-defense. But this withholding of body and emotion carries its own dangers. In Vickers's Freudian account of the male's traumatic encounter with the exposed woman's body, it becomes apparent that this moment is also necessary in order for desire to exist. Petrarch's poems focus on the remembered image, try and fail, ultimately, to "transmute it into an idol that can be forever possessed"—but the transgression, the seeing, is the necessary prelude to the loss that creates desire and fuels the poems. Belphoebe is never exposed to any man's eye; she controls her own heart and protects herself from vulnerability. Unlike Florimel, for instance, who is vulnerable, pursued, and finally, literally, iconized by the witch and her son, Belphoebe is an icon of her own volition. She seems to choose invulnerable perfection, a "Mask of Youth," rather than the body natural that in a woman's case is the "weaker vessel" to which the queen alluded in her speech at Tilbury.[14]

The subsuming of Queen Elizabeth's body natural into the rigid representation of her body politic might have unexpected repercussions in her subjects, in part because her sexual identity, conceived of as specifically feminine (with all that term implies for the Elizabethans), was an important component of their response to her.[15] Thus

14. "Diana Described," 103, 105.
15. Susanne Lindgren Wofford makes a connection between the queen's authority

we return to the implications of the language of desire that Elizabeth and her courtiers used. The Petrarchism of the Elizabethan court placed her in the position of desirable yet unobtainable lady, as did to a lesser extent the various goddess names applied to her (Diana, Phoebe, Cynthia). However, although tradition depicts such figures as Petrarch's Laura and the goddess of the moon as unobtainable, in fact it is clear that Elizabeth's subjects did regard their desires as in part obtainable through the manipulation of Petrarchan discourse. Elizabeth's courtiers used Petrarchan language to describe their very real attempts to gain favor, patronage, and preferment. An extreme example of the actual and pressing hope that might lie behind the Petrarchan mode of address may be found in Essex's letter to Elizabeth on September 6, 1600, a letter written from custody begging for audience. "Haste, paper, to that happy presence, whence only unhappy I am banished! Kiss that fair correcting hand," he wrote in an echo of Petrarch's "Ite, caldi sospiri, al freddo core!" (Go, burning sighs, to that cold bosom!)[16] He may be consciously or unconsciously echoing Petrarch here, but the hope (ultimately fruitless) that his Laura will fulfill his desire presses more urgently than Petrarch's hopes ever did.

The actual expectations that lie behind much of the Petrarchism in the Elizabethan court undercut the traditional Petrarchan formula in which the lady is—must be—unobtainable; just as absence is the prerequisite for desire, so on the level of plot the lady's "cold chastity" enables the poet's tortured, unrequited love and makes the sequence possible. However, as has often been noted, the abject position of the lover within the Petrarchan fiction is itself a fiction, since as the author the lover is actually controlling the sequence. No such underlying concession to male power exists in Elizabeth's court, and further-

---

and a feminine interiority that she finds in some characters in *The Faerie Queene*. She suggests that one anxiety underlying book 3 involves the poet's desire to represent this interior virtue without reifying and thus distorting it. Our readings share some of the same concerns but reach different conclusions, in that my focus is on the way Belphoebe exemplifies the anxieties and distortions resulting from a reification that the queen seems to have encouraged in her self-representation ("Gendering Allegory: Spenser's Bold Reader and the Emergence of Character in *The Faerie Queene* 3," *Criticism* 30 [1988]: 1–21).

16. Leonard Forster provides this example in *The Icy Fire: Five Studies in European Petrarchism* (Cambridge: Cambridge University Press, 1969), 141.

more, the patriarchal understanding of sexual roles demands that man's desire be answerable, ultimately, by female submission. Louis A. Montrose has discussed a dream recorded in the 1597 diary of Simon Forman, physician and astrologer, that suggests the way that Elizabeth's subjects' desire can take such a traditional sexual form. Forman dreamed of walking through the lanes of London in the company of the queen; he awakened just as she was becoming "very familiar" with him and seemed to "begin to love" him. Montrose shows how the dream reveals "mother, mistress, and monarch" present in the one figure, the queen, and desire for that figure is expressed, both in the terms of political and sexual desire, in the pun "to wait upon." Forman asks the queen if he may "wait on her" but then says, "I mean to wait *upon* you and not under you, that I might make this belly a little bigger." In Montrose's words, "the subject's desire for employment (to *wait* upon) coexists with his desire for mastery (to *weight* upon)."[17] Montrose uses the dream to show the doublings of political and sexual forms in Elizabethan culture—to suggest the way in which, under Elizabeth, the sexual and political are inextricably intertwined. But a further aspect of Forman's dream worth mentioning is the way in which the sexual character of his relationship with his queen is given primacy. Yes, the figure in the dream is *identified* by Forman in his diary as the queen, and the fact that she is old might identify her as a maternal figure. But most of the action of the dream depicts a sexual relationship between the two: the dreamer's jealousy when another man embraces her, his attempts to get her away and have her to himself, his sexual punning, and eventually (at the end of the dream) their dalliance as she becomes "familiar" with him. That the subject's desire for the queen has a strong sexual component or is expressed, at least unconsciously, in a clearly sexual language, along with our understanding that the political Petrarchism of Elizabeth's court bespeaks real desire for real preferment, provides us with a shift in focus when reading Spenser's Belphoebe. Perhaps Belphoebe is a threat not, like Diana, because of what she exposes, but rather because of what she keeps hidden.

17. "*A Midsummer Night's Dream* and the Shaping Fantasies of Elizabethan Culture: Gender, Power, Form," in *Rewriting the Renaissance: The Discourses of Sexual Difference in Early Modern Europe,* ed. Margaret W. Ferguson, Maureen Quilligan, and Nancy J. Vickers (Chicago: University of Chicago Press, 1986), 65–87; see also 65–68.

Belphoebe neither allows nor admits sexual desire: Spenser makes that very clear in her involvement with Timias, Arthur's squire. After she rescues him when he lies dying from wounds received in a fight with three foresters, he falls in love with her. Recovering from his physical wounds, he begins to waste away as a result of emotional wounds, the wounds of love he suffers in the presence of Belphoebe:

> O foolish Physick, and vnfruitful paine,
> That heales vp one and makes another wound:
> She his hurt thigh to him recur'd againe,
> But hurt his hart, the which before was sound.
>
> (3.5.42.1–4)

The poet implicitly criticizes Belphoebe for her "foolish physick," since she is the physician who both heals and wounds Timias.[18] Not only does Belphoebe fail to respond to Timias's love, but she does not even recognize the nature of his "malady," worrying rather that the original wound has failed to heal. Furthermore, the poet suggests that even had she understood that he loved her, she would not or could not have provided relief and fulfilled his desire:

> Many Restoratiues of vertues rare,
> And costly Cordialles she did apply,
> To mitigate his stubborne mallady:
> But that sweet Cordiall, which can restore
> A loue-sick hart, she did to him enuy;
> To him, and to all th'vnworthy world forlore
> She did enuy that soueraigne salue, in secret store.
>
> (3.5.50.3–9)

The choice of the word *envy* is telling here, implying as it does greed, a hoarding instinct rather than the virtue Spenser is supposedly praising in Belphoebe. The entire passage, which continues for six stanzas, while it seems a paean of praise for Belphoebe (and by analogy, for Eliz-

---

18. Judith Anderson points out another such implied criticism in the line (3.5.43.3), "Madnesse to saue a part, and lose the whole" ("The Queen of Spenser's Central Books," 52).

abeth's virginity), in fact subverts its own praise through the language used to depict Belphoebe's "fresh flowring Maidenhead" (3.5.54.6).

Belphoebe's virginity is in this passage suggested by the rose that she tenders "more deare then life"; she hides this flower from any threat, "lapped vp her silken leaues most chaire, / When so the froward skye began to lowre" (3.5.51.6–7). This rose, like the "sweet Cordiall" that could restore Timias, is withheld by Belphoebe, guarded "enviously" in the earlier stanza and "charily" here. Furthermore, all women are advised to embellish their beauty with this rose of virginity:

> To youre faire selues a faire ensample frame,
> Of this faire virgin, this *Belphoebe* faire,
> To whom in perfect loue, and spotlesse fame
> Of chastitie, none liuing may compaire:
> Ne poysnous Enuy iustly can empaire
> The prayse of her fresh flowring Maidenhead;
> For thy she standeth on the highest staire
> Of th'honorable stage of womanhead,
> That Ladies all may follow her ensample dead.
>   (3.5.54)

Several phrases and words used in this stanza are striking. The tone of the first two lines, with their emphasis on the adjective "fair," is difficult to identify. Judith Anderson finds it "insistent, even anxiously so" but also finds a logical reason for the repetition: to create a sense of the links between a series of steps, from fair ladies, to a generalized fair example, to the more exclusive form of virginity, and finally to Belphoebe herself.[19] Certainly she accurately describes the "steps" in this equation, and indeed Belphoebe's position on the highest stair is noteworthy for several reasons, among them the problematic connection thus implied between the kinds of chastity exemplified by the knight of chastity herself and the virgin huntress. If Belphoebe's virginity stands "on the highest staire," are we to understand that Britomart's movement toward holy matrimony is deficient, a somewhat lesser version of chastity? This would have to be our understanding of the matter if it were not for the fact that Spenser so care-

19. Ibid., 54.

fully undercuts all the praise he heaps with equal care on Belphoebe, his queen's avatar. Her position on the highest stair begins to totter if we hear an echo from *Amoretti* 58 in which the poet reminds his "proud fayre" that "he that standeth on the hyghest stayre / Fals lowest" (11–13). And to return to that troublesome "faire" in stanza 54: the link between the fair ladies whom Spenser addresses and Belphoebe, his paragon, is clear without a fourfold repetition of the word. I think we can also hear the hint of parody in the repetition of "faire," much as we can in Sidney's "With so sweete voice, and by sweete Nature so / In sweetest strength, so sweetly skild withall, / In all sweete stratagems, sweete Arte can show" (*Astrophil and Stella* 36, ll. 9–11). Both examples call attention to their own rhetoricity in a way that suggests a parody of the rhetoric of praise.

Another interesting thing about this stanza is the ambiguity surrounding the phrases "none liuing may compaire" and "follow her ensample dead." As Judith Anderson has shown, although Belphoebe's "ensample dead" refers to her example that will live on after her death, it may also suggest that her example, specifically her virginal example, *is* dead. Perhaps "none living" may compare to her because the example she sets better fits some otherworldly realm than it does human life on earth. Spenser's use of Penthesilia dead, rather than Penthesilia alive and fighting, for his simile at Belphoebe's introduction in book 2 strikes a similar note: Belphoebe is a lifeless rather than a vital figure. To take this analysis a step further, if all living ladies did follow Belphoebe's example, death would indeed be the result since procreation would stop. Such a reading may seem to veer into the ridiculously literal until we consider the placement of the stanza in question, which is at the very end of canto 5 and leads into the famous Garden of Adonis episode. The Garden of Adonis, seminary of all life, is carefully placed at the midpoint of book 3, a placement that indicates the importance of the fruits of sexuality to Spenser's understanding of chastity.

According to Anderson, "Spenser saw . . . clearly the temporal, human cost—to Belphoebe and Timias both—of the fully realized Petrarchan vision"—that is, the vision of the eternally unobtainable lady pursued eternally by her lover.[20] However, his treatment of Bel-

20. Ibid., 58.

phoebe seems to me far from sympathetic. The "cost" to Belphoebe of fulfilling the role of goddess-Petrarchan lady is not readily apparent; the cost to Timias is. By maintaining her impervious surface, Belphoebe loses nothing that she seems to desire. Timias, on the other hand, loses everything, including his vocation as Arthur's squire, in order to serve the object of his adoration who yet "envies" him the "soveraigne salve" of her love. Interestingly, later in the same passage, Spenser echoes his earlier choice of the word *envy* to describe Belphoebe's attitude toward her virginity: now he asserts, "Ne poysnous Enuy iustly can empaire / The prayse of her fresh flowring Maidenhead" (3.5.54.5–6). "Envy" is now "poisonous," closer to the "hatefull hellish snake" jealousy of canto 11 than to the "envy" that suggests guardianship. In fact, the former version of envy will characterize Belphoebe more accurately as we move into book 4 and find her turning on Timias because of his supposed unfaithfulness. Timias himself inadvertently wounds Amoret while trying to rescue her from Lust; then his attempts to comfort her lead to further disaster when Belphoebe finds him kissing her. The squire's service of his beloved seems only to embroil both himself and others in difficulties rather than producing the fruits of heroic deeds. Belphoebe is filled "with deepe disdaine, and great indignity" at the sight of Timias and Amoret together and considers killing them both, but contents herself with turning her face away from Timias after one oblique accusation ("Is this the faith") and fleeing away "for euermore" (4.7.36). Now the "envy" with which Belphoebe guarded her virginity in book 3 might occur to us in another context, although Spenser never uses the word again in relation to the virgin huntress. But certainly it is strange that Belphoebe, who could not even recognize a love so powerful that it was killing poor Timias in book 3, is quick to assume that the worst possible kind of "love" is being expressed in Timias's behavior toward Amoret in book 4. The recognizable historical allegory makes sense of this contradiction, at least in part: from his first appearance in relationship to Belphoebe, Timias clearly represents Sir Walter Raleigh (notice the reference to "diuine Tobacco" among Belphoebe's medicinal herbs in 3.5.32), and the episode involving Amoret is understood to allude to Elizabeth's banishment of Raleigh after he impregnated a lady of the court, Elizabeth Throckmorton, whom he married soon after. Elizabeth's "jealousy" of her court ladies who married her courtiers is legendary, and it is sometimes, although by no means universally, assumed that her anger at courtiers and ladies who became sexually involved with one another was motivated by her envy.[21]

Thus Belphoebe, and Elizabeth by implication, forbids desire not only for herself but for others as well. This power to forbid and deny is the focus in both episodes involving Timias, and both narratives detail his suffering, first because of his unrequited love for her, and then because of her rejection resulting from his supposed desire for Amoret. After Belphoebe leaves him in book 4 he becomes a wild hermit, completely solitary and silent, his hair long and matted, and his clothes torn to tatters. When Arthur encounters him in the woods he fails to recognize his erstwhile squire, and Timias does not enlighten him. Apparently, Elizabeth's power to deny, withhold, yet fatally attract leads to a silencing and emasculation of her courtiers: that is at least one way to understand Timias, who as a silent, dispossessed recluse has abandoned his noble calling of chivalry and the service of his lord. After Timias is reconciled to Belphoebe through the agency of the ruby shaped like a bleeding heart, these are the last words with which Spenser describes him in book 4:

> And eke all mindlesse of his owne deare Lord
> The noble Prince, who neuer heard one word
> Of tydings, what did vnto him betide,
> Of what good fortune did to him afford,
> But through the endlesse world did wander wide,
> Him seeking euermore, yet no where him describe.
> (4.8.18.4–9)

Timias may have regained Belphoebe's favor, but the poet does not appear to smile on this enterprise; in book 4 the last word on Timias is close to censure.

Spenser's depiction of Belphoebe suggests that Elizabeth's motto, *semper eadem,* contains an implicit threat because ultimately it does not permit male desire. Elizabeth is "always the same," an obdurate presence, the body natural of a woman transformed into an immutable public presence. Belphoebe's essence is power, particularly the

---

21. This allusion was first noted by J. Upton in his 1758 edition of *The Faerie Queene.*

power to resist, withhold, and remain the same. She will not, as Brito-mart did in Isis Church when she begins to grow great with child, bear the sign of male potency: she will not accommodate that desire as expressed in her subject's dream and let a male subject make his mark upon her body. The most Belphoebe "bears" is a sign of pity; it is Timias who bears the sign, the change, to the point that he is deformed and unrecognizable to the one who should properly be his master. Elizabeth's power is also in part the power to resist: Spenser appears to characterize her virginity as an "envious" withholding and to display an anxiety about her power to resist the desires of her courtiers. Elizabeth, like Belphoebe, exists outside the realm of ordi-nary human desires, and so she is outside of the realm of male power. Hilliard's "Mask of Youth," which reduces her features to a few sche-matic lines, renders her body natural always the same. That mask also suggests the way in which her body natural becomes an impor-tant component in the representation of her body politic, just as the language of erotic desire becomes an important part of the discourse of political relations in her court. As Spenser's portrait of Belphoebe suggests, such "political Petrarchism" poses a threat to masculine power. When the queen's body natural is reified, becoming an icon of the state, then within the discourse of eroticism she recedes beyond the reach of very real demands for favor and preferment. Such a po-sition attenuates both the immediacy of her human presence and the possibility of desire as well.

William Shullenberger

Love as a Spectator Sport in John Donne's Poetry

Because Donne seems to wish to banish from his amatory poems all the world excluded by the charmed circle of the lovers' arms, it is surprising how frequently he populates the poems with an observing third party. Donne seems to acknowledge something in the dynamic of desire that requires triangulation, the insertion of a potentially disruptive outsider in a love scenario hopefully scripted for two. A busy old fool, the unruly sun interrupts the lovers' sleepy waking rapture and occasions the petulant aubade of "The Sunne Rising." "The Canonization" develops the theme of love as sacred mystery, with the lovers as sacred types and intercessors, out of an initially direct and flustered defensive address to an unsympathetic interloper. "The Perfume" unfolds as a high stakes domestic intrigue, as the lovers, hemmed in on all sides by suspicious family and hireling spies, stealthily pursue forbidden courtship. Even poems that reach toward the most exalted and intimate expressions of love imply observers. A sense of the world watching conditions the advice of restraint and trust that the poet whispers to his beloved in "A Valediction: forbidding Mourning." The poet initially proposes that the lovers' parting is like a holy death scene in which the two lovers, represented as a "virtuous man" and his soul, are surrounded by confused sad friends (1–4). Histrionics of separation would give the holy secret of love away: "'Twere prophanation of our joyes / To tell the layetie our love" (7–8). In "The Exstasie," the poet imagines a hypothetical witness to the mystic and sepulchral stillness of the lovers' interinanimation; this

46

witness would be one "so by love refin'd / That he soules language understood, / And by good love were grown all minde" (21–23). The poet introjects this phantom acolyte at the moment when the poem's argument shifts from a physical to a metaphysical account of the ecstatic union, and reminds us of his screening and framing presence in the final stanza when the poet hopes to signal a move from ecstatic immobility to bodily presence and body language (73–76).[1]

Even the grave is not, for Donne's lovers, a fine and private place. "The Relique" depends upon the grave's being broken up, and the bracelet of bright hair signifies the lovers' union as having been salvaged from death as a relic worthy of spiritual devotion. The thought of death or of absence permits Donne's speaking voice a shift of position in the erotic triangle. He seems to take a particular cynical delight in projecting himself into the place of the third party, gaining paradoxically in spectral power by assuming the spectatorial role in witnessing his lover's faithlessness. In "A Valediction: of my Name in the Window," the inscription of the poet's name serves not only as a mnemonic focus for the beloved's thoughts of the poet after his real (or imagined) death but as proxy for the poet himself, installing the poet as an overseeing presence in the lover's conscience, thus effectively prohibiting any displacement of him in her affection. "The Apparition" brings the figure of the erotic spectator into chilling focus, as the poet imagines himself like some grim reaper rising from the dead to witness and to haunt the afterglow of his "murderous" mistress's faithless intercourse, and to terrify her into repentance.

What are we to make of the repeated intervention of a third party in the work of a poet who longs for a kind of absolute privacy in which "nothing else is" ("The Sunne Rising," 22), in which love "all love of other sights controules, / And makes one little roome, an every where" ("The Good-morrow," 10–11)? To say that Donne's poetry contains a strong voyeuristic component, which is frequently figured in the erotic spectator, is a critical truth more complicated than it initially seems. At the outset, let me try to defuse the contro-

---

1. All citations from Donne's love poetry in this essay are taken from John Donne, *The Elegies and the Songs and Sonnets,* ed. Helen Gardner (Oxford: Clarendon Press, 1965). All citations from his religious poetry are taken from John Donne, *The Divine Poems,* ed. Helen Gardner (Oxford: Clarendon Press, 1952). Poem titles and line numbers will be cited parenthetically in the text.

versy that might be generated by my employment of the concept of voyeurism, by stressing that I intend nothing morally or psychologically reductive by it. The eye is no doubt an element in forms of erotic activity that would hardly be called perverse and is certainly an element in representations of love prior to Donne's in medieval and Renaissance love lyric. The aubade tradition, for instance, to which we can relate "The Sunne Rising" and "The Good-morrow," depends frequently for its drama and its humor on an outsider who serves the lovers as a lookout. Ovid and Petrarch create paradigmatic narratives of desire that foreground seeing as both a potential threat and an instrument of imaginative and erotic control.[2] A longer essay would situate Donne's poetry in relation to the voyeuristic elements in prior Renaissance verbal and visual representations of the act and art of love. For now, I wish to call attention to the specific and characteristic ways in which Donne creates a visual field in his amatory poetry and stations an observer in relation to it. In order to understand this voyeuristic component, we need to study the way in which the activity of seeing, represented so frequently by the incursion of a third party, operates in the poetry as a social, psychological, and aesthetic phenomenon: socially, as an index of the conditions under which love could be made in the late Elizabethan and early Jacobean household; psychologically, as an expression of Donne's anxiety about being watched and longing to be watched; and aesthetically, as a way of implicating the reader and the act of reading in the poem.

The obsessive and metadramatic variations on spying scenes in Jacobean drama remind us of a social fact that conditions the dramatic structure of Donne's poems: in Jacobean living quarters, privacy was hard to come by, and making love in the interconnected semipublic rooms would be a problematic adventure fraught with suspicion, hesitation, and fear of the abrupt impingement of others. Architectural design reinforced a social structure that inhibited the expression of and satisfaction of private longing:

2. My colleague Wolfgang Spitzer of Sarah Lawrence College has provided insight and information on Donne's roots in the traditions of European love lyric. Nancy Vickers discerns the inversion of the myth of Actaeon in the poet-voyeur of the Petrarchan legacy in "Diana Described: Scattered Women and Scattered Rhyme," *Writing and Sexual Difference,* ed. Elizabeth Abel (Chicago: University of Chicago Press, 1982), 95–110.

The great houses of the fifteenth and sixteenth centuries had been constructed of interlocking suites of rooms without corridors, so that the only way of moving about was by passing through other people's chambers. . . . Always, at all times of day or night, servants were spying through cracks in the wainscoting, peering through keyholes, listening at doors to hear the rhythmic creaking of beds, and carefully inspecting the bed-linen for tell-tale stains.[3]

Replete with "seely plots, and pensionary spies," the crowded and suspicious households of the elegies, "The Perfume" and "Jealosie," are more a product of such social and architectural conditions than of a paranoid libertine imagination ("Jealosie," 32). Donne's positioning of outsiders anywhere from the remote periphery to the center of the poet's attention in the love scenario may be taken as an aspect of his realism, his imaginative registration of a social fact.

This persistent sense of social intrusiveness motivates his longing for a world elsewhere, an erotic paradise that obliterates all externals and bends time and space to its demand for pleasure. This may account for the repeated fantasy of royal power—"She'is all States, and all Princes, I, / Nothing else is" ("The Sunne Rising," 21–22)—a wish for the social authority to command a private space, or at least to be immune to the gaze of those attending. The space of writing, the poem, the "pretty roome" of a sonnet provides such a space, indeed the only pure space available ("The Canonization," 32). Yet Donne's realism grounds and hedges in his longing, preventing the formation of a romantic fantasy world at the expense of other social claims that exist in apparent contradiction to it. Donne's love poems, then, may be taken as early steps in the formation of a modern concept of privacy. They yearn for the private sphere of a totalizing sexual love that the culture has not yet invented; so the sublimity of love's potential self-absorption and self-completion is never completely cloistered from the intrusions of the sun, the racket of schoolboys and prentices, the well-meaning advice of friends, the stealth and abruptness of curious siblings, the threat of jealous husbands and fathers and eight-foot-

3. Lawrence Stone, *The Family, Sex and Marriage in England, 1500–1800*, Abridged Edition (New York: Harper & Row, 1979), 169–70. John Carey relates Donne's concerns about social intrusion to the tension and suspicion generated by Elizabethan tactics to enforce religious conformity (*John Donne: Life, Mind, and Art* [New York: Oxford University Press, 1981], esp. chap. 1, "Apostasy").

high iron-bound servingmen, or even the clownish protocols of the gravedigger.[4]

Donne responds to the experience of social infringement upon the amatory scene in several ways. One is to invoke the pressure and suspicion of others in order to heighten erotic suspense. In the game of erotic wit, the prospect of being caught adds to the adventure, as in "The Perfume" and "Jealosie," and a sense of being watched can intensify the erotic bravado. Second, like Freud's typical dreamer who absorbs and transforms intrusive external stimuli in the dream fabric, Donne assigns the intruder a role in the unfolding erotic scenario.[5] The busy old fool of a sun becomes first a scout for the lovers, keeping them informed of the activities and the inferior riches and pleasures of the world beyond their walls; then the *senex* takes his place as a groom of the chamber whose tasks are simplified to the cyclic ministration about the royal bed that is the new center of his universe. The nosey friend, whose chiding provokes the irritable opening stanzas of "The Canonization," eventually vanishes within the energetic exaltation of the speaker's love, to be replaced by the more reverent and anonymous devotees whose prayers of intercession to the poet and his lover have been coined by the poet himself.

Several of the poems develop this theme, transforming the private perfection of love into a religious mystery that is a public good. "The Canonization" and "The Relique" propose the beatification of love not only in order to insulate it from those claims that would disrupt it, but ultimately to recuperate and transform its social context. In these poems, the exaltation of the lovers above the physical concerns and evidences of "sublunary lovers" removes them from the threat of social intrusion ("A Valediction: forbidding Mourning," 13). The lovers assume intercessory and exemplary roles and transform the potential agents of that intrusion into devotees and beneficiaries of their "reverend love" ("The Canonization," 37). "A Nocturnall upon S. Lucies Day" provides a dark variation on the beatification motif.

4. Carey discusses the fantasy of royal power in relation to Donne's ambition in *John Donne,* chaps. 3 and 4. For the emergence of a modern conception of privacy in the seventeenth century, see Francis Barker, *The Tremulous Private Body: Essays in Subjection* (London: Methuen & Co., 1984).

5. *The Interpretation of Dreams,* trans. James Strachey (New York: Avon Books, 1965), 56–64.

As the somber energies of this confessional lyric circulate between the speaker and the thought of his dead mistress, they perform a liturgical *askesis,* an act of sacrificial devotion and esoteric instruction for the sake of the speaker's audience "who shall lovers bee / At the next world, that is, at the next Spring" (10–11). The speaker ritually sacrifices himself through the alchemy of love. By concentrating and sublimating within himself all the deadness and emptiness that afflict sublunary love, he becomes a redemptive agent of love, in effect an antimatter version of the philosophers' stone—"I am by her death, (which word wrongs her) / Of the first nothing, the Elixer grown" (28–29)—freeing other lovers for the generative life of love.

The liturgical and healing function is also implicit in "The Exstasie," where the implied witness "so by love refin'd / That he soules language understood" (21–22) will "part farre purer than he came" (28), the beneficiary of his attendance on the lovers' mystic encounter. This witness, "some lover, such as wee" (73), becomes an interpretative participant in the mystic "unperplexing" (29) of individual selfhood in the poem. His witness of the lovers delivers them from esoteric and sepulchral solitude by an act of erotic understanding that both ritually purifies him and "markes" (75) the action of the lovers as a socially verifiable and accessible experience. In these poems, then, by making over the potentially pesky intruder into a reverent audience, an initiate, Donne transfigures private encounter at odds with the world's curiosity and claims into public spectacle, even liturgy, and thus derives from the esoteric mystery of love a universal catechism. He thus refigures the social resistance to the private claims of love into social approbation, imagining a kind of Marcusean culture orchestrated on the expression and fulfillment of desire rather than on its repression.[6]

In order to understand something of the psychological function of the erotic spectator's role in Donne's poetry, we need to see that role in relation to the general dominance that Donne confers upon the act of seeing. Donne's poems frequently begin with a visual gesture or very quickly establish the visual as the primary mode of perception: "Marke but this flea" ("The Flea"), "I fixe mine eye on thine" ("Witchcraft by a Picture"), "Let me powre forth / My teares before thy face"

---

6. Herbert Marcuse, *Eros and Civilization: A Philosophical Inquiry into Freud* (Boston: Beacon Press, 1966).

("A Valediction: of Weeping"). In his various inventories of body parts, the eyes tend to be the first organs to be enumerated and assigned: "Send home my long strayd eyes to me" ("The Message," 1), "Here I bequeath / Mine eyes to Argus, if mine eyes can see" ("The Will," 2–3), "I never stoop'd so low, as they / Which on an eye, cheeke, lip, can prey" ("Negative Love," 1–2). Paradoxically, Donne establishes the dominance of seeing at the expense of visual information and imagery. The poet's word creates a world where vision dominates, yet the visual field fades into the phenomenology and psychology of seeing, where what is being seen is less important than that it is seen, or less important than the physical or imaginative sensation it elicits. We learn very little, for instance, about the physical beauty of the woman ordered about in the strip tease of the elegy "To his Mistris Going to Bed."[7] Although the act of seeing is implied as a counterpart to and a motivation for the poet's directions, the focus of the poem is on the pleasurable thrill that comes through the sight and on the control that both word and eye confer in the erotic scenario, rather than on particular information about what is seen.[8]

The most frequent specific image in Donne's visual repertoire is that of the lovers reflecting each other's image in the eye or in the tears welling out of the eye ("The Good-morrow," "The Sunne Rising," "A Valediction: of Weeping," "Witchcraft by a Picture," "The Canonization," and "The Exstasie"). This image seems to crystallize the erotic wish that motivates the poems: a moment of loving intensity that takes the loving self outside itself; both concentrates the self and dissolves it in the mirroring sight of the beloved. In this primary *mise en scene,* poet and beloved are suspended in the eye of the other in a moment of self-recognition and wholeness. This visual epiphany simultaneously brings the self into focus in an instant of totalizing desire and excludes the clamorous demands of the world beyond.

7. "He hardly seems to see the girl, though his appraising eye dwells on the clothes she takes off" (Carey, *John Donne,* 107).

8. William Kerrigan argues that the elegy, deliberately veering toward touch from the frustrating visual trajectory of the Petrarchan tradition, "announces a great turning point in the history of the Renaissance love lyric" ("What Was Donne Doing?" *South Central Review* 4 [1987]: 4–6). Thomas Docherty describes the poem as an instance of male colonization of female "otherness" (*John Donne, Undone* [London: Methuen & Co., 1986], 82).

Desire exceeds and arrests the sexual drive in a tremulous preverbal instant of mutual self-constitution:

> This Exstasie doth unperplex,
>   (We said) and tell us what we love,
> Wee see by this, it was not sexe,
>   Wee see, we saw not what did move:
>
> But as all severall soules containe
>   Mixture of things, they know not what,
> Love, these mixt soules, doth mixe againe,
>   And makes both one, each this and that.
>   ("The Exstasie," 29–36)

The patterns of negation, repetition, interruption, reversal, and re-dundancy in this passage, as well as the primarily monosyllabic dic-tion, intimate a condition of complete pleasure that is ultimately inef-fable or preverbal and, in a sense, pregenital ("it was not sexe"). The diffused and "mixt" condition of erotic intensity here is situated in the gaze and precedes the urgent sexual appeal to turn to the bodies that is the speaker's final persuasion (49–76).

We might associate this image of the lovers lost and found in each other's eyes with the psychoanalytic description of the moment of mirroring coherence when the infant discovers his or her wholeness in the image reflected in the mother's affectionate, totally absorbed, and absorbing gaze. In this instant, self-recognition coincides with a desire that is impossible to differentiate from the "desire of the other," so that one's constitution of a sense of self as a coherent subject is inseparable from the knowledge of self as a possessed object. It does not press Donne's poems too hard, I think, nor infantilize their wit, to recognize them as exuberant variations upon this moment of world making, or to suggest that the poetic tone of cozy intensity and of pure trust, the sense of erotic overfullness and of psychological com-pleteness, have their experiential basis in the totalizing and exclusive intimacy of mother and child. "The Good-morrow," whose tone is set by the leisurely afterglow of erotic satiation, opens by reference to past pleasures explicitly oral and infantile and proceeds to urge a steady condition of pleasure: "Let us possesse our world, each hath one, and is one" (14). Both "The Exstasie" and "A Valediction: of Weeping" refer to the moment of self-discovery in the lovers' gaze as an idealized surrogate of sexual generation in which conception, gestation, and birth occur simultaneously: "Pictures on our eyes to get / Was all our propagation" ("The Exstasie," 11–12); "For thus they [the poet's tears] bee / Pregnant of thee" ("A Valediction: of Weeping," 5–6). If the eye becomes the organ of reproduction at this moment, then the image of the self propagated there is implicitly fetal or infantile. The frequency and priority of these visual images suggest that one of Donne's deepest longings in the poems is not for genital satisfaction but for the security of absorption in a self-completing relationship whose earliest pattern is set in the intimacy between mother and child. Even as the poems spin about this moment of imagistic reproduction rather than of genital possession, Donne conditions their moments of fullness by suggesting the tenuousness and fragility and brevity of this visual world, ephemeral as a tear, eclipsed with a blink or a loss of attention, and vulnerable to the intervening gaze of others.[9]

For Donne knows the romantic evanescence of love's sweet fullness; such love allows only a momentary reprieve from an anxiety about being watched that may partly conceal a longing to be watched. The ambivalent logic of exposure conditions Donne's construction of love scenes. We have considered the social factors that might affect such construction; the persistent appearance of an observer who intrudes on the scenes suggests some kind of internal necessity at work here as well. If the anxiety about being observed expresses itself in a furtive sense of guilt over being witnessed at a forbidden activity, the longing to be watched expresses the need for recognition, for the confirmation of an existence, that stakes itself most utterly, for Donne, in the gamble of selfhood in love making. This complex of guilt and longing structures the religious poetry as well, in confessional scenes exposing the soul's naked sinfulness before God.

Critics have long recognized that the categorization of Donne's poems

9. Anna Nardo calls attention to the frequency of "face-to-face encounters" in Donne's poetry and their recollection of the mutuality between mother and child ("John Donne at Play in Between," in *The Eagle and the Dove: Reassessing John Donne,* ed. Claude J. Summers and Ted-Larry Pebworth [Columbia: University of Missouri Press, 1986], 159). See also Jacques Lacan, "The mirror stage as formative of the function of the I as revealed in psychoanalytic experience," in *Ecrits: A Selection,* trans. Alan Sheridan (New York: Norton, 1977), 1–7.

into "devotional" and "erotic" verse is blurred by the appearance of common themes, strategies, images, and existential concerns, which preoccupy Donne in all his work. The latent content of a religious lyric may be as erotic as the latent content of an amatory poem; even one as bawdy as "The Flea" may be theological. The devotional lyrics provide further evidence for Donne's poetic consistency in articulating a triangular pattern of desire, constituted by an anxious speaker, the various "false mistresses" that the world offers, and an onlooking God. The explicit identification of the observer figure in the religious poetry may provide us an indirect way of accounting for his more shadowy, anonymous presence in the amatory poems. Ocular motifs dominate the religious poems, for God's gaze is inescapable, and the poet quakes with fear and shame to return that look. In the religious poetry, God is most frequently situated in the position reserved for the erotic spectator, impassive yet unshakably stern in his witness of the poet's frenetic and furtive liaisons with "the world, the flesh, the devil" ("This is my playes last scene," 14), "pleasure or businesse" ("Goodfriday, 1613," 7), or "Fame, Wit, Hopes, (false mistresses)" ("A Hymn to Christ, at the Authors last going into Germany," 28). The gaze of God, "whose feare already shakes my every joynt," is omniscient and threatening ("This is my playes last scene," 8). Yet Donne cultivates the thought of that punitive gaze as a means of correction, a way to break the poet's illicit contracts and contacts with the false mistresses that the world and the devil have to offer and restore the divine image in him.[10]

The act of rightful possession by God would be an act of erotic violence, a punitive and purgatorial ravishing that would "breake, blowe, burn, and make me new" ("Batter my heart," 4). In "Goodfriday, 1613," the soul-searing gaze of Christ from the Cross is in itself sufficient to "Burne off my rusts and my deformity" (40) and to

---

10. See Carey (*John Donne,* 37–46) and Docherty (*Undone,* 147–86) for recent treatments of the convergence of theological and erotic motifs in Donne's poems. M. Thomas Hester makes a suggestive case for the love lyrics as a site where Donne, still sympathetic to Recusant rhetoric and theology, can covertly entertain it. See Hester, "'This Cannot Be Said': A Preface to the Reader of Donne's Lyrics," *Christianity and Literature* 39 (1990): 365–85; also Eugene Cunnar, "Donne's Witty Theory of Atonement in 'The Baite,'" *SEL* 29 (1989): 77–99. On the terrifying image of God's gaze in Donne's divine poems, see Richard Strier, "John Donne Awry and Squint: The 'Holy Sonnets,' 1608–1610," *MP* 86 (1989): 373, 378.

"Restore thine Image, so much, by thy grace, / That Thou may'st know mee, and I'll turne my face" (41–42), thus to accomplish the metanoia that the poet both longs for and dreads. The poet turns his back on Christ here "but to receive / Corrections, till Thy mercies bid Thee leave" (37–38), like a four-year-old boy awaiting punishment from his father. A divine possession which is punitive would give Donne the kind of recognition that his guilt over transgression requires, the assurance of love through chastisement an insecure child would understand: "O thinke mee worth thine anger, punish mee" (39). The structural homology between erotic and devotional poetry would lead us to expect that the voyeur's position reserved for God in the devotional poetry is occupied by a potentially judging, punitive father in various guises.

An overzealously psychoanalytic schema would align the figure of the erotic spectator in Donne's poetry with the formation of the superego: the father's inquisitive and inquisitorial stare interrupts the pre-oedipal communion in which mother and child are lost in each other's gazes. One might even guess at the traumatic origins of this circuit of desire in Donne's loss of his natural father at age four: the shock, anger, and guilt occasioned by that loss could account for the transgressive impulse of the poems, the recurring wish to be absorbed, enclosed, and protected by the all-encompassing gaze of the mother, and the nervous admission of a spectator whose disapproval, threat, or punishment would be at least a form of paternal recognition.[11] Such a model could account for certain aspects of certain poems, but it risks flattening out the textures of the poems and streamlining their variety. In certain but not all cases, the voyeur could be associated with a spectral father. There are certainly evidences of a confused oedipal struggle with the father, not only in the religious poems but in such elegies as "The Perfume" and "Jealosie" (where the sickly jealous husband is a comic father figure), and in the punning of "The Sunne Rising." In these poems Donne exposes the erotic spectators as paternal

11. See R. C. Bald, *John Donne: A Life* (Oxford: Clarendon Press, 1986), 35–36. Carey stresses Donne's guilty correlation between the sight of God and the oversight of a father whom he imagines glorified, in Satyre III and in the Holy Sonnet, "If faithfull soules be alike glorifi'd" (40). Dennis Flynn provides a less tendentious account of Donne's anxieties in "Donne the Survivor," *Eagle and the Dove*, 15–24. Anthony Low has reminded me that Donne's guilt over his survival of his brother might well have intensified the longing for purgative chastisement that is a feature of the religious lyrics.

Loss of his father (56)
causes quiet!

substitutes, satiric *senex* figures, whom the speaker proceeds mockingly to dismiss, outwit, or render impotent. That the sun is assigned the position of a *senex* figure and stripped of the conventional attributes of royal and religious power in "The Sunne Rising" suggests a witty role reversal by the poet. In "Goodfriday, 1613," Christ on the Cross as "a Sunne" that "by rising set, / And by that setting endlesse day beget" (11–12) is granted the x-ray gaze customarily associated with the Father in the Holy Sonnets. These poems hint at the displacement or disabling of the father as spectator, and at the role confusion involved in assuming the father's proprietary and authoritative position as judging and punitive spectator.

Perhaps a more flexible psychoanalytic account of the triangulation of desire in Donne's poems would suggest that, as the original maternal position in the circuit of desire establishes a site where various forms of intimacy with and control over women could be entertained, the original paternal intervention in that circuit establishes a site where the struggle with various male others would repeatedly be enacted. This could account for the shifting of positions within the circuit of desire in "The Apparition." This strange poem gathers its uncanny power by its entertainment of Donne's greatest anxieties about sexuality—inconstancy and exposure. Here the poet visually and dramatically realizes and focuses these anxieties by removing himself from center to periphery of the sexual scene, as if he realizes that there is more power, or at least more control, to be had in being the scene's observer and intruder than in being its male participant. His imagined role as spectral and spectatorial revenger seems overdetermined, a figure familiar to us from Shakespearean and Jacobean tragedy as well as Donne's poetry, as if it were materializing not just Donne's anxieties but the anxieties of a patriarchal culture in crisis. Driven by Othello's prurient compulsion to imagine "ocular proof," Donne's speaker also takes on the fear of infidelity and the longing for revenge expressed by Hamlet's father's ghost. In the schema of Donne's poetry, he occupies the site reserved for the punitive God in the devotional lyrics.[12]

12. For an account of the English dramatists' exploration of male anxiety and its relation to theatrical spectatorship, see Katharine Maus, "Horns of Dilemma: Jealousy, Gender, and Spectatorship in English Renaissance Drama," *ELH* 54 (1987): 561–83.

Despite its supernaturalism, "The Apparition" is as naturalistic as
Donne gets. In tone and texture as in dramatic situation, the poem
inscribes a primary scene for film noir. The betrayed lover will rise up
from the dead to confront the guilty bad girl with her crimes in the
moment of her postcoital languor. Postcoitus is an especially vulnerable moment, as the ego, burst momentarily in the little death of orgasm, seeps back into the fleshly coordinates of the undefended body
drifting toward sleep. At this moment, which is too late for alibis, the
poet will reclaim her by confronting her with her crime and his judgment. His powerful retributive gaze is a moment of photographic
arrest and reification, fixing the exposed woman's body and erotically exalting it into an icon of guilty female sexuality, "bath'd in a
cold quicksilver sweat" (12) like the body of the gilded woman in the
James Bond film *Goldfinger.* This is a rare moment in Donne's visual
repertoire, as the body of the woman is glimpsed whole and naked,
yet stylized, even glamorized by the poet's paralyzing gaze: at once
one of Donne's "metal girls," and all fluid, shimmering in the ghastly
pallor of erotic guilt exposed.[13]

Donne's speaker savors this high tension moment of erotic transgression and revelation with a grim glee. By positioning himself as
spectator, he is able to savor the transgressive action of sexuality
while escaping culpability, occupying the site of retribution against
it.[14] He cuts the scene at the moment of the mistress's exposure by a
refusal to speak until the imagined scene is enacted:

> What I will say, I will not tell thee now,
> Lest that preserve thee; and since my love is spent,
> I'had rather thou shouldst painfully repent,
> Then by my threatnings rest still innocent.
>
> (14–17)

If the poet's goal is to ensure the mistress's fidelity, this is an odd
bit of self-defeating bluster. He reveals instead the rather perverse

13. Carey, *John Donne,* 138–39.
14. "[Voyeuristic] Pleasure lies in ascertaining guilt, . . . asserting control, and sub-
jecting the guilty person through punishment or forgiveness" (Laura Mulvey, "Visual
Pleasure and Narrative Cinema," *Screen* 16 [1975]: 14).

goal of confirming her infidelity. Why should this be? By catching his "murd'ress" in some indeterminate future with her pants down, the poet imagines reversing the power relations that motivate the poetic outburst in the first place. She has refused and defeated him, and her scorn will eventually murder him; he confesses that even now "my love is spent" (15). Although the arresting and punitive gaze becomes a figure for his recovery of power over her in death, words are the organs of potency in this poem as in all poems. Donne's withholding of the retributive words at this moment of anticipation may be a current necessity disguised as a choice, for if his love is spent, what is left for him to say? The expectation that the words will come to him at the moment of his postmortem apotheosis as avenging spectator is a transformation of his own current impotence into a future vengeful power, which draws its energy from the poet's shift of position in the erotic triangle.

The situating of the mistress in "The Apparition" as the auditor of a discourse yet to be spoken accords with other poems in which Donne stresses the role of the beloved as auditor of a directive or even as reader: "Marke but this flea" ("The Flea," 1); "Stand still, and I will read to thee / A Lecture, Love, in loves philosophy" ("A Lecture upon the Shadow," 1–2); "I'll tell thee now (deare Love) what thou shalt doe / To anger destiny, as she doth us / . . . Study our manuscripts, those Myriades / Of letters, which have past twixt thee and me, / Thence write our Annals" ("A Valediction: of the Booke," 1–2, 10–12). In "A Valediction: of my Name in the Window," the name of the poet engraved in the window glass provides the basis for an extended admonition and instruction on the nature of reading, and remembering. The name serves as visual cue to conscience. The inescapable sight of it will be sufficient to conjure the poet's psychic presence as censor over his vacillating mistress's thoughts and acts, particularly over her act of writing. The poet's inscription is an act of permanent entitlement, which ensures that his mistress will be unable to behold her own image in the window glass, gaze out upon another lover, read his solicitations or write in response to them without discovering the poet's "name alive" (47), and active in commanding her attention and affection. Donne thus identifies the scene of lovers' confidences with the scene of reading. As the poems at their highest pitch erode boundaries between the lovers, at their most self-conscious they erode boundaries between the reader of the poems and the characters, who are represented by the poems frequently in the very actions that typify a reader's response. In this perspective, the subject of the poems and their potential beneficiary is the reader, and the erotic persuasion is directed as deliberately, although perhaps more subtly, to the reader as it is to the mistress. The poet addresses his "thou" simultaneously to the beloved implied within the representational structure of the poem and to the actual reader whose visual and interpretative engagement with the poem brings it to virtual "life."

In the first part of this essay, I suggested that the erotic spectator assumes a surrogate function for Donne: in the perspective of the third party, most ideally represented in "some lover, such as wee" (73) of "The Exstasie," private love is mediated for public good, esoteric encounter becomes socially therapeutic, such that the spectator "parts farre purer than he came" (28). This function of interpreter, acolyte, and beneficiary, can be better explained by reference to the place of the reader in the dynamics of the poem than to the place of the disguised superego, which I investigated in the middle section of the essay. In introducing the third figure, Donne thus introjects the public discourse of the poem into the apparently private and privileged discourse of the poem's love making. Although we have been conditioned to reflect on the "implied reader" of a text, the reader is more "actual" in substantiating the action of a poetic text than the beloved to whom it is ostensibly addressed. It is the beloved who is "implied" by the act of poetic speech and by the reader's response, and it is the reader who is the actual object of the poet's rhetorical self-display, both the admirer and the judge of the play of wit, both the "thou" being addressed and the silent observer whom Donne variously resists, browbeats, condescends to, cultivates, and purifies.[15]

Reading can be aligned with voyeuristic activity in several ways.

---

15. Wendy Wall shows how elaborate prefatory metaphors and engravings in Elizabethan publications serve to titillate and implicate the reader as potential voyeur ("Disclosures in Print: The 'Violent Enlargement' of the Renaissance Voyeuristic Text," *SEL* 29 [1989]: 52–53). Although Donne practiced the gentleman's prerogative of retaining his poetry in manuscript, the elements of exposure, exchange, and circulation disclosed by Wall in marketable publications become a part of the writing game that he plays as well. Perhaps because his erotic disclosures are not for sale, Donne's texts tend to incorporate images of potentially faithless mistresses rather than of the whores that figure prominently in the marketable Elizabethan texts.

Donne — and even his
readers — engage in
"voyeuristic activity"
"with a minimum of
genital risk" (61)

deferral of consummation"

Sight establishes visual intimacy even as it protects against physical commitment or engagement, for the voyeur's project involves "the wish both to be and not to be in the presence of the object of interest." Reading as an activity originating in sight parallels voyeurism by its participation in an imagined scene of pleasure from which one is at the same time physically detached. As a voyeuristic activity, reading promotes and variegates a generalized erotic stimulation with a minimal genital risk; even as it enables imaginary participation, it assures at least a minimal distance from the scene where love is being staged, and thus protects one from the dissolution of the boundaries of self toward which genital sexuality drives. The reader as voyeur is situated in a place that allows for maximum imaginative mobility and physical intactness, with an indefinite deferral of consummation, because the visual and imaginary mode of stimulation is not the one-way street of physical touch. Reading, like voyeurism, thus promotes a "cool" eroticism—"For ever warm and still to be enjoy'd, / For ever panting, and for ever young," as Keats would put it—by its insulation of the subject from the literal enactment of desire. Physical detachment assures psychic mobility, as the vision or imagination of the erotic scene in its totality from outside it, rather than from a specific location determined within it, permits the shifting of imagination between the positions of pleasure-giving and -receiving, active and passive, male and female: "Through the willing surrender to the active / passive alternations of reading, readers (subjects who become objects) play within and also escape the confines of voyeurism and exhibitionism."[16]

Donne inserts an erotic spectator in so many of the love poems, then, for several reasons, not the least of which is to inscribe within the fictive speech a reminder to the reader that the pleasure of the text is a voyeuristic pleasure. This is a gesture perhaps less confrontative but no less striking than Baudelaire's turn to his "hypocrite lecteur!— mon semblable,—mon frere!" familiar to English language readers from T. S. Eliot's appropriation of it for *The Waste Land*.[17] That

16. Joel Rudinow, "Representation, Voyeurism, and the Vacant Point of View," *Philosophy and Literature* 3 (1979): 176; Keats, "Ode on a Grecian Urn," in *The Poems of John Keats*, ed. Jack Stillinger (Cambridge: Harvard University Press, 1978), 26–27; Robert Con Davis, "Lacan, Poe, and Narrative Repression," *MLN* 98 (1983): 988.

17. *The Waste Land* in *The Complete Poems and Plays, 1909–1950* (New York: Har-

Donne is a highly self-regarding poet, whose pleasure is in the dazzle
of wit, seems beyond dispute. That he would give his attention in the
writing of a poem to the genesis and stimulation of reader response
seems a likely supposition, even if the acts of marking, observing,
reading, interpreting, and writing were not repeatedly inscribed in
the stage directions of the poetry. Donne thus produces lyrics with a
palpable and self-conscious design on the reader, who is introjected
as "mon semblable, mon frere," initially, perhaps hypocritically resis-
tant, potentially a rival in the interpretative possession of the body of
the text,[18] but ultimately the poet's double in the scene of seduction
and acolyte in the sacred arts of love. In a poem, Donne knows, desire
finds its fulfillment in the play of language. The verbal pleasure in
making poetry and in its being read becomes so intermixed with the
pleasure in the love scenarios it conjures as to absorb or supersede the
specifically sexual pleasure that is the ostensible goal and subject of
the poetry. Textuality, textual performance, becomes the source of
its own pleasure, but Donne knows that that pleasure is completed by
a witness, one whose imaginative participation in the text makes it
as real as it will ever be. Donne is both canny enough and generous
enough to his actual readers—perhaps more generous than to his
implied mistresses—to include us in the show.[19]

court, Brace & World, 1952), 76. "The pleasure of the text" refers to Roland Barthes,
The Pleasure of the Text, trans. Richard Miller (New York: Hill and Wang, 1975).

18. The theme of rivalry could provide another source for the introjection of an intrusive male observer in Donne's poetry. The courtier world and its representation on the
Renaissance stage provides ample evidence of the contentious social context for Donne's
expression of the theme. Rene Girard argues that "mimetic desire" establishes rivalry at
the very heart of social life, for what is desired gains in value and intensity by its being the
object of another's desire. For Girard, even the love object is potentially less a goal in
herself than a pretext for conflict. This might account in part for the frequency with
which Donne's engagement with the intruder exceeds his attention to the beloved. See
Girard, *Violence and the Sacred,* trans. Patrick Gregory (Baltimore: Johns Hopkins University Press, 1977), 145–49.

19. Eve Kosofsky Sedgwick explores English literary tradition for the ways in which
the figure of woman may provide a mediating text for male bonding. Sedgwick's insight
may provide an approach to the place of women in the exchange of texts between the
young wits of Donne's circle. See *Between Men: English Literature and Male Homosocial Desire* (New York: Columbia University Press, 1985). On the social context and
function of Donne's lyrics, see Arthur Marotti, *John Donne, Coterie Poet* (Madison:
University of Wisconsin Press, 1986); and Ted-Larry Pebworth, "John Donne, Coterie
Poetry, and the Text as Performance," *SEL* 29 (1989): 61–75.

Stella P. Revard

The Sapphic Voice in Donne's "Sapho to Philaenis"

Donne's elegy, "Sapho to Philaenis," has been a poetical conundrum, either ignored or until recently deplored by critics, who have puzzled over its genre, style, voice, and its very presence in the canon of one of the most aggressively masculine of English poets. Despite strong manuscript authority and its inclusion in both the 1633 and 1635 volumes of Donne's poems, both Helen Gardner and Herbert Grierson regard the poem with suspicion, questioning whether it is an elegy or an epistle and whether, indeed, Donne wrote it at all. In her edition of Donne's elegies and the *Songs and Sonets,* Gardner relegates it to the "Dubia," as "too uncharacteristic of Donne in theme, treatment, and style to be accepted as unquestionably his."[1] Assuredly, "Sapho to Philaenis" with its female persona and plaintive tone gives us Donne in an unusual mood and voice; as a dramatic monologue, however, it resembles Donne's other elegies and contains much that is characteristically Donnean in sentiment, style, and development.

Almost certainly, the initial inspiration for the elegy is Ovid's letter, "Sappho to Phaon," hence, probably, both Grierson's and Gardner's conviction that the poem is "an Heroicall Epistle," not an elegy. But although Donne bows here and there to the Ovidian model, his aim, I

---

1. John Donne, *The Elegies and the Songs and Sonnets,* ed. Helen Gardner (Oxford: Clarendon Press, 1965), xlvi. All quotations of Donne's poetry are from this edition. Grierson, although designating the poem a heroical epistle, remarks that it has a closer relation to the elegies than to Donne's other epistles and "must have been composed about the same time" (*The Poems of John Donne,* ed. Herbert J. C. Grierson, 2 vols. [Oxford: Clarendon, 1912], 2:91).

believe, is to adopt the voice of the original Sappho, rather than that of Ovid's poetical Sappho. Glancing at Sappho's own verse, he attempts to imitate the woman-loving Sappho of the extant poetry rather than the Sappho of Roman tradition, who had committed suicide after her thwarted love affair with Phaon. Moreover, Donne's poem goes beyond the Ovidian model and explores some of the attitudes toward love notable in Sappho's poetry. Whether or not we see Donne's Sappho as an erotic double of the ancient Greek poet, she is a person with a distinctive voice that may be set beside the dramatic personae of Donne's other elegies.

Although both Gardner and Grierson express strong reservations about "Sapho to Philaenis," recent critics have not only embraced the poem as authentically Donne's but have argued that it gives extraordinary insight into Donne's views of human sexuality. Janel Mueller argues that Donne was ahead of his time in his sympathy for the lesbian point of view. Similarly, Elizabeth Harvey in a recent article reviews the critical history of Ovid's epistle and argues that Donne, in contrast to Ovid, espouses the erotics of the feminine voice in a positive manner. James Holstun, however, takes a different line, stating that whereas Donne does not condemn lesbianism, he does view it from the male patriarchal perspective as a primitive sexual state no longer viable in society and made obsolete by human history. According to these critics, Donne should be looked at as the founding father of the sexual revolution, for long before his time he dared to explore what most poets in the Renaissance acknowledged only obliquely— the sexual love of one woman for another.[2]

Before, however, we consider Donne's attitudes toward lesbianism, we must ask how much of Sappho's poetry was available to Donne. Sappho had been printed for the first time by Henri Estienne in the

2. Mueller, "Lesbian Erotics: The Utopian Trope of Donne's 'Sapho to Philaenis,'" *Journal of Homosexuality* 23 (1992): 103–34, simultaneously published in *Homosexuality in Renaissance and Enlightenment England: Literary Representations in Historical Context,* ed. Claude J. Summers (New York: Haworth Press/Harrington Park Press, 1992). See also Janel Mueller, "Troping Utopia: Donne's Brief for Lesbianism in 'Sapho to Philaenis,'" *Sexuality and Gender in Early Modern Europe: Institutions, Texts, Images,* ed. James Grantham Turner (Cambridge: Cambridge University Press, 1992); Elizabeth D. Harvey, "Ventriloquizing Sappho: Ovid, Donne, and the Erotics of the Feminine Voice," *Criticism* 31 (1989): 115–37; James Holstun, "'Will you rent our ancient love asunder?': Lesbian Elegy in Donne, Marvell, and Milton," *ELH* 54 (1987): 835–67.

1550s and had been imitated by both male and female poets in France in the sixteenth century.[3] Did Donne know either Sappho's poetry or that of her imitators? Is this why he made a deliberate choice in his elegy to adopt her voice and to adopt it not as Sappho complains—as she does in Ovid's heroical epistle—to a boy who has abandoned her, but as she does in her own poetry to a young female. If so, he rejected his own favorite Ovid as a poetical model and courted the ancient Greek female poet who came before and taught so much to the Roman world from Catullus through Ovid not only about desire, but also about how to write poetry.

In seeking the role of the Sapphic voice in Donne's elegy, I am not denying the importance of Ovid's letter, "Sappho to Phaon," number fifteen, which, as Elizabeth Harvey points out, had been restored to its place in Ovid's *Heroides* only in the Renaissance.[4] There are clear structural, thematic, and imagistic links between Donne and Ovid, as well as the important differences in attitude and treatment. Ovid's poem is a complaint in a seminarrative style, epistolary in form and almost (at 220 lines) four times as long as Donne's sixty-four-line elegy. In it Sappho addresses Phaon directly recalling their love, but she also bewails her other misfortunes, recounting in sequence her exile, the death of her father, her estrangement from her brother, her concern for her daughter, and concluding with her despair over her love for Phaon, the last and the most bitter of her miseries. Descriptions not only of past events but also of present happenings enter her letter. As she writes, she weeps and rends her robe. Finally, she recounts her vision of a naiad who rises from the water and tells her to go to the Leucadian cliff and cast herself off. The conclusion of the

3. Henri Estienne first published Sappho as an appendix to his edition of the anacreontea in 1554. He published Sappho next in 1560 in the second volume of the two-volume set of Greek lyric poets. The fragments and poems of Sappho next appear in a text of Greek lyric poetry edited by Laurence Gambara: *Carmina Novem Illustrium Feminarum* (Antwerp: Christophor Plantin, 1568). The text not only contains Sappho's poetry with facing Latin translations but also fragments from other Greek women poets (Erinna, Corinna, Myrtis, to name a few) and the poetry of other lyric poets. Gambara also includes epigrams about Sappho, as well as descriptions of her and her work in the writings of ancient grammarians and other writers. For commentary on the imitations of Sappho by Ronsard, Louise de Labe, and other French poets in the sixteenth century, see Joan DeJean, *Fictions of Sappho: 1546-1937* (Chicago: University of Chicago Press, 1989).
4. "Ventriloquizing Sappho," 117-18.

poem, in keeping with its letter style, is a plea that Phaon return or at least write to say why he flees from her.

Donne's Sapphic monologue has few of Ovid's expository and narrative techniques, resembling more closely his other elegies in its poetic and dramatic strategies. It shares, however, a plaintive opening and enough images to show that Donne at least began with Ovid in mind. Donne's Sappho takes both her fire and tears from her Ovidian counterpart. Both find the fire of passion threatened by tears. Ovid's Sappho tells Phaon that she has abandoned lyric for elegiac verse because elegy is more suited to weeping. Tears blot the page as she writes and mingle with the kisses she remembers. Her passion, however, continues hot as Aetna.

> Scribimus, et lacrimis oculi rorantur obortis;
> adspice, quam sit in hoc multa litura loco![5]
> (97–98)
>
> I write and my eyes are dewy with springing tears,
> see how many blots are in this place!

For Ovid the images of fire and water look forward to the drowning of Sappho's passion in the foredoomed leap from the Leucadian cliff into the watery depths of the sea. In Donne's elegy fire is not just the fire of Sappho's sexual passion but also that of her poetic talent: "Where is that holy fire, which Verse is said / To have, is that inchanting force decai'd?" (1–2). The watery tears may have quenched her poetic but not her passion's fire; its flames threaten the image of the beloved in her heart: "Onely thine image, in my heart, doth sit, / But that is waxe, and fires environ it" (9–10). As in Ovid's epistle, tears mingle with kisses: "When I would kisse, teares dimme mine *eyes*" (56). Love for both the Ovidian and the Donnean Sappho is a violent

---

5. Ovid, "Sappho to Phaon," *Heroides and Amores,* ed. and trans. Grant Showerman, 2d ed., rev. G. P. Goold (London: William Heinemann, 1977), 186. An edition of Ovid with the *Epistolae* was printed in London in 1594 by John Harison. In the argument before the epistle there is a biographical resume of Sappho, citing that there were two women in antiquity of this name: one the poet, the other a prostitute. An account of Sappho's love for Phaon follows.

passion that alternates between the metaphoric opposites of fire and water.

Despite these imagistic borrowings, Donne very soon leaves the lovelorn, heterosexual Sappho of Ovid's epistle behind. Though plaintive in tone, Donne's is no mere love complaint but an introspective monologue that explores passion as it pleads its case. Key to the difference is Donne's effort through the Sapphic voice to define homoerotic love. Donne was not insensitive to the special relations of woman to woman, as other poems in his canon testify. In the 1635 edition of Donne's poetry, "Sapho to Philaenis" is included among the letters immediately after "To the Lady Bedford" ("You that are she and you that's double she"), which is also a celebration of the friendship of women, in this case Lady Bedford and her newly deceased cousin, Lady Markham. The cousins, like the lovers in "Sapho to Philaenis," find identity in one another: "Shee was the other part, for so they doe / Which build them friendships, become one of two" (3–4).[6]

Like his verse epistle to Lady Bedford, Donne's "Sapho to Philaenis" is sympathetic to the bonds of woman to woman. Nothing, however, in the first twenty-five lines identifies the elegy's dramatic voice as uniquely feminine. The tone is very like that of the typical male Elizabethan lover, who complains of neglect by his mistress. Sappho regrets her declining poetic power, laments that her "Verse that drawes Natures workes, from Natures law" (3) is inadequate to describe her loved one, Nature's best work, and fears that Philaenis's image dwelling in her heart melts from her passion, hence depriving her of "Picture, Heart, and Sense" (12). Remembering Philaenis's beauty, Sappho even toys with the sonneteer's comparison game:

> What shall we call thee than?
> Thou art not soft, and cleare, and strait, and faire,

6. In the first edition of Donne's poems (1633), "Sapho to Philaenis" is printed neither with the other elegies nor with the verse epistles but is placed after "An Epitaph upon Shakespeare" (149) before a series of religious poems, beginning with "The Annuntiation and Passion" (168–85) (see *Poems, by J. D.* [London, 1633]); hence its inclusion in the second edition (1635) with the verse epistles seems significant. See John T. Shawcross, ed., *The Complete Poetry of John Donne* (Garden City: Doubleday, 1967), 249–50. On the friendship of Lady Bedford and Lady Markham as expressed in Donne's poems, see Claude J. Summers, "Donne's 1609 Sequence of Grief and Comfort," *Studies in Philology* 89 (Spring 1992): 211–31.

> As Down, as Stars, Cedars, and Lilies are,
> But thy right hand, and cheek, and eye, only
> Are like thy other hand, and cheek, and eye.
>
> (20–24)

There is even, as she briefly alludes to Phao, a recognition that she doted similarly upon Phao when she loved him. Love's idolatry would seem to be above sexual differentiation: "Here lovers swear in their Idolatrie, / That I am such" (27–28). In brief, the hesitations, doubts, passions, even tears of the female lover are very like those of Donne's typical male lover. The second part of the elegy, however, turns away from the accents of heterosexual to those of homosexual love. The turning point, in fact, is that very moment when Sappho remembers the passion she felt for Phao. Here Donne even offers us a recollection of Ovid's Sappho who, like Donne's, worries lest "Griefe" discolor her and mar her beauty, making her less worthy of her lover. It is no accident that most of the echoes of Ovid's imagery are confined to the first part of the elegy.

In turning from plaint to an intellectual exploration of the difference between male and female sexuality, Donne departs from Ovid as a model and attempts to come to terms with the poet Sappho and her treatment of love. If Donne knew Sappho directly, he probably came to her in Henri Estienne's octavo text that prints her extant poems with those of the other Greek lyric poets. Although this book is not listed in Donne's library, Estienne's edition of the Greek lyric poets was widely available; other texts of Sappho's poetry were not.[7] The Sapphic canon in the sixteenth century was significantly smaller than it is today, having been augmented since the Renaissance by poems and fragments that come from papyri and other sources unknown then. Estienne's octavo contains Sappho's complete poetry in Greek, as the Renaissance knew it, with a facing Latin translation; its sixteen pages consist of two complete odes, fragments of other poems, and quotations about Sappho from other writers, who in citing her work, preserved it for posterity. Estienne also printed an abridged

---

7. For a list of Donne's extant books, see Geoffrey Keynes, *A Bibliography of Dr. John Donne*, 4th ed. (Oxford: Clarendon, 1973), 258–79. I have consulted Sappho in Estienne's 1567 edition of the nine lyric poets: *Carminum Poetarum Novem, lyricae poesews principum, fragmenta*, 2 vols. (Antwerp: Christophor Plantin, 1567), 2:17–34.

version of the sixteenth-century life of Sappho by Lilio Gregorio Giraldi. Reading Sappho in Estienne's edition is a curious experience, for the poems and fragments are presented through the eyes of the grammarians who quote Sappho, frequently illustrating how through metaphor and allusion she has earned her place as the foremost voice of passion in antiquity. Hence, as Donne read Sappho's poetry in Estienne's text, he would have found, inseparable from it, literary criticism from ancient writers who presumably knew Sappho's complete canon. Renaissance critics drew on these ancient commentaries as they attempted to assess Sappho's accomplishments as a love poet. Her odes, says Julius Caesar Scaliger, best celebrate not only love but the difficulties of love.[8]

Underlying Donne's elegy, I believe, is the Renaissance rediscovery of Sappho as one of the leading lyric voices of erotic literature. Donne seems to be alluding indirectly in his elegy to the extant poems and fragments that depict, however briefly and obliquely, Sappho's attitudes toward young girls and toward love. Unknown to him in all probability were the two lyric letters to Atthis that would have been the closest models for the kind of verse elegy in semiepistolary style that "Sapho to Philaenis" is. In these Sappho tells of her passionate longing for her absent friend. Donne probably knew, however, the two fragments to Atthis: in one Sappho remembers her friend as a graceless child and in the other berates her for pursuing Andromeda and neglecting her. She defines love as that limb-loosening Eros who makes her tremble with desire, helplessly bound to a bitter-sweet passion:

> Ἔρος δηὖτέ μ' ὀ λυσιμέλης δόνει,
> γλυκύπικρον ἀμάχανον ὄρπετον.
> (238 [40–41 B., 137 D.])[9]

---

8. *Poetices Libri Septem* (1561), 41. Torquato Tasso also commends Sappho as a love poet and cites "φαίνεταί μοι" in full in Greek (*Delle Rime del Sig. Torquato Tasso,* 2 vols. (Brescia, 1592), 1:57–58).

9. I cite the poems and fragments of Sappho's poetry by number from *Lyrica Graeca Selecta,* ed. D. L. Page (Oxford: Clarendon, 1973). The texts of the poems, unless otherwise indicated, are from Page. Translations, unless otherwise indicated, are mine. I have checked the modern versions of Sappho against the readings in Estienne's 1567 edition for any marked differences in text.

> Love, loosening my limbs, shakes me:
> bitter-sweet, helpless, abandoned.

The fragment catches both passion and painful ambivalence, the very ingredients so prominent in Donne's elegy. Donne has chosen, however, for the name of Sappho's beloved neither Atthis nor any other of the girls the original Sappho named, names Ovid alludes to in his epistle. Instead, he calls Sappho's beloved Philaenis, the name of a Hellenistic poet, who is first cited without connection to Sappho, in several epigrams of the Greek Anthology, and thereafter, as Harvey has pointed out, by Martial and Lucian.[10]

Many of the fragments of Sappho that Donne might have known tell nothing directly about her relationships with women but are wonderfully evocative. The famous night piece attributed to her describes her longing and loneliness:

> δέδυκε μὲν α σελάνα
> καὶ Πληιάδες, μέσαι δὲ
> νύκτες, παρὰ δ' ἔρχεθ' ὥρα,
> ἐγὼ δὲ μόνα καθεύδω.
> (468 [52 B., 94 D.])[11]

> The moon and the Pleiades have set;
> It is the middle of the night,
> And the hour comes;
> But I go to bed alone.

This fragment supplies in a way the subtext for Donne's elegy, for Donne's Sappho is also alone in her longing, able to express her passion but unable to fulfill her desires. Other fragments catch fleeting feelings, images, and thoughts—many of them contradictory.[12] She describes the nightingale not just as the messenger of spring (as Ben

10. For a discussion of the identity of Philaenis see Harvey, "Ventriloquizing Sappho," 123–25.

11. Page places this poem among the "Fragmenta Adespota." The poem is found in Estienne, *Sapphus Carmina* in *Carminum Poetarum Novem,* 32.

12. The second century A.D. writer Pausanias remarked that Sappho sang many contradictory things of love (*Sappho,* ed. and trans. Willis Barnstone [New York: Anchor Books, 1965], 173, 16 n. 146).

Jonson does in his imitation of this fragment), but as the voice that stirs desire: "ἦρος ἄγγελος ἱμερόφωνος ἀήδων."[13] She likens the stirring of love in her heart to the effect of the wind in the mountains as it stirs the oak trees (204 [42 B., 50 D.]). Regretting the passing of her girlhood, she creates a dialogue in which she questions why maidenhood has left her:

> παρθενία, παρθενία, ποῖ με λίποισ' ἀποίχηι;
> οὐκέτι ἤξω πρὸς σέ, οὐκέτι ἤξω.
> (230 [109 B.,131 D.])

> "Virginity, virginity, why have you left me?"
> "Never will I return to you, never return."

It would be difficult for Donne or for that matter any reader to construct from these fragments a coherent notion of their context, but it is impossible not to feel their power. In one, for example, Sappho cries out, "I wish to speak, but shame prevents me" : "θέλω τί τ' εἴπην, ἀλλά με κωλύει αἴδως" (243 [Alc.55,2+Sa.28 B.,Sa.149 D.]). Does the Sapphic voice in this fragment not express something very like what Donne's Sappho feels, wishing to speak and express her love but overcome with the shame and anguish of her situation? In fact, if there is any mood that the fragments of Sappho's lyrics express, again and again, it is that of insatiable longing whether Sappho is speaking, as it were, in her own voice or in the voice of a young girl awakening to love. One famous fragment is the cry of the girl to her mother that she cannot ply the loom, for Aphrodite has tamed her heart with longing: "γλύκηα μᾶτερ, οὔτοι δύναμαι κρέκην τὸν ἴστον, / πόθωι δάμεισα παῖδος Βροδίναν δι' Ἀφροδίταν" (221 [90 B.114 D.]).[14]

Sappho's two lyrics, quoted more or less complete by Longinus and Dionysius of Halicarnasus, were celebrated in antiquity and in the Renaissance for their eroticism. The first and second selections in Estienne's edition both tell of Sappho's pursuit of young girls and both speak of unrequited desire. The first is addressed to dappled-throned, deathless Aphrodite, "ποικιλόθρον' ἀθανάτ' Ἀφρόδιτα" (191

---

13. *Sappho,* ed. and trans. Barnstone, 16 n. 146.
14. Not contained in Estienne, but found in Hephaistion's *Handbook,* cited by Estienne for the Atthis fragments.

[1B.et D.]), and is a prayer to the goddess to come to Sappho and to relieve her longing. Set in the form of a ritual hymn, it portrays the goddess in an intimate, affectionate, and even somewhat amused relationship with Sappho, who pleads with her not to crush her with sorrow, but to come, as she did once, in response to her cry of anguish. "What do you want this time, Sappho?" Aphrodite asks the poet and without waiting for an answer promises her that the girl she loves will not continue to scorn her attentions; she will not only reciprocate Sappho's love but will also become the pursuer, not the pursued. We hear some accents of Sappho's hymn in Donne's elegy, for Donne's Sappho is just as impatient to capture her beloved, just as insistent by merely wishing it that she can change the beloved from indifference into a willing, indeed an eager, reciprocal partner in love.

The second lyric, "Φαίνεταί μοι κῆνος ἴσος θέοισιν"—"That man seems to me equal to the gods" (199 [2 B.et D.])—was imitated by Catullus in antiquity and echoed also by Ovid. Longinus cites the poem as evidence of Sappho's power to convey poetically the physical effects of passion:

> Is it not wonderful how simultaneously she summons the soul, body, hearing, tongue, sight, flesh, all as separate things distinct from herself, and by contrary elements, she both freezes and burns, is mad and sane, she is afraid or she is nearly dead; thus not only one passion is evident but a whole assembly of emotions; for all these things happen to lovers, and her taking the best of the emotions, as I said, and joining them together, produces the excellence of this passage.[15]

Both the poem and Longinus's commendation have an impact on Donne's elegy, for he tries to evoke both situation and the emotions that Sappho describes. Sappho imagines that a young man sits opposite her beloved; in her mind she takes his place and experiences the emotions she might feel were she to be in her loved one's presence: her voice fails, her ears pound, sweat pours over her, fire runs through her veins, and she feels close to dying. Donne's Sappho entertains a similar flight of fancy, as she imagines a young boy in Philaenis's company, playing with her, or as she compares Philaenis's beauty to the

---

15. *Sappho,* ed. and trans. Barnstone, 171.

gods: "Thou art so faire, / As, gods, when gods to thee I doe com-pare, / Are grac'd thereby . . . What things gods are, I say they'are like to thee" (15–18). Donne is both alluding to the dramatic situation in Sappho's poem and echoing Sappho's famous opening line, "That man appears to me equal to the gods," applying, however, the godlike fortune to the beloved, not the spectator. In the process he also re-stores the poem to the female voice. In Donne's elegy female speaks to female, not male to female as in Catullus's imitation, or female to male as in Ovid's.

Donne's Sappho begins by expressing her jealousy that a man sits opposite her beloved and then proceeds to describe her feelings, thus creating a poetic picture and then reacting to it. She imagines first the "soft boy," who plays with Philaenis, an adolescent whose "chinne, a thorny hairy'unevennesse / Doth threaten" (33–34). She dispraises the male in order to argue the superiority of the female lover: "Why shouldst thou than / Admit the tillage of a harsh rough man?" (37–38). Sappho's choice of the metaphor of "tillage" to dispraise mas-culine love is a particularly apt one, for both in ancient and Renais-sance love poetry the female is often viewed as the fertile soil that the male "plows," subjugating her both sexually and societally to his use. Sappho's love brings with it no thraldom. Instead, she would restore the female to the freedom she had in the golden age, for her body, like the world then, is a "naturall Paradise, / In whose selfe, unmanur'd, all pleasure lies" (35–36). Contrary to the ancient theory present in the Renaissance that the female was by virtue of her sex defective, Sappho proclaims that Philaenis is perfect in herself, nor needs per-fecting by a man. In this passage, Sappho promises that through love the lost perfection of the human race will be restored in the promised return of the age of gold; there female lovers, superior to their male-female counterparts, will reap golden rewards. Not only will the free-dom but also the innocence of the golden age return, where untainted by the sin that male-female dalliance has produced, females will be free and innocent in their love as fish in streams and birds in the air. Repeating the word *all*, Sappho proposes that female love creates the best of all possible worlds because the two lovers can create between them all the sweetness that "Nature yields, or Art can adde" (44). I cannot agree with James Holstun that the paradisal state Sappho argues for is either archaic or passed. Throughout the seventeenth

century, poets proposed the return of the golden age and with it
societal equity and freedom in love. Donne accords no more to the
lesbian lovers of this poem than what he pleads for heterosexual lovers
in many of his other poems. Through love the golden age promised in
both classical and Christian literature will come again. The paradise
that his Sappho envisions for herself and Philaenis is more idealized
and less libertine than that which a heterosexual lover like Carew in
"The Rapture" urges as the ideal state for lovers, free from society's
constraints.

Donne in fact permits Sappho to idealize lesbian love as a meeting
of like and like, which has a peculiar exclusivity. In loving one of the
same sex, Sappho loves the "likenesse" of herself. She imagines that, as
she looks at a likeness of herself in a mirror, she is looking at Philaenis:

> Likenesse begets such strange selfe flatterie,
>   That touching my selfe, all seemes done to thee.
> Myselfe I'embrace, and mine own hands I kisse,
>   And amorously thanke my selfe for this.
>   (51–54)

Donne is trying to do two things: to express Sappho's emotions and
to analyze how a woman's love for another woman is different from a
man's for a woman. Yet in the process Donne's treatment of Sapphic
transport becomes somewhat academic. The original Sappho's description of passion emphasizes her physical and emotional reactions and
stresses the universal in her experience: what she feels for her beloved
transcends male or female. Donne dissects rather than describes emotion. He implies also that the female in making love to a female is
experiencing something somehow different from what she might feel
for a male. In her loved one, the female lover finds herself; the second
female is her glasse, her other world: "My halfe, my all, my more"
(58). In this, the female lover argues that she and her loved one come
near a perfection unknown to their male-female counterparts. Their
likeness binds them together, and they are kept from imperfection,
sickness, and the change that lesser lovers less united experience, rising by similitude above mortal constraints. But they can so triumph
only if, as Sappho pleads, Philaenis restores Sappho to herself by join-

ing her in this sublime similitude. Donne seems to plead here what is a curious composite of ideas about love drawn from Sappho's and his own poetry. To an extent he succeeds in portraying love, as it is often portrayed in the original Sappho, as a "loving madnesse," an obsession, charged with the most intense emotions. But he has not made us feel, as we so often feel with Sappho herself, that in describing the love of one woman for another, he has described the quintessential nature of passion.

Despite its effort then to exploit the Sapphic voice and attitudes, Donne's "Sapho to Philaenis" speaks in more deliberate tones than those we associate with the extant lyrics of Sappho. It lacks Sappho's seemingly artless intensity, her passionate abandon, and her lyric simplicity. Like the other elegies of Donne, "Sapho to Philaenis" is an intellectual exercise, marked by Donne's peculiar dissection of motive and exploitation of conceit. He makes Sappho pause in the midst of her loving madness to reflect—in the Donnean way—on the philosophical underpinnings of her love, to intellectualize what she feels. He makes her speculate, like Plato's Aristophanes in *The Symposium,* that a woman seeking another woman is seeking her other half; that the two, joined in a kind of cosmic union, experience a subliminal, almost platonic love.

In the central section of the elegy, Donne has permitted Sappho to argue that homosexual lovers are somehow different from heterosexual ones; at the conclusion, however, he brings the homosexual and heterosexual lovers together. Donne's Sappho in fact echoes the sentiments of the heterosexual lovers of Donne's own lyrics. Like the lover in "To his Mistris Going to Bed," Sappho imagines her loved one's body as a paradise. Like the lover in "The Canonization," she boasts the transcendent perfection of her beloved: "So may thy mighty, 'amazing beauty move / Envy'in all women, and in all men, love" (61–62). Like the lovers of "A Valediction: forbidding Mourning," soaring above those dull sublunary lovers who experience change, she says that her love for Philaenis raises both of them above change: "And so be change, and sickness, farre from thee, / As thou by comming neere, keep'st them from me" (63–64). Repeatedly, just like the Donnean lover of the *Songs and Sonets,* she longs for oneness with the loved one. With her, too, that often repeated word *all* is the leitmotif of her desire.

Ultimately then, "Sapho to Philaenis" shares as much, perhaps more, with other poetry in the Donne canon in its intellectual play, in its extension of conceit, as it does with Sappho's lyrics. Donne began his elegy with the serious motive of looking through Sappho's eyes. We must not blame him that he only succeeded in looking over her shoulder. Other poets of the age who knew Sappho's poems—Jonson, for example—did no more than to borrow a notable line or image. Donne initiates a dialogue with the ancient poet, going further than others had in attempting to fathom the love of woman for woman that inspired her lyrics. Finally, however, this dialogue breaks down into a Donnean monologue, so marked by the characteristic intellectual curiosity of his other poetry that it persuades us that this elegy clearly belongs to his canon with as unique a voice as that of the ancient lyric poet that it purports to imitate.

Theresa M. DiPasquale

Donne's Catholic Petrarchans
The Babylonian Captivity of Desire

Donne establishes the ruling conceit for the first part of "Satyre III" when he praises "our Mistresse faire Religion": men's denominational preferences are as various as their tastes in women. Crants the Calvinist (49–54) loves a nutbrown maid; Anglican Graius (55–62) settles for the fiancée his "Godfathers" pick; and the ecumenical Graccus (65–69) is "The Indifferent," who will commit himself only to variety. Given these characterizations, we might expect the Roman Catholic Mirreus to be in love with a whore, a painted papal moll like Duessa, and indeed his mistress is clothed in the "brave" frippery to which Protestants "will not be inthrall'd" (49). But as it turns out, she is not much of a seductress; her lover is having trouble tracking her down:

> Mirreus
> Thinking her unhous'd here, and fled from us,
> Seekes her at Rome; there, because hee doth know
> That shee was there a thousand yeares agoe,
> He loves her ragges so, as wee here obey
> The statecloth where the Prince sate yesterday.
> (43–48)

Mirreus's pursuit of an evasive mistress has distinctly Petrarchan overtones. His beloved has, like Daphne, "fled" the place in which her beauties might have been profaned; so he is led "far astray . . . pursuing her who has turned in flight" (*Rime sparse*, 6). Like Petrarch, he fetishizes his lady's apparel and adores an absent presence.[1]

The satire's parallel between Catholicism and Petrarchism points to a related analogy in Donne's love poetry, where the attitudes and utterances of unrequited lovers are often reminiscent of specifically Roman piety. Donne finds that the religion of love has more than one denomination, and his Petrarchan speakers—faced with the rejection of their faith in favor of sexual pragmatism, jolly promiscuity, or mutual devotion—speak in defensive counter-Reformation accents. Their discourses of desire uphold a creed of nonfulfillment, assert the efficacy of erotic relics and sacraments, and proclaim invalid any love doctrine that challenges the orthodoxy of frustration. Indeed, some of the most stubbornly Petrarchan personae in the *Songs and Sonets*—the speakers of "Loves Deitie," "The Funerall," and "Twicknam Garden"—redefine both love and desire in order to uphold the ways of their tradition-bound faith.

For Donne, I would argue, Petrarchism is love's papistry, the Babylonian captivity of desire. But Donne himself was "raised Catholic" (to use a phrase many academics and stand-up comics rely on today), and in another sense, he was raised Petrarchan. Thus, in his love poems, as in his Protestant polemics, Donne anatomizes a tradition that he knows from within. As we will see, he helps explain the unnerving inner logic of frustrated desire and shows how that logic shapes and defines erotic discourse.[2]

The speaker of "Loves Deitie" is in a mood to challenge Petrarchan discourse on the most fundamental level; he wants to redefine its vocabulary: "It cannot bee / Love, till I love her, that loves mee" (13–14). His frustrated desire is defined as love only since the perverse young "god of Love"—backed by "custome" (6)—imposed the "des-

1. Donne, *The Satires, Epigrams and Verse Letters*, ed. W. Milgate (Oxford: Clarendon, 1967). All quotations of Donne's poetry are taken from this edition and from *The Elegies and the Songs and Sonnets*, ed. Helen Gardner (Oxford: Clarendon, 1965). Cf. *Rime sparse* 16, where Petrarch compares himself to an old man who wanders away "to Rome, following his desire" to gaze on a true icon of Christ; similarly, Petrarch seeks Laura's "longed-for true form" (*Petrarch's Lyric Poems*, trans. and ed. Robert M. Durling [Cambridge: Harvard University Press, 1976]; all quotations of Petrarch are taken from this edition).

2. Cf. Dennis Flynn, "Donne's Catholicism," *Recusant History* 13 (1975): 1–17, 178–95; Thomas Hester, *Kinde Pitty and Brave Scorn: John Donne's Satyres* (Durham: Duke University Press, 1982); and N. J. C. Andreasen, *John Donne, Conservative Revolutionary* (Princeton: Princeton University Press, 1967).

tinie" of unrequited passion upon him. Thus, he wishes to return to the practices of those who "dyed before" the bad little boy was born; "hee, who then lov'd most" never "Sunke so low, as to love one which did scorne" (3–4). If contemporary lovers rose up to "ungod" the willful Cupid, the speaker thinks, they could return to the nobler ways of the ancients (20). He no sooner proposes that they overthrow the deity's "Tyrannie," however, than he recants his rebellious words. In the final stanza, he declares that he would be "loth" to see his lady requite him since she already loves another, and "Falshood is worse then hate" (27).

N. J. C. Andreasen reads the poem as affirming the values Petrarch himself embraces at the end of the *Rime sparse,* when he acknowledges Laura's moral rectitude and admits that her acquiescence would have destroyed them both. Donne's speaker, Andreasen argues, "accepts traditional morality through his recognition that [the lady's] infidelity would be worse than rejection, however much he might long for reciprocity" (138). The central contest of the poem, seen in these terms, is that between moral and immoral impulses. But Andreasen's discussion is rich with the language of Reformation controversy: the lover rebels against "tradition by appealing to the earliest era of love"; he will recognize "only the early apostolic era as the proper precedent" and maintains this "mood of iconoclasm" until the sudden reversal of the final stanza; the whole is "a contrast between . . . tradition . . . and reformation" (137, 138). According to this reading—which is, I would stress, based upon the terms that the poem itself establishes—the "custome" that the speaker finally reaffirms is not "traditional morality" but traditional religion, which is, in a Protestant milieu, not the same thing at all. The speaker has not struggled onto moral high ground; rather, he has made an unsuccessful attempt to abjure the distinctly Catholic tradition of Petrarchan desire.

Central to the speaker's un-Reformed love religion is the spurious pontifical authority of the love god himself. The speaker's indictment of the deity resembles Donne's Protestant analysis of papal history: the Pope's claims to universal primacy are based upon the teachings of pious men who could not realize how their doctrines would later be twisted; for "the Ancients spoke of many . . . things controverted now . . . [and] never suspected that so impious a sense would have been put upon their words, nor those opinions and doctrines so mis-

chievously advanced, as they have been since."[3] In the poem, the
speaker is "Sure, [that] they which made [Cupid] god, meant not so
much" (8) as to have him preside over frustrated desire; but, with a
display of popelike ambition, this "moderne god will now extend /
His vast prerogative, as far as Jove" (15–16). Like the Bishop of Rome,
the love god does have a legitimate ecclesiastical role to play, and
when "in his young godhead" he "practis'd" only his duly appointed
function (9), he fulfilled the same role as the legendary Bishop Valen-
tine, uniting male and female, lover and beloved: "when an even flame
two hearts did touch, / His office was indulgently to fit / Actives to
passives" (10–12).[4] But now, having brought under his rule many
things that have nothing to do with weddings—resentment, uncon-
secrated desire, letters sent from afar, poetry of formal compliment
and complaint, and all courtly or Petrarchan situations that make
men "rage . . . lust . . . write . . . commend" (17)—this renegade
Cupid is a pope who grasps at secular authority and abuses the
faithful.

Thus, when the speaker of "Loves Deitie" recants his protestations
and renews his allegiance to the Petrarchan love god, he is plunging
back into erotic recusancy. Both he and his lady ought, he feels, to
persevere in the faith that they currently profess:

> why murmure I,
> As though I felt the worst that love could doe?
> Love might make me leave loving, or might trie
> A deeper plague, to make her love mee too,
> Which, since she loves before, I'am loth to see;
> Falshood is worse then hate; and that must bee,
> If shee whom I love, should love mee.
>
> (22–28)

As the speaker sees it, a relationship founded on female infidelity
would be a "plague" worse than either ongoing frustration or the

---

3. *The Sermons of John Donne,* ed. George R. Potter and Evelyn Simpson, 10 vols.
(Berkeley: University of California Press, 1953–1962), 3:316. All quotations from the
Sermons are taken from this edition and cited by volume and page number.
4. Donne, "Epithalamion . . . on the Lady Elizabeth, and Count Palatine," in *The Epi-
thalamions, Anniversaries, and Epicedes,* ed. W. Milgate (Oxford: Clarendon, 1978).

quenching of his own ardor. Self-interest, no less than respect for the "moral order," determines his feelings: when considered in light of the speaker's fear that he has not yet "felt the *worst* that love could doe" (23), the thought "Falshood is *worse* then hate" (27) implies a concern for his own welfare, a precaution lest he himself become the victim of her infidelity.

He is convinced that duplicity and betrayal "must bee" his lot if she requites him, for he assumes that if he is her first paramour, he will not be her last. Implicit in his preference for unrequited passion is a smug logic: as long as one remains frustrated, one will never sprout the cuckold's horns. In "The Indifferent," a libertine Venus condemns to inevitable cuckoldry those "Heretiques" who "thinke to stablish dangerous constancie"; the Cupid of "Loves Deitie" enforces a bitterly monogamous Petrarchan faith that is in some respects exactly opposed to his mother's religion of "sweetest . . . Variety." But mutual devotion is anathema in both erotic denominations, and the speaker of "Loves Deitie" is thus convinced that female reciprocity is a bad thing. Any "Rebell and Atheist" who tries to break free from the creed of nonfulfillment will, he concludes, get what is coming to him; the only way to avoid the "worst that love could doe" is to stay within the One True Church of frustrated desire.

The language of Petrarchan poetry helps to ensure that lovers will do just that; it is a discourse that perpetuates the dubious pleasures of unconsummated longing. In a verse letter to the Countess of Huntingdon, Donne promises the Protestant lady whom he addresses that he will not "vexe [her] eyes" with a cruciform verbal icon, the "crosse-arm'd Elegie" of Petrarchan suffering. Such utterances are, he insists, perversely effectual; they generate the very frustration they purport to lament: he "Who first look'd sad, griev'd, pin'd, and shew'd his paine, / Was he that first taught women, to disdaine" (35–36). This mock foundation myth proposes that Petrarchan art is a self-fulfilling prophecy and identifies Petrarchan desire as "love . . . with such fatall weaknesse made, / That it destroyes it selfe with its owne shade" (33–34). Congenitally flawed, "made" weak from the start, the lover's dark exhalations are reflexively fatal; his anguished state both originates in and is destroyed by its own utterance, "that thing [which] whispers it selfe away" (30). The inverse of seduction poetry, Petrarchan lament ensures that no sexual persuasion will take place, for those pursuing

"The right true end of love" ("Loves Progress," 2) the faint moans of "whining Poëtry" prove worse than useless.

But is any poetry worth writing? The speaker of "Satyre II" has his doubts:

> Though Poëtry indeed be such a sinne
> As I thinke that brings dearths, and Spaniards in,
> Though like the Pestilence and old fashion'd love,
> Ridlingly it catch men; and doth remove
> Never, till it be sterv'd out; yet their state
> Is poore, disarm'd, like Papists, not worth hate.
>
> (5–10)

The lines associate poverty-stricken rhymers with both Catholicism and the maladies of Petrarchan desire; their self-defeating "sinne" weakens England and makes it vulnerable to the extravagant fashions and ultra-Catholic aggressions of Spain, while they themselves are afflicted with the plaguelike disease of "old fashion'd love": pitiable and impotent, they suffer its "Ridlingly" paradoxical symptom of icy fire, fever and chills.

The speaker mocks every kind of poet from the professional playwright to the dilettante lyricist, but most important as a guide to the *Songs and Sonets* is his comment on the writer who "would move Love by rimes" (17). Such efforts are useless, he argues, for "witchcrafts charms / Bring not now their old feares, nor their old harmes" (17–18). Donne plays upon a popular Reformation theme—compare Corbett's "Faeryes Farewell"[5]—which associated the Catholic past with a now defunct magic. The writer of feeble Petrarchan pleas finds himself thwarted in the pursuit of sex because he trusts in the poetic equivalent of "hocus-pocus"; his superstitious mumblings make no impression on the women of the satirist's reformed and enlightened age.

In "The Funerall," we see in action a Romish Petrarchan's efforts to use "witchcrafts charms." The speaker's lady has denied him sexual grace; she has refused to "save" him from the death of frustration (24); and although she has given him a "subtile wreath" of her hair (3), he

---

5. *The Poems of Richard Corbett,* ed. J. A. W. Bennett and H. R. Trevor-Roper (Oxford: Clarendon, 1955), 49–52.

cannot be certain just "What . . . shee meant by'it" (17). He does, however, have his own use for the token: since the woven circlet is all that he has of the lady, he makes a fetish of it.[6] Calling it her representative, he insists that it be treated with all the reverence due to her:

> Who ever comes to shroud me, do not harme
> > Nor question much
> That subtile wreath of haire, which crowns mine arme;
> The mystery, the signe you must not touch,
> > For 'tis my outward Soule,
> Viceroy to that, which then to heaven being gone,
> > Will leave this to controule,
> And keepe these limbes, her Provinces, from dissolution.
> > (1–8)

In referring to the bracelet as the "viceroy" of his body's spiritual monarch, the lover proclaims it the absent presence both of his own soul and of the lady whose "controule" over him the bracelet signifies and exercises.

As the poem proceeds, his attitude becomes more and more recognizably idolatrous and, from the perspective established in "Satyre III," Romanist. Mirreus and his coreligionists call the Pope Christ's vicar and revere him as the regent of the King who has "to heaven . . . gone." And they commit idolatry in adoring the Sacrament, for in doing so they "worshippe the giftes in steede of the giuer himselfe."[7] Similarly, this lover honors the inanimate "Viceroy," his beloved's gift to him, as he would the lady herself. Indeed, he deals with frustration precisely as does the Catholic of "Satyre III": he loves his mistress's "ragges so, as [subjects] obey / The statecloth where the Prince sate yesterday" (47–48). But the speaker feels that his monarch has condemned him to death. By withholding herself from the speaker and

6. I use the term *fetish* in its anthropological sense. Cf. John Freccero, "The Fig Tree and the Laurel: Petrarch's Poetics," *Diacritics* 5 (1975): 34–40. Freccero draws on the work of Yehezkel Kaufmann, *The Religion of Israel,* trans. and abr. Moshe Greenberg (Chicago: University of Chicago Press, 1960), who identifies "the Jews' conception of idolatry as a kind of fetishism" (37).

7. John Calvin, *The Institution of the Christian Religion,* trans. Thomas Norton (London: Vautrollier for Humfrey Toy, 1578), 4.17.36. All quotations of the *Institutes* are taken from this translation and cited by book, chapter, and section.

granting him only an empty sign of the grace that might have saved him, the lady has killed him.

In the final stanza, then, he seeks revenge. He reinterprets the wreath of hair once more and, with insolent disregard for the lady's intended meaning, works his own will upon the sign:

> What ere shee meant by'it, bury it with me,
>   For since I am
> Loves martyr, it might breed idolatrie,
> If into others hands these Reliques came;
>   As 'twas humility
> To'afford to it all that a Soule can doe,
>   So, 'tis some bravery,
> That since you would save none of mee, I bury some of you.
>
> (17–24)

At first, it would seem that the lover here develops Protestant scruples about the idolatrous veneration of the bracelet. But his Reformation sentiments appear deeply ironic, given the idolatrous attitude underlying the opening stanza, where his reification of the sign allowed him to feel that he was revering the lady in revering it. In the final lines, that same literalism—what the Protestant theologians would call a "carnal" understanding—makes him gloat over the violence he can do to the symbol that represents her.

Reformers accused the Roman clergy of a gross disregard for God's intentions in instituting the Eucharist, and they detected in the doctrine of eucharistic sacrifice a hubristic desire to control the Giver of the sign: to make Him and then slay Him through the magic of the Mass, to entomb Him through the reservation of the Host.[8] The speaker of "The Funerall" is guilty of just such "bravery." The lady has given him a sign of herself, and "What ere shee meant by'it," he can use it to love her to death. His talisman will be wrapped into his winding sheet and lie with him forever in the grave.

The speaker hints at the emotional logic underlying his spite when he speaks of the wreath as something that can reproduce. He insists

---

8. For example, Donne's *Sermons* 5:135; 7:267, 429 and the account of a 1548 debate on the Eucharist in John E. Booty's edition of the 1559 *Book of Common Prayer* (Charlottesville: University Press of Virginia, 1976), 363–64.

that the ring of hair be buried with him lest it "breed idolatrie" in others; it has already bred that semiotic sin in him. The spiritual adultery he has committed in his fetishistic relation with the signifier is the only kind of sex he has been allowed. But like most Renaissance lovers, he is uncomfortable with the idea that he might not be the only one. Thus, in taking precautions to ensure that his beloved object does not "breed" with someone else, he is protecting, not the other men who might handle it, but himself. Their idolatry would give them as much of the lady as he has possessed, and he will brook no rivals.

In "The Funerall," then, the lover's attitude toward other males is purely defensive. The arch-Petrarchan of Donne's love poetry, however, is the speaker of "Twicknam Garden," who puts erotic recusancy on the offensive and—with a wily Jesuitical gesture—offers successful lovers a eucharist of suspicion; he seeks to drive a wedge between requited men and the women they love. Satisfying his desire by subverting consummated love, he pushes the doctrine of nonfulfillment to an alarmingly aggressive extreme.

In the first stanza, he associates his own frustrated longing with a perverse sacramentalism. The "spider love" that torments him is a priest performing poisonous magic: it "transubstantiates all, / And can convert Manna to gall" (6–7). Under the influence of such a powerful force, the speaker himself becomes an agent of corruption; the garden into which he has entered now "may thoroughly be thought / True Paradise" for he has "the serpent brought" (8, 9). As both a phallic symbol and an emblem of primal envy, the snake image establishes an alarming affinity between ruthless *invidia* and frustrated masculine desire. The remainder of the poem plays upon the implications of that affinity.

In the second stanza, the lover objects to the joys of springtime itself. His feeling that it would be "wholsomer" for him if "winter did / Benight the glory of this place" (10–11) is often compared with Petrarch's sensation in the well-known "Zefiro torna," and the parallels are valid as far as they go: in each lyric, the speaker contrasts his own emotional state with the sweetness of the season.[9] But in Petrarch,

---

9. Cf. Andreasen, *Conservative Revolutionary,* 133; John E. Parish, "Donne as a Petrarchan," *Notes & Queries* 4 (1957): 377–78; and Bernard Richards, "Donne's 'Twickenham Garden' and the *Fons Amatoria,*" *Review of English Studies* 33 (1982): 181–83.

the poet's subjectivity is powerful enough to ruin the spring for him; objective reality is of no concern to him, and he does not desire to work quasi-magical alterations in the realm outside his own consciousness. Donne's speaker has a state of mind less powerfully detached, and he shows more aggression; still able to perceive the beauties around him, he *wills* that they might be marred. Petrarch feels "the singing of little birds, and the flowering of meadows, and virtuous gentle gestures in beautiful ladies are a wilderness and cruel, savage beasts" (310.12–14). His perceptions are utterly distorted, and social reality is flattened out into a backdrop for autonomous subjectivity; the ladies' gestures become a static part of the landscape upon which the author's feelings are projected. In Donne's poem, the process is reversed; the landscape is invested with quasi-social characteristics, and the trees become insensitive onlookers whose derision fuels the speaker's anger and resentment. He sees in the garden's beauty the laughing faces of others who have no sympathy for him, and he responds with the dark wish "that a grave frost did forbid / These trees to laugh, and mocke mee to my face" (12–13).

In order that he "may not this disgrace / Indure" (14–15), he asks that Love, that powerful transformer of substances, change him into

> Some senslesse peece of this place . . .
> Make me a mandrake, so I may grow here,
> Or a stone fountaine weeping out my yeare.
>   (16–18)

The request would at first seem to be a retreat from the petty malevolence in the first half of the stanza, a move toward a more conventional Petrarchism. For in the *Rime sparse,* metamorphosis is the ultimate effect of love's agonies; mythic transmutation allows the poet to express his emotion through richly significant forms. Indeed, as a mandrake, the speaker of "Twicknam Garden" might be beneficial to other lovers, since the plant is traditionally believed to function as an aphrodisiac and fertility charm.

It is on the fountain form that he settles, however, as he elaborates his fantasy in the final stanza:

> Hither with christall vyals, lovers come,
>   And take my teares, which are loves wine,

And try your mistresse Teares at home,
For all are false, that tast not just like mine;
    Alas, hearts do not in eyes shine,
Nor can you more judge womans thoughts by teares,
    Then by her shadow, what she weares.
O perverse sexe, where none is true but shee,
Who's therefore true, because her truth kills mee.

(19–27)

By choosing to become a fountain, the speaker completes an ironic analogy—first hinted at in the opening stanza—between himself and Christ. He has come, grief stricken and anguished, to his own Garden of Gethsemane, and he now parodies the Savior's eucharistic self-offering.[10] Like Jesus, the speaker would give "loves wine" to those seeking Truth, but his tears are the eucharistic drink neither of Christianity nor of fulfilled eros. Shed in pain and possessed of magical properties, they are the sacramental outpourings of unrequited desire; but their flavor, he insists, is that of authenticity itself. Thus, he can offer his lachrymal wine to requited lovers as a means of testing ladies' fidelity.

Men of reformed love religion—those who have rejected Petrarchan superstition and embraced the joys of mutual desire—must resist jealous qualms. In "The Good-morrow," the lovers' waking souls "watch not one another out of feare" (9); and the speaker of "The Anniversarie" aspires to a love stronger than any anxiety: "True and false feares let us refraine" (27). Donne's requited lovers are by no means blind to the possibility that a woman may be unfaithful—they forget it no more than Renaissance Protestants do the danger of idolatry, but they nevertheless confirm their faith in mutual truth, confronting head-on the spectral threat of infidelity. Such speakers treat both their ladies' tears and their own poetic utterances as sacramental witnesses or seals of commitment. Their ears are "fed with true oathes,"

10. Cf. discussions of the sacramental imagery in Judah Stampfer, *John Donne and the Metaphysical Gesture* (New York: Funk and Wagnalls, 1970), 173–74; Andreasen, *Conservative Revolutionary,* 146–48; Richards, "'Twickenham Garden' and the *Fons Amatoria,*" 182; Sallye Sheppeard, "Eden and Agony in 'Twicknam Garden,'" *John Donne Journal* 7 (1988): 70; and Terry G. Sherwood, *Fulfilling the Circle: A Study of John Donne's Thought* (Toronto: University of Toronto Press, 1984), 111, 213 n. 7.

and their eyes are nourished by the flow of "sweet salt teares" ("The Anniversarie," 15, 16).

But the speaker of "Twicknam Garden" ministers bitter tears, and his wine feeds suspicion rather than faith; he encourages lovers to cater to their doubts. With the disruptive spirit that the English saw in Jesuit missionaries, he tries to disturb the faith of those who have entered into true love's communion and to replace it with the spurious sacramentalism of the old dispensation. He urges them to collect "loves wine" in "christall vyals" so that they may carry it home and use it as an elixir of truth.[11]

In a sermon, Donne critiques Catholic churchmen who sell the "merchandises" of Rome, proclaiming "the value, and efficacy of uncertain *reliques,* and superstitious charms, and incantations." Such vendors are "Ambassadours to serve their own turns, and do their owne businesse." The Anglican clergy, by contrast, offer free of charge "no other *reliques,* but the commemoration of [Christ's] Passion in the *Sacrament*" (*Sermons* 10:126, 127). Those who deal in trinkets and potions supplant the central mysteries of faith for their own gain, and that is precisely what the Twicknam lover does. For, in the *Songs and Sonets,* consummated love has its own central mystery—the reflection of one lover's face in the other's eye, and the trust that "true plaine hearts doe in the faces rest" ("The Good-morrow," 16). The Twicknam lover discredits this core of emotional faith when he insists, "Alas, hearts do not in eyes shine" (23). In its place he offers magical assurance: conveniently portable tears for fears. According to the telling logic of Donne's sermon, then, this charm peddler must be an ambassador to serve his own turn; he must be making a profit of one sort or another.

So what does the Twicknam lover have to gain by offering a truth potion to fulfilled lovers? It would at first seem that he gets nothing more than the chance to vent his resentful feelings toward women:

11. The imagery calls to mind abuses of the Eucharist that Protestants saw as an ongoing threat. The first Edwardian Prayer Book proscribes communicants' taking communion in the hand lest they take the bread and convey it "secretelye awaye" to use as a magic charm (*The First and Second Prayer-Books of King Edward the Sixth* [New York: E. P. Dutton, 1910], 230). Cf. Keith Thomas, *Religion and the Decline of Magic* (New York: Scribner, 1971), 34–35, and a 1584 treatise by Reginald Scot, *The Discoverie of Witchcraft* (New York: Dover Publications, 1972), which catalogues "Popish" superstitions and abuses, including the use of consecrated wine to cure a cough (148).

"O perverse sexe, where none is true but shee, / Who's therefore true, because her truth kills mee" (26-27). His anger is generated by a refusal to perceive the true use of a thing—a refusal that from a Protestant perspective is characteristic of Roman sacramentalism.[12] The speaker insists upon defining feminine fidelity not as a positive expression of love for one man, but rather as a weapon of malice to be used against him. In the first stanza, he identifies the only "True Paradise" as that which harbors a serpent; here, he can conceive of no Edenic lady, no woman who is one man's *hortus conclusus,* except by accounting for her behavior as an expression of malice. Thus, like "the spider love" itself, he "convert[s] Manna to gall." For in the horn-mad Renaissance, a lady's fidelity is the heavenly white bread that sustains her lover, but with his perverse interpretation the speaker flavors sweet devotion itself with bitterness.

The craving for certainty about a woman's truth—the fatal appetite of the "curioso impertinente," as Cervantes calls him—provides the speaker with a guaranteed market for his tearful wine. It will be difficult for men to ignore the offer of an elixir that detects infidelity, for it nourishes a fear already latent in their hearts.[13] The speaker's assertion that "none is true but" the one he loves is, in essence, a challenge; he dares those who think themselves happy to test the validity of their contentment. And for one lover, the man to whom the Petrarchan's unattainable lady is true, the challenge is a particularly insidious trap. For according to the closing couplet, that man alone will find that his mistress is true; however, in so doing he will learn also that his lady is the object of the speaker's devotion and that she is faithful to him only out of spite toward another.[14]

The speaker's formulation redefines the Petrarchan love triangle in a way that marginalizes the requited male; it casts him as the sexually neutral catalyst of a chemical reaction in which the Petrarchan and

---

12. Cf. Calvin, *Institutes* 4.17.37 and 18.7–8, as well as the twenty-fifth of the *Thirty-Nine Articles:* "The Sacraments were not ordained of Christ to be gazed upon, or to be carried about, but that we should duly use them" (qtd. from E. Tyrrell Green, *The Thirty-Nine Articles and the Age of Reformation* [London: Wells, Gardner, Darton, 1896]).

13. Cf. *Orlando Furioso* 42.98–104.

14. The Wine of Truth will poison him. Cf. a story of priests killing a king with a poisoned host (*Sermons* 7:295; 9:302); as Thomas Browne tells it, the chalice is tainted, so the victim "receive[s] his bane in a draught of his salvation" (*Pseudodoxia Epidemica,* ed. Robin Robbins, 2 vols. [Oxford: Clarendon, 1981], 1:607).

his cruel fair are, ironically, the active ingredients. The overt misogyny of the closing stanza masks the speaker's real agenda: a redefinition of requited love that places it in the service of the Petrarchan nonrelationship and the poetry of frustration.

In "Twicknam Garden," Donne puts Petrarchan metamorphosis to work as a disguised instrument of aggression; he recontextualizes in a social milieu Petrarch's insistence that he has lived "without any envy; for if other lovers have more favorable fortune, a thousand of their pleasures are not worth one of my torments" (*Canzoniere* 231.2–4). This claim, made in isolation from those whom it deflates, is fairly straightforward grandstanding. The disavowal of envy is part and parcel of the claim to infinite superiority of feeling; Petrarch dwells apart in a universe whose very structure differs from that of the worldly lovers of whom he has spoken in the third person. In Donne's poem, however, the speaker addresses requited lovers directly, song becomes social discourse, and the distance breaks down. Having precipitated an encounter between himself and those who have succeeded in love, the speaker must avail himself of new strategies. Uprooted from their self-absorbed and self-reflecting isolation, Donne posits, the utterances of Petrarchan frustration cannot sustain their gemlike perfection. In a direct confrontation with the fulfilled sexuality of requited love, the Petrarchan's claim to a suffering so sublime as to be beyond envy degenerates into a mean-spirited act of sabotage: the fox spreads a rumor about pesticide poisoning among those beasts who *can* reach the grapes.

The speaker's announcement that "all are false, that tast not just like mine" (22) has the ring of a dogmatic hubris that, Donne the preacher insists, Protestants must avoid. They must not, he explains, harbor a "peremptory prejudice upon other mens opinions, that no opinion but thine can be true, in the doctrine of the Sacrament." Rather, he tells his congregation, "Exercise thy faith onely, here, and leave . . . disputation to the Schoole" (*Sermons* 7:291). The speaker of "Twicknam Garden" gives lovers the opposite advice. Like a Roman Catholic controversialist, he insists upon his sacrament as the only efficacious alternative to a system of barren, even deceptive signifiers; for, in order to impress upon requited lovers their need for his truth-telling tears, he declares that "hearts do not in eyes shine" (23) and that one can no more "judge womans thoughts by teares, / Then by her shadow, what she weares" (24–25). The speaker thus denies the sacramental validity of female tears, insisting that there is no correspondence between the outward signs and the inward reality that the woman would have her lover believe they represent. He urges his listeners to delve into the nature of the mystery he has impugned, and in so doing he tempts them to a "Carnality in the understanding" or "concupiscence of disputation" (*Sermons* 2:84) that Donne sees as a characteristic fault of Roman Catholics.

In a sermon, Donne cites Saint Gregory's description of this masochistic inquisitiveness: "The mind of a curious man delights to examine itself upon Interrogatories, which, upon the Racke, it cannot answer, and to vexe it selfe with such doubts as it cannot resolve" (2:84). In "The Blossom," Donne links such self-torture to frustrated sexuality when the speaker addresses his heart as "thou which lov'st to bee / Subtile to plague thy selfe" (17–18). But the sadistic Petrarchan of "Twicknam Garden" satisfies his desire in a slyly complementary way: he facilitates the self-torture of requited hearts, finding his delight in making Iagoesque suggestions.

The poem is an exploration of Petrarchism's darker recesses. But Donne attacks only the things he knows well enough to turn inside out. The Jesuitical wit of *Ignatius His Conclave* fights counter-Reformation fire with fire. The elaborate arguments of *Biathanatos* reveal suicidal preoccupations in the author of *Pseudo-Martyr,* and a poem like "Twicknam Garden" tells us perhaps more than we would like to know about how a psyche prone to frustration and resentment anatomizes such feelings.[15] Years after Donne became an Anglican divine, we can find him playing games with the many different levels of masculine jealousy. As a preacher, he uses precisely the same strategy as does his Twicknam speaker to warn the benchers of Lincoln's Inn about the dangers posed by—what else?—Jesuits:

> There is a snare laid for thy wife; Her Religion, say they, doth not hinder her husbands preferment, why should she refuse to apply her self to them? We have

15. Cf. Dennis Flynn "Irony in Donne's *Biathanatos* and *Pseudo-Martyr,*" *Recusant History* 12 (1973–1974): 49–69; and Arthur Marotti, *John Donne, Coterie Poet* (Madison: University of Wisconsin Press, 1986), 214–18, who discusses "Twicknam Garden" as an expression of Donne's ambivalence toward literary patronage.

used to speak proverbially of a Curtain Sermon, as of a shrewd thing; but a Curtain Mass, a Curtain *Requiem,* a snare in thy bed, a snake in thy bosome is somewhat worse. I know not what name we may give to such a womans husband; but I am sure such a wife hath committed adultery, Spiritual Adultery, and that with her husbands knowledge; call him what you will. (*Sermons* 4:138–39)

What are we to make of such tactics? Like those employed in "Twicknam Garden," they play less upon desires—sexual or spiritual—than upon fears.

In a much later sermon, Donne defines the preacher's role in terms of earnest and heartfelt wooing: "True Instruction is a making love to the Congregation, and to every soule in it; . . . Wee have no way into your hearts, but by sending our hearts" (9:350). But this direct approach would not work if those most in need of "Instruction" were not present, and in the sermon on spiritual cuckoldry, addressed to the male professionals and students of Lincoln's Inn, that is precisely the case. Questioning the Protestant fidelity of the lawyers' crypto-Catholic wives, the preacher is faced with a distinctly Petrarchan problem: female absence. The women are, presumably, not on hand to hear the Anglican love-songs of Dr. Donne, and thus we find him resorting to the devious strategies of the Twicknam speaker.

The discourses of frustrated desire turn out, then, to be inseparable from the aggressive maneuvers of envy, and Donne's Catholic Petrarchans have found but one of many ways to play out the drama of invidious sexuality. Throughout the *Songs and Sonets,* Donne explores the deep affinity between the bewitchment of love longing and the voodoo strategies of malice. Even an apparently requited lover can fear that his mistress will work "Witchcraft by a Picture," burning his image in the light of her eye or drowning it in the salt water of her tears. It becomes clear that only the man who can "keep off envies stinging" ("Song," 6) can believe himself requited by "a woman true, and faire." In some of the greatest of Donne's love lyrics, couples achieve such confident unassailability; they choose—as do the lovers of "The Anniversarie"—to "refraine" from fears both "True and false." But there are also those like the Twicknam speaker, caught up in a frustrated, spiderlike desire, who come to find envy itself erogenous and who satisfy their desire by pricking others with its sharp little sting.

Anthony Low

Thomas Carew
Patronage, Family, and New-Model Love

Coming from the direction of the twentieth century, a reader might not notice what is perhaps the most radical quality in Thomas Carew's love poetry, since that quality consists in an absence: the virtual absence, for the first time since Wyatt, of the Petrarchan tradition in any of its moods and variations. True, from the beginning, English Petrarchists, like their Italian predecessors, indulged in mockery and undermined the tradition with cynical demurrals and pragmatic insertions. Even in the hands of iconoclasts like Donne, however, the basics persisted: distorted, mocked, fought against, yet ultimately still a determining force.[1] As in politics, so in love: as Donne rails against the patronage system, so he rails against Cupid's "vast prerogative" but finds no substitute. With Carew, however, the discourse of desire undergoes a fundamental change, as a new-model courtier, client, and lover appears. None of Carew's lovers stays faithful to a haughty, refusing mistress, none pines away with unsatisfied desire, none is killed, even in jest, by submission to superior disdain. The absence of a whole complex of originally feudal or courtly attitudes, although Carew was a consummate courtier, has its roots, as I shall argue, in his family situation and experience with the patronage sys-

---

1. See Arthur Marotti, *John Donne, Coterie Poet* (Madison: University of Wisconsin Press, 1986); and Anthony Low, "Donne and the Reinvention of Love," *English Literary Renaissance* 20 (1990): 465–86.

tem.[2] Like Donne, Carew learned by disgrace. A destructive confrontation with father, family, and culture forced him to find other forms of patronage and love that were not feudal in principle.

Carew's youthful expectations were high. His family on both sides were successful city people who moved among circles at the porous border between trade and gentility. His mother and grandmother both were daughters of Lord Mayors; his father practiced law, proceeded Master in Chancery in 1576, and was among the crowd of successful men knighted by King James in 1603. Carew's family by blood and marriage also included members of the government and the nobility. But just as he left Oxford for the Middle Temple in 1612, pursuing the usual course of a younger son hoping to rise in the world, his father, Sir Matthew, suffered financial reverses and, as a letter of 1613 reveals, had to turn to his prominent nephew-by-marriage, Sir Dudley Carleton, Ambassador to Venice, for assistance:

> My very honorable good Lord,
>
> There hathe passed many a drearye and sorowfull daye over my head sence my last writeng unto your lordship, many griefes, mich sorrow, and great mishaps. . . . My self to be cozened and deceaved, of all my land, wheruppon I had levyd my whole estate, and brought my self in debt for it. Where I was in hope to have left my son a thowsand pound land per annum, I am not lyke to leave him anye.[3]

Sir Matthew had two sons whom he hoped to launch in life: the elder to receive his land; the younger, Thomas the future poet, to be given a good start up the ladder of a professional or public career. But things were not working out as hoped. Sir Matthew's financial reverses were compounded by the refusal of either son to cooperate with his plans: "[My] twoe sons, the one roneth up and downe after houndes and hawkes, the other [Thomas] is of the midle temple, where he hath a chamber and studye, but I feare studiethe the lawe very litle, so as I am neither happye in my self nor my children" (xviii).

---

2. See, especially, Guy Fitch Lytle and Stephen Orgel, eds., *Patronage in the Renaissance* (Princeton: Princeton University Press, 1981); and Robert C. Evans, *Ben Jonson and the Poetics of Patronage* (Lewisburg: Bucknell University Press, 1989).

3. *The Poems of Thomas Carew*, ed. Rhodes Dunlap (1949; repr. Oxford: Clarendon Press, 1964), xvii-xviii. Further quotations from Carew are from this edition; contractions are expanded and the use of *u, v, i,* and *j* silently modernized.

Thomas Carew's case was apparently resolved when Sir Dudley agreed to employ him. Since Carleton held a government post, by taking service with him Carew assumed his first position in the complex of patronage networks, formed by personal relationships and political allegiances, that ascended ultimately to court and throne. As his father's fortunes waned, his own brightened. He served with Carleton in Venice, Florence, and Turin, and accompanied him to the Netherlands in March 1616. There, shortly after reaching his majority, he slipped. Like Donne, he offended his patron mortally and, through him, the whole system. His sin was to set down in his private writings something severely offensive to Sir Dudley and Lady Carleton.

At first, Carleton kept the matter quiet. He sent Carew back to England under pretext of seeking better service. There Carew courted his cousin Lord Carew, recently of the Privy Council, and the Earl of Arundel, whom he had met in Florence. In September 1616, Carew wrote probably his earliest surviving compositions: three "suitors' letters" to Carleton, to use Frank Whigham's term.[4] Though they seem to have many purposes—reporting on Carew's suits for employment, paying his respects, passing on bits of news and gossip—it is fair to say that all three letters are among the most careful of all his writings, and that they are subordinated entirely to a single end: the all-important pursuit of advancement and place in the world to which he belonged by birth. The concluding rhetoric of the first letter in which he reports his failure to elicit a definite response from Lord Arundel—not yet knowing that Carleton's promised recommendation will never arrive and that he is already irredeemably disgraced in the eyes of past and future patrons, but clearly suspecting that something has gone badly wrong—may best indicate his terrible predicament. A single long, graceful, beautifully crafted but increasingly desperate sentence ends the letter and tails into a complimentary close and signature:

> Your Lordships letters to my Lord of Arrondell, because it was necessarie for me to wayte uppon my Lord Carew, and could at no time see him but with the King from whose side he seldome moveth, I left with Master Havers to be

4. "The Rhetoric of Elizabethan Suitors' Letters," *PMLA* 96 (1981): 864–82; see also Whighams's *Ambition and Privilege: The Social Tropes of Elizabethan Courtesy Theory* (Berkeley: University of California Press, 1984).

delivered to him, of whome I learned that he was as yet unfurnished of a
Secretarie, wherefore according to your Lordships instructions my fathers
councell and my owne inclination I will labour my admittance into his service, wherein I have these hopes, the present vacancie of the place, the reference my father had to his Grandfather and the knowledge which by your
Lordships meanes he had of me at Florence, wherein if neede be and if Master
Chamberlane shall so thinke good I will engage my Lord Carew, and where-
unto I humbly beseech your Lordship to add your effectuall recommendation,
which I knowe will be of more power then all my other pretences, which yow
will be pleased with your most convenient speede to afforde me, that I may at
his returne hether (which will be with the Kings some 20 dayes hence) meete
him with your Lordships letters and that I may in case of refusall returne to
your service the sooner, from which I profess (notwithstanding all these fayre
shewes of preferrment) as I did with much unwillingness depart, so doe I not
withowt greate affliction discontinue; my thoughts of their proper and regular
motion not aspiring higher then the orbe of your Lordships service, this irreg-
ular being caused by your self whoe are my *primum mobile,* for I ever accounted
it honour enough for me to *correre la fortuna del mio Signore* nor did I ever
ayme at . . . greater happiness then to be held as I will allways rest / Your
Lordships / Most humbly devoted / to your service / Thomas Carew. (202–3)

Carew's impending disgrace throws a sharp light on his words.
Notice his awareness of intricate and demanding family linkages; so
many people must be placated. He approaches Arundel at the behest
of his cousin-by-marriage and his father, invokes a connection between
his father and Arundel's grandfather, thinks of bringing to bear (if
prudent advice permits) the influence of his other noble cousin. In
another letter to Carleton he writes that, while waiting for the promised recommendation, he has "had leysure to see my sister Grandmother and other my frends in Kent, whoe remember their most
affectionate services to your Lordship and my Lady" (206). But all
depends on the arrival of Sir Dudley's letter; without it (for it is as
much a release as a recommendation) he cannot shift allegiance from
one member of his extended family circle to another. True, he bravely
asserts that he acts at "my owne inclination." We may doubt this
assertion, however, by the evidence of the letter itself—except insofar
as any loyal servant must conform his will to his master's, as closely as
a devout man conforms his will to God's. Carew's language increasingly approaches religious fervor as he professes a chivalric desire to
reattach himself to his former master and follow him into any danger,
attributing to Sir Dudley the God-like power of a *primum mobile.*

Such was the pitch to which Carew rose, but he failed. Called to a meeting with his father and confronted with his offense, he stubbornly refused to apologize in acceptable form. As a result he was cut off permanently from his own extended family. Lady Carleton was Sir Matthew's niece by blood. The connection that got Carew his position now worsened his guilt. Sir Matthew died two years later, at the age of eighty-five, still grumbling of ungrateful sons; Dame Alice, the poet's mother, lived two more decades yet omitted all mention of the prodigal from her will. The evidence suggests a complete break between Carew and his family. The result of his slip was to drop him clear out of the patronage network.

His disgrace proved critical to his career and poetry. As Kenneth Burke often observed, writers are affected by their cultures, times, historical situations, family and individual circumstances, in ways both social and psychological. A particular poet shares characteristics with his contemporaries but possesses, or is possessed by, others peculiar to himself. Carew's development of a radically new kind of love poetry in England—libertine, anti-authoritarian, almost wholly disconnected from the Petrarchan traditions that even Donne felt obliged to parody and dispute—was closely related to the crisis of his career and the psychosocial forces it unleashed.

Of course, Carew later became a successful courtier, able to look down from a secure position at still struggling young friends like Suckling. He rose by assuming an attitude and a style of living diametrically opposed to what his family intended for him. Preferment in the service of Carleton or Arundel represented filial obedience and dutiful use of the kinship network. His refusal to apologize severed those connections. It is risky to psychologize on slight evidence; still it seems the break in Carew's career represents a typically youthful revolt against father, family, and social system, all combining to represent authority to him.

This scenario of mutually destructive intergenerational warfare, familiar alike in Freud, history, and our experience, might have ended the story had it not been for later public events. In 1625 James's court gave way to Charles's. There was a distinct change in tone and a repudiation of former styles and values. Whether the new court was better or worse than the old is arguable. At any rate, it thought itself different. In 1630, against strong competition, Carew was named

Gentleman of the Privy Chamber Extraordinary and Sewer in Ordinary to the King. He obtained these posts and the honor and security they represented by finding his own patrons unconnected with his family: chiefly Kit Villiers, younger brother of the Duke of Buckingham, who represented par excellence not the use but the abuse of favor. Arundel, whose favor his family had urged him to court, was a bitter opponent of Buckingham's, so Carew's transfer of allegiance could hardly have mended his bad relations with former friends. Villiers, Carew's new patron, got as far as he did, despite his frequent drunkenness and other scandalous behavior, only because his brother was the most successful *parvenu* in all of British history. Carew wrote several poems for this patron and his family and further helped Villiers, who had small wit or polish, to court and win a rich wife. From a position in the patronage network that was filial and duteous, Carew moved to a position of mutual advantage as the hired wit to a King's favorite.[5]

This transformation in Carew's stance toward the world, resulting in his invention of a new manner in poetry, went through three observable stages. First he rebelled utterly against his family and against any hope of regaining family patronage. His father, in a series of letters to Carleton intended to repair the breach, but which must only have made matters worse, vividly described the nadir of Carew's career. Thomas, he wrote, "haveng geven over al studye here eyther of lawe or other lerning, vagrantlye and debauchedlye takethe no maner of good but al lewde courses, with the which he will weary me and al his other frendes, and run hym self into utter ruyn." He further reported that his son "lieth here syck with me of a new disease" (xxvii), which, Rhodes Dunlap and others speculate, was that syphilis about which Carew's friend Suckling was to jest so indelicately in his poem "Upon T. C. having the P." Then Carew evidently pulled himself together sufficiently to accompany Sir Edward Herbert to France, an arrangement that may be interpreted either as a temporary exile or as

---

5. On the Villiers connection, see Rhodes Dunlap, xxxiv–xxxv; and Michael P. Parker, "Carew, Kit Villiers, and the Character of Caroline Courtliness," *Renaissance Papers* (1983): 89–102. Arundel and Buckingham not only differed in character but were political foes: see Kevin Sharpe, "The Earl of Arundel, his circle, and the opposition to the Duke of Buckingham, 1621–1628," in *Faction and Parliament: Essays on Early Stuart History,* ed. Kevin Sharpe (Oxford: Clarendon Press, 1978), 209–44.

a somewhat tentative step toward rehabilitation. That rehabilitation could not have proceeded smoothly, however, for Carew's next certainly documented action in pursuit of his career was to turn to his family's political enemies for advancement.

Carew may have had other help. Rhodes Dunlap recounts the scandalous tale about Henrietta Maria: "Thomas Carew, Gentleman of the Privy Chamber, going to light King Charles into her chamber, saw Jermyn Lord St. Albans with his arm round her neck;—he stumbled and put out the light;—Jermyn escaped; Carew never told the King, and the King never knew it. The Queen heaped favours on Carew" (xxxv). The tale, as Dunlap notes, may be apocryphal, for it seems almost too good to be true; yet at least it tells us the kind of image a contemporary attached to Carew. He arrived by using his wits and his new friends, not his family connections. He learned that insolence, rebellion, and libertine behavior, gracefully indulged, might be not impediments but actual helps to advancement and honor.

Carew's central image for the ideal courtly stance, in his poem comforting Kit Villiers's widow on the death of her husband, as Michael Parker points out, is not a Jonsonian circle with a firmly fixed center, as we might expect of a Son of Ben, but an eddy dancing in a stream:

> He chose not in the active streame to swim,
> Nor hunted Honour; which, yet hunted him.
> But like a quiet Eddie, that hath found
> Some hollow creeke, there turnes his waters round,
> And in continuall circles, dances free
> From the impetuous Torrent; so did hee
> Give others leave to turne the wheele of State,
> (*Whose restlesse motion spins the subjects fate*)
> Whilst he retir'd from the tumultuous noyse
> Of Court, and suitors presse; apart, enjoyes
> Freedome, and mirth, himselfe, his time, and friends,
> And with sweet rellish tastes each houre he spends.
>   ("To the Countesse of *Anglesie*," 57–68)

As Parker further notes, an eddy "moves contrary to the direction of the tide or current." To model one's life on such a motion "demands an unceasing awareness and an 'active grace,'"[6] qualities suggestive of Carew, not Villiers. To be an eddy is to give oneself to the stream and take one's energy from it yet at the same time to move, covertly, to a counter impulse. In this apparent surrender to the social current, a skillful courtier gains "freedome," and with that freedom or space for independent movement he enjoys "mirth," "time," "friends," and (above all) "himselfe." We see in this image an early adumbration of the growth of modern independent subjectivity.

No doubt Carew felt real gratitude to the man who restored his career: "But all his actions had the noble end / T'advance desert, or grace some worthy friend" (55–56). Still, in describing such a "new-model courtier,"[7] Carew based his ideal principally on his own experience and not that of his unfortunate friend. The eddy was his own solution to the social and family impasse in which he had earlier been caught. He projected his ideal courtly stance onto the figure of his dead benefactor, who was notorious for his lack of courtly finesse and outward delicacy and who—when he suffered disgrace and banishment for having, like Carew, offended his patron—never recovered.

For a man of Carew's time, personal identity was largely a product of social position, and personal psychology closely depended on one's place in the patronage network and experience in getting there; so a convergence of psychological and cultural forces importantly affected his life and poetry. We see just such a convergence in the image of the eddy, which reveals to a postmodern reader how the independent subject may grow out of the social self. In different historical circumstances, Ralegh and Sidney learned the politics of desire for an unobtainable object, desire that, Arthur Marotti shows, was an inextricable mixture of frustrated religious, political, and amatory ambitions. The political experience of these earlier courtier-poets reverberated with and reinforced a Petrarchan stance in their love poetry. Carew's psychosocial circumstances, to the contrary, taught him a politics and an amatory strategy based on cynicism, libertinism, and scorn for authority. The stream of authority and society, he evidently recognized, was too strong to be wholly resisted, but consummate courtly

6. "Carew, Kit Villiers," 96.
7. Ibid., 102.

abilities could enable a skillful practitioner to dance in it and achieve a precarious but real degree of personal freedom and pleasure.[8]

The result is a new kind of English love poetry. In "To A. L. Perswasions to love," the lover represents a new-model amatory servant, ready to abandon his mistress for another who will reward him better. If she plays hard to get, he warns her, she will only defeat herself:

> And what will then become of all
> Those, whom now you servants call?
> Like swallowes when your summers done,
> They'le flye and seeke some warmer Sun.
> (45–48)

The right sort of patron, he learned from painful experience, needs supportive clients just as clients need a generous patron. So, he tells A. L., choose a suitor who will be useful and reward him appropriately:

> Then wisely chuse one to your friend,
> Whose love may, when your beauties end,
> Remaine still firme: be provident
> And thinke before the summers spent
> Of following winter; like the Ant
> In plenty hoord for time of scant.
> Cull out amongst the multitude
> Of lovers, that seeke to intrude
> Into your favour, one that may
> Love for an age, not for a day;
> One that will quench your youthfull fires,
> And feed in age your hot desires.
> (49–60)

Thus Carew implicitly presents himself as a client who can help his patroness to what she wants, giving a new twist to the age-old carpe-diem theme on which he bases the poem. He also offers a cynically pragmatic version of the perennial desire for eternal love, which here

8. See "'Love Is Not Love': Elizabethan Sonnet Sequences and the Social Order," *ELH* 49 (1982): 396–428.

becomes sexual gratification drawn out by mutual convenience into old age: seize the day—and prolong it.

"Ingratefull beauty threatned" takes Carew's newfound knowledge that the patronage relationship cuts both ways and creates a triple equivalence between the poet and his subject, the lover and his mistress, the client and his patron:

> Know *Celia,* (since thou art so proud,)
>   'Twas I that gave thee thy renowne . . .
> . . . .
> That killing power is none of thine,
>   I gave it to thy voyce, and eyes:
> Thy sweets, thy graces, all are mine;
>   Thou art my starre, shin'st in my skies;
> Then dart not from thy borrowed sphere
> Lightning on him, that fixt thee there.
> Tempt me with such affrights no more,
>   Lest what I made, I uncreate.
>   (1–2, 7–14)

He has "made" her as he made Villiers. If ill-treated he will simply go elsewhere and make someone else, letting her sink back into nonentity. As becomes more evident in a context of social mobility and clientage for hire, no mistress has "killing power" over a lover prepared to leave her service if provoked.

My reference to Carew as a "hired wit" was lightly employed. Yet his behavior as client and lover may well have been influenced not only by the particulars of family circumstance and court personalities but also by the rise at midcentury of a market economy. Everywhere feudal service was giving way to labor for hire, a fundamental change beginning to produce an increasingly mobile society more responsive to individual financial reward than extended-family loyalty. A similar mobility is found in Carew's "Good counsell to a young Maid":

> When you the Sun-burnt Pilgrim see
>   Fainting with thirst, hast to the springs,
> Marke how at first with bended knee
>   He courts the crystall Nimphe, and flings

His body to the earth, where He
Prostrate adores the flowing Deitie.

But when his sweaty face is drencht
    In her coole waves, when from her sweet
Bosome, his burning thirst is quencht;
    Then marke how with disdainfull feet
    He kicks her banks, and from the place
That thus refresht him, moves with sullen pace.
                                    (1–12)

"So," he concludes, "shalt thou be despis'd, faire Maid, / When by the sated lover tasted" (13–14). The politics of desire and ambition in a situation of too much stasis give way to a politics of satiation and disillusionment in a situation of too much change.

Even rejection by the mistress takes a new direction (though with some precedent in Wyatt). In "A deposition from Love," Carew tells us that he "was foretold" (presumably by Petrarchan authorities) and long believed that all the "plagues" of love are at its entrance. If only the lover can win his mistress, his troubles are over. Experience teaches otherwise. Although he has managed to "enter, and enjoy, / What happy lovers prove," to "kisse, and sport, and toy, / And tast those sweets of love" (11–12, 13–14), these pleasures only increase his unhappiness later when his mistress abandons him. The Petrarchan lover, Carew concludes, loses what was never his,

But he that is cast downe
From enjoy'd beautie, feeles a woe,
Onely deposed Kings can know.
                        (28–30)

Thus opportunism cuts two ways and undermines the very basis of the political and amatory orders. If clients are empowered to seek out new patrons with impunity, and lovers new mistresses—or even subjects new kings—then all victors in games of preferment risk being dropped if a better client or apter lover appears on the scene.

As the psychologies of amorous and political disenchantment converge, constancy of service becomes less a reliable ideal than a rhetorical weapon to be wielded and dropped at will. *"True love can never change his seat,"* Carew urges in "Eternitie of love protested," but his other poems belie that ideal. To *"correre la fortuna del mio Signore,"* the chivalric vow he once addressed to Sir Dudley, is now recognized for what it always was: a polite foreign anachronism. In "Boldnesse in love," Carew again applies his new experience, hard-learned in the wars of patronage, to love:

> Marke how the bashfull morne, in vaine
> Courts the amorous Marigold,
> With sighing blasts, and weeping raine;
> Yet she refuses to unfold.
> But when the Planet of the day,
> Approacheth with his powerfull ray,
> Then she spreads, then she receives
> His warmer beames into her virgin leaves.
>
> (1–8)

Petrarchan sighs and tears, begging and dutiful subservience, only fail. To succeed, the suitor must drop old pieties, boldly lie, and help himself. As the title even of the apparently old-fashioned poem "Eternitie of love protested" suggests, the Petrarchan ideal of unconditionally faithful love, like the feudal ideal of loyalty until death, becomes more a protestation or a piece of rhetoric than something put into practice once the mistress is persuaded. Eternity is no more than a word the successful lover speaks, not a commitment to be acted on.

Of course, there is more to Carew's love poetry than opportunism. Since I have focused on the crisis of his early career, which forced him into an alternative route to prosperity and a reinvention of himself, I have focused on the related employment in his poetry of libertinism, pragmatism, and self-interest in the pursuit of love. Sometimes love has for Carew a more positive side. Along with the general stripping away of dead Petrarchan conventions, which no longer suit the new age and his new experience in courting patrons, come the blessings of less of that crawling or enforced subservience which results when love, patronage, and family go wrong, of greater mutuality and equality between lovers, of more recognition that love is a two-way transaction.

It might be hoped that there could be other ways of arriving at mutuality less painful and disillusioning, less dependent on bringing the other person down in estimation and more on raising oneself. Perhaps these glum results follow naturally from Carew's having begun the revision of his career by anticipating that root modernist practice, "killing the father." Still, in "To A. L.," cynical though Carew's address is, we find a connection between his new-found irreverence and the possibility of mutuality and equality in love:[9]

> Did the thing for which I sue
> Onely concerne my selfe not you,
> Were men so fram'd as they alone
> Reap'd all the pleasure, women none,
> Then had you reason to be scant;
> But 'twere a madnesse not to grant
> That which affords (if you consent)
> To you the giver, more content
> Then me the beggar; Oh then bee
> Kinde to your selfe if not to mee.
>
> (17–26)

Again Carew's redefinition of love and patronage relates to economic change. Love is reduced to a "thing," to sexual "pleasure," which in turn is a commodity to be reaped, given, or begged. This achievement of mutual benefit through the pursuit of mutual selfishness reminds us of the familiar paradox of the profit motive in the early modern political economy, which, though not yet fully worked out, was already implicit in the changing agricultural marketplace that Carew's reaping metaphor calls to our attention. Self-interest and individualism, like enclosure and labor for hire, are just beginning to be seen in progressive circles not as violations of the general welfare but as efficient ways of increasing the total stock to the ultimate good of all.[10]

9. On mutuality in "To A. L." see Renée Hannaford, "Self-Presentation in Carew's 'To A. L. Perswasions to Love,'" *SEL* 26 (1986): 97–106; for a divergent view, see Kevin Sharpe, *Criticism and Compliment: The Politics of Literature in the England of Charles I* (Cambridge: Cambridge University Press, 1987), 117. On the life and politics, see Joanne Altieri, "Responses to a Waning Mythology in Carew's Political Poetry," *SEL* 26 (1986): 107–24; and Diana Benet, "Carew's Monarchy of Wit," in *"The Muses Common-Weale": Poetry and Politics in the Seventeenth Century,* ed. Claude J. Summers and Ted-Larry Pebworth (Columbia: University of Missouri Press, 1988), 80–91.

10. See Anthony Low, *The Georgic Revolution* (Princeton: Princeton University Press, 1985); and Joyce Oldham Appleby, *Economic Thought and Ideology in Seven-*

Libertinism or free love is analogous to the free market just as the extended family is analogous to feudal politics. Indeed, they are more than analogous. Politics and family in a feudal or an early Renaissance patronage system are inextricably interdependent. A man without family—by marriage or by formal or informal adoption if not by blood—cannot expect to gain patronage. As family feelings and obligations shape the political network, that network in turn shapes courtship, marriage, and family. But in a free-market economy (and, even more, in the industrialized society that results) extended family ties become impediments rather than benefits to the smooth working of the system and to individual success. Mobility and utility rather than stability and loyalty, mutual advantage rather than mutual giving, become the prime virtues. Impartial trade replaces the give-and-take of familial relationships. People move where they are most needed, and where they can find most advantage, in a constantly shifting social system that encourages no more than temporary allegiances between masters and servants, patrons and clients, mistresses and lovers. At the same time lover and mistress, or as we would now call them, lover and lover, meet on terms of greater equality in the general breakdown both of patriarchal social authority and the now waning courtly authority of the etherialized lady-mistress. Equality is gained, permanence lost. These are, of course, only tendencies, which, several hundred years later, still spasmodically work themselves out among us.

teenth-Century England (Princeton: Princeton University Press, 1978). Further on Carew and the new economics see my "Agricultural Reform and the Love Poems of Thomas Carew; With an Instance from Lovelace," in Culture and Cultivation in Early Modern England: Writing and the Land, ed. Michael Leslie and Timothy Raylor (Leicester: Leicester University Press, 1992), 63–80.

M. L. Donnelly

The Rack of Fancy and the Trade of Love
Conventions of *Précieux* and *Libertin*
in Amatory Lyrics by Suckling and Carew

Even allowing for the unflagging inventiveness of the human mind, the repertoire of brute expression available to erotic desire is not much more extensive than that possessed by humbler appetites, limited as it is by physiology and mechanics. Far from similarly limited, however, is the kaleidoscopic array of cultural expressions in which the erotic impulse may clothe itself. The poets of the Cavalier love lyrics of the 1620s and 1630s could choose from an enormously diversified range of literary models, generic vehicles, and stylistic registers afforded by their predecessors. Standing at the end of a long European literary tradition, they commanded a perspective survey of an exceptionally rich topography of conventionally coded expressions, each of which carried its considerable load of cultural, ideological, and more or less popularized philosophical baggage.

An English court poet of the Caroline years might know firsthand not only the poems of contemporary European writers like Marino, Chiabrera, Battista Guarini, Saint-Amant, Des Barreaux, and Theophile de Viau, but he might well be familiar with the social scenes of their production as well. Inevitably in a culture that sets as much store by self-consciousness and mastery of roles and manners as court culture does, familiarity with a growing repertoire of literary gestures intensifies aesthetic distance and critical awareness of how each genre figures as a representation of the world. The sophisticated Car-

oline courtier-poet who has seen the great courts and cities of Europe
while serving abroad on military or diplomatic missions has acquired
an extended sense of possibilities, of roles, of pure theatrical *scène*.
Awareness of the possible range of roles and self-representations begets
a slightly ironic distance, an amused *disinvoltura*. It is easier to see life
as a masque, as a scenic display, as a phenomenal play of "what-if."
Acceptance of such a view of oneself as at once performer and spectator in an arbitrary text engenders an extraordinary freedom and
insouciance of manner in one's role, a manner that is not a seventeenth-century one per se, but rather a court character.[1]

Within the familiar repertoire of his free range, the court poet
found the obvious polarities of stance available for the representation
of the sentiment of sex and for capturing the excitements of eroticism
at the Caroline court to be the *libertinism* of the Taverns and the
préciosité of the acolytes of the Hôtel Rambouillet.[2] Each position
evokes and, indeed, demands the other: brute natural facts, egoistic
desire and will, provoke the elaborate *précieux* strategies of transcendence that, in their turn, cry out for the deflation and reductionism of
libertin assertion. Specifically, Queen Henrietta Maria ostentatiously
supported the *précieux*. Her vigorous championing of "Platonics,"
and her own and her husband's aggressive representation of their
relation as a paragon of chastity and ideal marriage certainly con-
spired to heighten the potential social value of the literary exploitation of *précieux* ideas and models.[3] Just as certainly, to some, this

1. For an outline of what is known of Suckling's earlier career, travels, and experiences, see *The Works of Sir John Suckling: The Non-Dramatic Works,* ed. Thomas Clayton (Oxford: Clarendon Press, 1971), xxx–xxxv. All references to Suckling's poems will
be given parenthetically in the text to this edition, by number of the poem and line numbers. On Carew's early career and exposure to the social and literary culture of European courts, see Rhodes Dunlap, ed., *The Poems of Thomas Carew* (Oxford: Clarendon
Press, 1949), xvi–xxxii. Dunlap asserts that Carew was not only familiar with "the ped-
antry of Malherbe," but also with "the poetry of the Pleiade and their successors," and
may have known personally Giambattista Marino, "who resided at Paris from 1615 to
1623, [and] was regularly to be seen at the Hotel de Rambouillet and at court" (xxxii).
Citations of Carew's poems will be given parenthetically in the text by line numbers from
Dunlap's edition.
2. On libertinism in seventeenth-century French literature, see F. T. Perrens, *Les Lib-
ertins en France au XVIIe Siècle* (1896; repr. New York: Burt Franklin, 1973); on the
précieux mode, see Odette Des Mourgues, *Metaphysical, Baroque, & Précieux Poetry*
(Oxford: Clarendon Press, 1953). See also Fletcher Orpin Henderson, "Traditions of
Précieux and *Libertin* in Suckling's Poetry," *ELH* 4 (1937): 274–99.
3. Cf. Kevin Sharpe, "Cavalier Critic? The Ethics and Politics of Thomas Carew's

posturing amounted to a challenge issued on behalf of artifice against nature, evoking an enthusiastic response in the form of direct, parodic, or ironic counterdiscourses.

Two key voices between them embody these polarities within the discourses of desire that answered to the fashionable sensibilities of the Caroline court: the voices of Thomas Carew and Sir John Suckling. Contrasting in many ways, overlapping in others, these two nevertheless define the field and dominant stances of Cavalier amatory verse.[4] Both, but especially Carew, command a variety of poetic-erotic gestures and genres and play with various *libertin* stances. No significant English poetic voice is to be wholly identified with *préciosité*.[5] However, Carew in his most representative poems delights in mobilizing (and sometimes subtly ironizing) the exquisite and curious refinements of his coterie. In so doing, his art takes in some of the vocabulary and affectations of *préciosité*. His poetry delights in its complete mastery of conventionalized gesture and polite repartee, its utter command of the right words and postures. He fully grasps the arbitrariness, the conventionality of the devices and allusions he employs. He is too sophisticated to believe that there is any other way for a cultured, civilized man to write or live. Suckling, on the contrary, at *his* most characteristic manifests the opposite affectation of utter offhandedness and disdain of art—"easy, natural Suckling," as Milla-

Poetry," in *Politics of Discourse: The Literature and History of Seventeenth-Century England,* ed. Kevin Sharpe and Steven N. Zwicker (Berkeley: University of California Press, 1987), 132, 136. See also chap. 4 in vol. 1 of Stephen Orgel and Roy Strong, *Inigo Jones: The Theatre of the Stuart Court,* 2 vols. (Berkeley: University of California Press, 1973). On Platonic love and *préciosité* at the Caroline court under the patronage of Henrietta Maria, see especially Erica Veevers, *Images of Love and Religion: Queen Henrietta Maria and Court Entertainments* (Cambridge: Cambridge University Press, 1989).

4. In such an identification, I follow in the wake of contemporary opinion: "Madam Mericke to Mrs Lydall" from Wrest, dated 21 January 1638/9 (of which Rhodes Dunlap remarks, "apparently a literary exercise" [Dunlap, *Poems of Thomas Carew,* xxxviii, n. 3]) mentions the two together as "best wittes of the time" (Public Record Office, S.P. 16/409:167). Robert Baron, in *Pocula Castalia* (1650) "couples [Carew] with Suckling ('the glory of the Bower') as a master of love and lovers," and Jo. Leigh, in commendatory verses addressed to Humphrey Moseley for bringing out Cartwright's *Comedies, Tragi-Comedies, with Other Poems,* 1651, applauds Moseley for having brought out editions of both "brave Suckling" and "melting Carew, who so long / Maintain'd the *Court* with many a charming Song" [sig. (*)^r] (Dunlap, *Poems of Thomas Carew,* xlvii).

5. Cf. Alfred Harbage, *Cavalier Drama* (New York: Modern Language Association of America, 1936), 36.

mant so quotably sums him up—an appeal to "nature" that, coupled with a swaggering dismissal of *précieux* postures, keynotes the *libertin* ethos.

In his amatory lyrics, Suckling's typical stance insists on discarding conventional posturing and glossing and taking life on the simplest terms, ostensibly its own, which is to say, nature's. Of course, this pretence is itself another conventionalized posture. At the same time, it serves as a device for asserting one's superiority to ordinary people who are taken in by conventions and proprieties, or as a way of claiming control over one's milieu by declaring one's own freedom from the bondage of convention that governs others. The trouble with this stance is, in pretending to see through the accepted conventions of life and art that blind one's fellows with illusion, in its insistence on being unillusioned, it must perforce be *dis*illusioned. The extreme reach of Suckling's skeptical stance discovers either that there is *really* nothing there at all beneath the manners and the fancy dress, or that whatever there is to be found of an unadulterated "nature" beneath art and convention is nothing that can finally satisfy human need. Further complicating Suckling's situation is the fact that his own superior status and reputation are themselves to a certain extent built on conventional and social distinctions, which, however, he and his coterie might insist were, in fact, "natural."

Texts like Suckling's, produced and distributed within a small, known circle of acquaintance, attractive beyond that circle to postulants and admirers of its manners and scene, always have a double function. There is the representation of the ostensible subject, the issue, theme, situation, or character treated, and there is the representation of the author, part of whose self-representation or role such a production inevitably must be. In Suckling's case, this latter function seems to bulk unusually large. Despite his accustomed pose of downrightness and blunt frankness, it is not merely the needs of "bare, unaccommodated man" that his lyric verse addresses. As courtly gentleman and wit, Suckling always has one eye cocked toward self-regard: how do I *look*? Is my performance appropriate to the superior, courtly, casually self-assured role I adopt? If it were not so, he would not have to *insist* so on his possession of those qualities of person and attitude. Besides, Suckling's own gentility and aristocratic connection is not of spotless integrity, which may help to account for the hectic nature of his pursuit of the role of swashbuckling, courtly gentleman-gamester and knight. Of old Saxon stock active in public affairs (but not ennobled) on his father's side, he derived his maternal bloodlines from rich and ambitious London merchants; his mother's brother, Lionel Cranfield, was the *arriviste* Lord Treasurer of England under James I.

To be sure, he was largely successful in the role he embraced, for to his age Suckling was primarily noted not for his uncompromising reductionist naturalism, but rather as the model of the witty, worldly, and elegant social companion. Personality undoubtedly had much to do with his contemporary reputation, but the valuation of his verse above that of other gentlemen-wits seems to be based equally on his offhandedly apt style, and his consciously projected posture of superior knowingness.[6] For example, in his poem, "The Wits" (a.k.a. "A Sessions of the Poets"), when called to stand in competition for the laurel crown, Suckling

> did not appear,
> And strait one whisperd *Apollo* in's ear,
> That of all men living he cared not for't,
> He loved not the Muses so well as his sport;
> And
> Prized black eyes, or a lucky hit
> At bowls, above all the Trophies of wit.
> (71.73–78)

Here, by asserting in his typical carelessly apt verse a brashly masculine preference for sex and gaming (equally "sport"), and his indifference to the laurels that might crown approved "cultural" performance, the gentleman-poet maintains his superiority to certain kinds of cultural pretension that he sees as effeminate. Although the words

6. Humphrey Moseley, the bookseller, maintains in his "The Stationer to the Reader" prefixed to *The Last Remains of Sr John Suckling* that the genuineness of the works included may be quickly determined by "any Judicious soul" who will "seriously consider the Freedom of the Fancie, Richness of the Conceipt, proper Expression, with that air and spirit diffus'd through every part," and insists on the "generous rise" of "this Gentile and Princely Poet . . . *from the Court*" (*Works of Suckling,* ed. Clayton, 6; emphasis mine).

are presumably Humphrey Moseley's and not Suckling's, it is pertinent to note how shrewdly the address "To the Reader" in *Fragmenta
Aurea* (1646) plays on certain of these elements of Suckling's chosen
role. The intended audience (now, for a printed text, clearly expanded
beyond the original circle, but flatteringly projected as including them)
is a masculine world made up of "knowing Gentlemen" who already
"honour these posthume Idæa's of their friend" and of other men who
aspire to improve their own "Civility and Understanding" by con-
templating the gentleman-poet's transcendent wit and variety. The
selling points of the collection are inextricably bound up with Suckling's social superiority and status as worldly wit and courtly ornament of his age. Only those who are like him can appreciate him: that
is, "they that convers'd with him alive, and truly, (under which notion
I comprehend only knowing Gentlemen, his soule being transcendent,
and incommunicable to others, but by reflection)," and those that "by
looking upon these Remaines with Civility and Understanding . . .
may timely yet repent, and be forgiven" for not having made the acquaintance of so great an ornament of the age before.

> The name that leadeth into this Elysium [of his surviving works printed in
> *Fragmenta aurea*], is sacred to *Art* and *Honour,* and no man that is not excel-
> lent in both, is qualified a *Competent Judge:* For when Knowledge is allowed,
> yet Education in the Censure of a Gentleman, requires as many descents, as
> goes to make one; And he that is bold upon his unequall Stock, to traduce this
> Name, or Learning, will deserve to be condemned againe into Ignorance his
> Originall sinne, and dye in it.

So says the bourgeois bookseller, astutely calculating his market for
the wares of the lately dead mirror of "art and honor."[7]
    Moseley's references to knowledge and learning in these praises of
Suckling suggest that the poet's insistence on a superior discernment
had registered with contemporaries no less than his personal charm
and gentlemanly bearing. The nature of that knowledge and discernment claimed by the poet is conveniently illustrated by "Loving and
Beloved" (No. 62). This lyric about love at court articulates a world-
liness that, while demonstrating mastery of the rules of the game, also

---

7. *Works of Suckling,* ed. Clayton, 3.

sees through the social masque and masks and asserts a knowledge of the way things truly are. Without blanching from the unvarnished truth (in contrast to the foolishness or hypocrisy of polite lovers), Suckling maintains with typical assertive gusto, "There never yet was honest man / That ever drove the trade of love." "It is impossible," he vows, "nor can / Integrity our ends promove." Insisting on the duplicity of fashionable courtship, Suckling constructs the poem as a series of double entendres. Their improper suggestions not only demonstrate his worldly sophistication, but they also embody the double vision imposed by the polite lover's sublimated account of his position. "Promove" means "to advance or encourage" (this passage is cited in OED to illustrate this sense), but also "instigate or incite"—hence, integrity cannot advance or promote our ends when we love (for the real end we desire is to orthodox manners and morals discreditable), and it is not integrity (ours or our object's) that incites our "ends" (*membrum virile*) to be "moved" (to readiness for action). The reader whose wit discerns the joke has implicitly aligned himself with Suckling's position, recognizing a "base" meaning (in one sense from the moralist's point of view, in the other from the libertine naturalist's) that is glossed over in the Platonizing excuse that what we really are moved to love is virtue. When he adds as the warrant for his reductionist view an analogy to the great world of politics, Suckling evokes a further article of the libertine manifesto: that it refuses the homage of respect to all received ideas and conventional verities, social and political as well as religious—"For Kings and Lovers are alike in this / That their chief art in reigne dissembling is." The gesture is that of a man speaking among men, aware of a shared knowledge of the world that excuses calling a spade a spade.[8]

"Loving and Beloved" may be read as implicitly a criticism of the polite rituals of courtship established by *précieux* convention—"grouse shooting with the grouse removed," in Alfred Harbage's apt phrase.[9] "Here we are lov'd, and there we love" then becomes, "Here, in the courtly game and ritual, we earn appreciation for the art with which we go through our paces, but *there,* in a dark corner or a stolen tryst,

8. Unlike his successor in the role, Rochester, Suckling never pursues further the political skepticism implied by his libertine naturalist stance. Perhaps the virtuous image of his king afforded him no immediate concrete ground for the application of theory.
9. *Cavalier Drama,* 36.

we love in deed." "Good nature now [playing along with the ladies' courtly game, being a good lap dog] and passion [real physical desire and its satisfaction] strive / Which of the two should be above" [have mastery, rendered in an only slightly veiled metaphor for *positio coitionis*], "And laws unto the other give." "So we false fire with art sometimes discover" [the Platonic ardors artfully couched in the language of refined courtly love philosophy are not the true *flammas Veneris*], "And the true fire with the same art do cover" [perhaps because the *true* fire, in contrast to the affectations of Platonic *précieux* role playing, is regarded as shameful, dishonorable, something to be kept hid].

> What Rack can Fancy find so high?
>   Here we must Court, and here ingage,
> Though in the other place we die.
>   (62.13–15)

The spatial terms, *here, here, the other place,* complicate the suggestiveness of the verse and enforce the libertine's duplicity of vision, seeing the natural and private behind or beneath the public conventions, and calling the former "the real": "here" is "where we are loved" (but do not love in return, or get the "right true end of love"), therefore, "here" points to the *précieux* realm of courtly representation, the "here" that is public, locus of observed looks and gestures and promises of lips, site of all the acts and assurances compassed under words like "countenance," "give countenance to," "put such-and-such a face on things," and "save face." "The other place" becomes both a spatially discrete location—private as opposed to public, the boudoir or chamber as opposed to the court—and a metonymy for what is acted in those private places, as opposed to the public actions of the ritual game played on the courtly scene. It is further a physiological discrete place, not the head, or countenance, or face, but the other end, locus of the act designated by the timeworn Renaissance pun on "to die."

In "Loving and Beloved," the tension so wittily handled between the real love that must be hidden and the false love that must be acted out also enforces a disjunction between the head and the body, the calculated roles played by the public persona and the urgencies of the pudenda. Having inscribed this gap, Suckling's libertine stance is baffled to bridge it; his dilemma issues in a flight or renunciation, an issue that in fact might be marked as a characteristic of Suckling's whole manner: confronted with intolerable conflicting demands of nature and social convention, troubled by contradictory but imperative claims, he takes refuge in flight—flight into frivolity, flight into irresponsibility, flight into a reductionism that denies the reality of the gap.[10] He throws up his hands, with ominous levity foreshadowing his final tragic throwing in his hand when means ran out and necessity closed in:

> Since it is thus, God of desire,
>   Give me my honesty again,
> And take thy brands back, and thy fire;
>   I'me weary of the State I'me in:
> Since (if the very best should now befal)
> Love's Triumph, must be Honours Funeral.
>   (62.19–24)

The set heroic play conflict between Love and Honor, which can be rehearsed in many registers and keys, is always more or less present and implicitly played against whenever the more aware Caroline poets rise above the playful jocularity of tavern games exemplified by Suckling's riddle, "A Candle." The Love-Honor conflict, however, is only the favored expression in the court culture of the implicitly underlying antinomy of Nature and Convention, the Natural and the Artificial. However, neither term is clearly and unambiguously aligned with one of the underlying terms and not the other. As socially constructed concepts, when approached from varying philosophical or ideological commitments, Love and Honor are each variously denounced as being wholly unnatural strictures artificially imposed on behavior and hence appropriately defied by truly noble or heroic souls. (Virtually every one of these terms and qualifications ought to be italicized to mark their ambivalence or contested sense.) On the other hand, they are each extolled as natural manifestations of a superior,

---

10. For a comparatively slight but striking example, see "[Loves Offence]," No. 55.

"noble" character type. Theorizing love and honor in a courtly context entails recognizing and exploring exhaustively the complex connections of each term, as well as their complicated relations with each other. This consciousness is not merely the product of the modern critic's perspective. Whenever any kind of social frame is drawn around its subject, whenever any context fleshes out the substance of Cavalier song, the antinomy of nature and convention lurks uneasily beneath the smooth reflecting surface of easy, polite, and courtly verse, an ominous shadow.

The libertine courtly poet finds himself caught in a nasty bind "when Honour's at the stake." As courtly gentleman, the tag end of a European tradition of the warrior-aristocrat, his two chief occupations as defined by the mythology of his culture were amorous and military, and "honor" was a key word in both spheres of action. But as a self-proclaimed sophisticate, as a man who knew the world, especially as one who toyed intellectually with libertine naturalism, his pose insists that he see *through* the increasingly artificial, exotic, and fantastically labored conventions of his order, the *précieux* affectations, the playing of roles derived from the mannered fancies of Greek romance.

A further impetus to doubleness of vision and ambivalence for the aggressively masculine courtier-poet arises from the fact that the mythology of his class is partly generated and certainly codified by literature—poetry and romances—that is assiduously cultivated and advanced by the ladies. The arbiters of culture are, to a great extent, those who are in real terms in the society relatively powerless, legally and economically, and their attendant "servants," clients, and flatterers, like Wat Montague, who are equally powerless in terms of what is called today real-world "clout."[11] But the social prestige of the myth is great; it possesses the power of glamour. Essex and Buckingham in turn tried to be the next Sidney: Astrophel, the dashing knight, the accomplished courtier, the romantic hero, "the soldier's, scholar's,

11. On the "feminism of Cavalier drama," see Alfred Harbage, *Cavalier Drama,* 39. The well-known role of the wives of the local bankers, doctors, and lawyers as the traditional arbiters of culture in midwestern American bourgeois life may be a relevant analogy. See also Thorsten Veblen, *The Theory of the Leisure Class,* introduction by John Kenneth Galbraith (Boston: Houghton Mifflin Company, 1973), esp. 46ff., 65–73, 77–80, and 211ff.

courtier's eye, tongue, sword." In Suckling's verse, his sometimes stridently masculine pose expresses its resentment of the social power of the cultural myth as nurtured by the queen and her party not least in the extent to which it often presents women and ladies' men as objects of condescension or even contempt.[12]

From the leadership of the queen, Henrietta Maria, on down through the court circles, the ladies and ladies' men largely set the official tone of society, and established the standards of *politesse* and high culture. Since civility, courtesy, and some dexterity in amorous flirtation and courtly compliment were part of the expected equipment of the gentleman-courtier, it was necessary to traffic in the fashionable roles and dialect of courtship, the currency that bought reputation as such. Even Sir John Suckling occasionally prostitutes his muse to affect the Platonicks.[13]

His more characteristic posture, however, is the *reductio* that sweeps away all posturing, convention, and social constructs in favor of an implicit appeal to "nature." That complex word with all its attendant associations in classical and modern thought usually comes down, for Suckling, to the libertine meaning of self-gratification, the fulfillment of natural appetite.[14] In this sense, the obvious figure for sexual ap-

12. Cf. the withering scorn administered in "[The Wits]" (No. 71, often called "A Sessions of the Poets") to Sir Toby Mathew (57–64) and "two or three" who came in bringing "letters (forsooth) from the Queen" (65–72).

13. Poems in which he seems without irony to present a conventional pure and idealized (or at least unconsummated) love include: No. 26. "*Non est mortale quod opto:* Upon Mrs. A. L."; No. 34. "Love's Burning-glass"; No. 38. "Detraction execrated"; Nos. 44. "[To his Rival I]" and 45. "To his Rival [II]"; No. 46. "To a Lady that forbidd to love before Company"; No. 47. "The Invocation"; and No. 53. "[Love's Sanctuary]." No. 27. "Upon A. M.," with its two versions, one of which is debatably Platonic, would seem another sort of thing entirely, since even in the version that takes "Yeeld not, my Love" as categorical, the purpose of the coyness urged is the sensualist's motive to lengthen out and increase the joys of anticipation, which, it is implied, will always exceed the mere gratification of satiety; cf. No. 40. "Against Fruition [I]" and especially No. 41. "Against Fruition [II]."

14. Cf. the persistent employment of analogies between the use of a woman and the use of food, or a riding horse, and the comparison of the confinement of love in marriage to a quagmire or prison, assuming the necessity of change, in "*A Letter to a Friend to diswade him from marrying a Widow which he formerly had been in Love with, and quitted*" (No. 51[a] and "*An Answer to the Letter,*" in *Works of Suckling,* ed. Clayton, 155–56, 157–58); the correspondent has traditionally been identified as Thomas Carew, but Clayton thinks that the similarities in both compositions to Suckling's expressions and concerns in other works suggest that both are his. On the complexity of the word *nature* see Raymond Williams, *Keywords: A Vocabulary of Culture and Society,* rev. ed. (New York: Oxford University Press, 1985), 219–24.

petite is appetite for food; for example, a discourse of appetite and feeding underlies the military tropes Suckling deploys in No. 67, "'Tis now since I sate down before." In "Of thee (kind boy)" (No. 51), he jettisons entirely the hoary conventions of traditional love poetry and couches his argument in terms of consuming foods, the lowest common denominator presented as bluntly and nakedly as possible:

> There's no such thing as that we beauty call,
>   it is meer cousenage all. . . .
>
> (9–10)

The poet will not be tied to love's conventional rosy lips and snowy skin "though some long ago / Like't certain colours mingled so and so," for "'Tis not the meat, but 'tis the appetite / makes eating a delight, / and if I like one dish / More then another, that a Pheasant is" (17–20)—though another might call it potted hare or old mutton. The end in view is purely self-regarding, self-gratifying, a mechanical release that refuses to acknowledge any objective standard of value; it matters not who gives ease to the perpetual itch:

> What in our watches, that in us is found,
> So to the height and nick
>   We up be wound,
> No matter by what hand or trick.
>
> (21–24)

Indeed, viewed in such raw terms, it is no wonder that it all seems a trick, "meer cousenage all." Beneath the swagger, one senses a sardonic self-contempt; the mind is superior to the old game, but the senses and the appetites demand that the mind's resources join the match once more.

In the two poems "Against Fruition" (Nos. 40 and 41), Suckling pushes his posture of cynical realism still further toward an ultimate reduction. The first turns on the equation of women with other objects of consumption—"Romances read," plays whose plot is known—or objects of aesthetic contemplation (simply another kind of self-affirming consumption)—"sights once seen," "Prospects . . . Where somthing keeps the eye from being lost, / And leaves us room to guesse." The final assessment here concludes with an endorsement of the proverbial wisdom that by being forced to recognize its limits, possession that knows the extent of its goods has been impoverished:

> They who know all the wealth they have, are poor,
> Hee's onely rich that cannot tell his store.
>   (40.29–30)

However, the second poem "Against Fruition" descends further into nihilism, denying that "that obscure object of desire" has any real existence at all; it is a fantastic, chimerical hope, an empty projection of an imagined perfection of bliss:

> Then fairest Mistresse, hold the power you have,
> By still denying what we still do crave:
> In keeping us in hopes strange things to see
> That never were, nor are, nor e're shall be.
>   (41.23–26)

Again Suckling's worldly knowingness is ironized: even as he announces his awareness that the hope his mistress lingers out by denial is a vain thing, empty of content, he seems to acquiesce in being fooled by the game again, if it is played well enough ("keeping *us* in hopes").

These poems strike a further sardonic note, as Fletcher Orpin Henderson long ago pointed out, by urging the same suspension of carnality that was erected into a dogma by Platonic and *précieux* love theory, but wittily grounding their similar counsel on the diametrically opposed principle of the most refined sensuality.[15] However, the ethos of materialist, sensualist naturalism is a dead end, uncovered in A. J. Smith's frustration with the metaphysical results of ratiocination

---

15. "To write against fruition by advancing 'libertine' arguments at a time when the subject was being treated more or less seriously by other court poets, is part of the wit of Sir John which has not been fully appreciated" (Henderson, "Traditions," 296).

and predication in Cavalier love lyrics.[16] The result is a recognition that love can exist only in anticipation, that once enjoyed, the object falls from value and estimation in an instant while the insatiate fancy must rove to seek a new projection of desire. Such knowledge commits the disappointed sensualist to an endless cycle of consummations that consume his dream: the ultimate masculine sexual damnation of an endless, restless Don Juanism, running through indistinguishable objects and repetitive acts that never finally satisfy and teach nothing but disgust and disillusion.[17] One thinks of Baudelaire, approvingly quoting Stendhal: "*Le Beau n'est que la promesse du bonheur*," "Beauty is the promise of happiness," with its sad premise, "promises worth making are never kept." Suckling himself at times seems like a character Stendhal might have created—that "*esprit impertinent, taquin, répugnant même.*"[18]

"[Loves Feast]" (No. 54) starts with less violence than "Fye upon hearts that burn with mutual fire" (No. 41). However, the unillusioned weariness that underlies its opening polite refusal springs from bleak recognition of the absence of lasting value or a real object in the game announced in the other poem. His heart "will not do its part," says the poet,

> For through long custom it has known
> The little secrets, and is grown

16. See "*Among the Wastes of Time:* Seventeenth-Century Love Poetry, and the Failure of Love," chap. 4 in *The Metaphysics of Love: Studies in Renaissance Love Poetry from Dante to Milton* (Cambridge: Cambridge University Press, 1985).

17. Cf. Charles L. Squier, *Sir John Suckling* (Boston: Twayne Publishers, 1978), 153: "Both Suckling and Herrick share an undeserved reputation for being more superficial than they really are. A certain darkness, an intense dissatisfaction with reality, a disappointed idealism, is beneath the surface of both poets." For a more light-hearted (but fundamentally serious) argument that Suckling's wit is more than froth or "a scum of ungodliness from the seething pot of iniquity," see "'At Bottom a Criticism of Life': Suckling and the Poetry of Low Seriousness," by Thomas Clayton in *Classic and Cavalier: Essays on Jonson and the Sons of Ben,* ed. Ted-Larry Pebworth and Claude J. Summers (Pittsburgh: University of Pittsburgh Press, 1982), 217–41; the characterization as a "scum of ungodliness" is quoted by Clayton (233) from *A Mappe of Mischiefe* (1641), 5.

18. R. P. Blackmur quotes Baudelaire on Stendhal in "The Charterhouse of Parma," *Kenyon Review* 26 (1964): 211; cf. also the aptness to Suckling's ethos of the terms Blackmur deploys in analyzing Stendhal's poetics in the novel: "*puntiglio,* honor, rashness, hysteria, intrigue" and "the politics of grand opera to follow on the histrionic" (224).

> Sullen and wise, will have its will,
> And like old Hawks pursues that still
> That makes least sport, flies onely where't can kill.
>
> (54.6–10)

The image of the old hawk, wise from experience, combines imagery of appetite and imagery of violence, the chase, the kill, analogous to the Petrarchan imagery of warfare in "'Tis now since I sate down before" (No. 51). The old hawk's choice of quarry also recalls the resolution of that poem to go seek an easy conquest—a decision supported by the recognition of No. 51 that the mechanism of ecstasy will go off like a clock, no matter who winds it to the nick. But how we are to respond to this worldly recognition is made far more ambiguous by the image that conveys it this time. "Sullen and wise," the old hawk's wisdom is rather like that of Bacon's ant, the exemplar of "Wisdom for a man's self"—"a shrewd thing in a garden." Flying at the base, slow target, acting for itself, not the falconer, and eschewing the excitement of the chase of sporting prey, the old hawk makes a strangely unsavory comparison for the poet's persona. And what are we to make of this repeated assertion of the wisdom of being content with easy conquests and unresisting victims, in contrast to the equally axiomatic assertion in "Against Fruition [II]" that "no *brave* spirit ever cared for that / Which in down beds with ease he could come at" (41.17–18; emphasis supplied)?[19]

Similarly ambivalent is the gormandizing conceit in "[Loves Feast]" where the poet presents himself in a curiously double-edged comparison to the "youth" who, "think[ing] perchance the pain's the glory," will "*mannerly* sit out Love's Feast" while

> *I* shall be carving of the best,
> *Rudely* call for the last course 'fore the rest.
>
> (54.14–15; emphasis supplied)

19. Among innumerable instances of the assertion that honor is earned in love, as in battle, only by difficult conquests, cf. Carew's lines in "Truce in Love entreated," which urge Cupid to leave tormenting the too vulnerable poet and dare "equall combat try": "And alas! that conquest gaines / Small praise, that only brings away / A tame and unresisting prey" (4–6).

While, by behaving boorishly, the speaker enjoys the best cuts before anyone else is served (or passes directly to the pièce de résistance without pausing for the appetizers), the terms of description characterize the contrasted youth with the favorable epithet of polite society, "mannerly," even as the protagonist is self-confessedly "rude." To be sure, this is a libertine poem, and therefore the affectations and punctilios of polite society are intended as objects of mockery and scorn; are not nature and appetite the only criteria of value? But the language and the rhythms are more complex than that pat formula comprehends: an undercurrent of regret, a darker tone pervades the ending of this poem:

> And oh! when once that course [the "last course"] is past,
> How short a time the Feast doth last!
> Men rise away, and scarce say grace,
> Or civilly once thank the face
> That did invite, but seek another place.
>
> (16–20)

Even as it asserts in double entendre once again that it is not the face but another place that lovers seek, this final stanza, perhaps surprisingly, seems to voice a sigh at the mutability and evanescence of human connection and the feebleness of the rituals of civility that bind us to one another. The conclusion to "[Loves Feast]" conveys at once an unblinking recognition of the way of the world, the Cavalier's typical knowing stance, and a note of regret that is far from the usual bright, hard-edged naturalism of the libertine attitude. Suckling, ordinarily not a complex poet, reveals the greatest density and ambivalence of which he is capable in such a lyric. As usual with him, the complexity of suggestion comes less from conscious manipulation of literary poses or generic assumptions, than from the implications or suggestions set in motion by what is said, from the reader's reflection upon the range of experience and response that is tacitly omitted, and occasionally from jarring notes when a word or an image introduces standards of judgment or stimulates emotional responses seemingly in conflict with the avowed ethos of the speaker. The complicating overtones in such cases are usually the result of oblique suggestion of the standards of convention: conventional honor and personal fastidiousness, or conventional bonds and standards of civility. When this kind of thing happens in Suckling, it is usually difficult to tell whether he intended the undercutting of his proclaimed stance, or whether his jocular libertinism has simply been betrayed, either by his own boasted facility, or by the duplicity and resonance of language itself.

The capacity of the duplicity and resonance of language to evoke discordant and complex emotional and intellectual responses is nowhere more evident in Caroline erotic lyric than in the conclusion of Thomas Carew's poem "The Rapture." Unlike Suckling, however, Carew seems to exploit fully the contradictions into which he plunges his reader; in fact, he insists on calling attention to his sophistical manipulation of value-laden words. While a vague undertone of dissatisfaction with his professed roles and avowed values occasionally haunts the cadences of Suckling's lyrics or jumps to the reader's mind from a word or phrase without direct acknowledgment by the poet, in "The Rapture" Carew's more analytical and reflective mind draws on stage into a direct confrontation the conflicting and incoherent competing values buried in his civilization's conceptualization of *eros*.

Suckling was concerned to represent himself striking an appropriately rakish attitude, rejecting conventions and forms rather than be mastered by them; Carew masters conventions and forms through his playful, distanced participation in them. In "The Rapture," whole systems of conventional values are rejected and scoffed at only to have their components disingenuously insinuated into the argument to support propositions inimical to the conventional. Mingled allusions to the tonally disparate worlds of Renaissance pastoral, Ovidian epyllion, and Roman and Donneian love elegy ultimately clash not only with each other but also with the "reality" that each tries to select from, transform, or assuage. The whole performance finally calls into question the very fictions of art that have so dazzlingly composed the substance of the poem.

Confronting the problem posed by the conflicting ways the Renaissance aristocratic convention of honor works as applied to the two sexes, Carew introduces "the Gyant, Honour" (3) at the very outset as the great obstacle to untrammelled erotic bliss and natural, sensual enjoyment. At the poem's end, he returns to Honor to exclaim:

> nor is it just that Hee
> Should fetter your soft sex with Chastitie,
> Which Nature made unapt for abstinence;
> When yet this false Imposter can dispence
> With humane Justice, and with sacred right,
> And maugre both their lawes command me fight
> With Rivals, or with emulous Loves, that dare
> Equall with thine, their Mistresse eyes, or haire:
> If thou complaine of wrong, and call my sword
> To carve out thy revenge, upon that word
> He bids me fight and kill, or else he brands
> With marks of infamie my coward hands,
> And yet religion bids from blood-shed flye,
> And damns me for that Act. Then tell me why
> This Goblin Honour which the world adores,
> Should make men Atheists, and not women Whores.
>   (151–66)

"Human justice" and "sacred right" have been scoffed at before in the poem, while their vocabularies were perverted to the service of libertinism and a distinctly non-Platonic religion of love. Suddenly they now appear in a very different light. It is assumed that, however ambiguously Honor may be regarded at this point in the poem, Justice, law, sacred right, and religion still retain a great deal of their conventional moral weight and automatic association with good; so the giant Honor is now presented as a perverter of those goods. Indeed, Honor itself is accorded more of the complication of its range of usages: no longer simple female chastity, as it was at the outset of the poem, it now embraces also the gentlemanly code that demands satisfaction for supposed insults or affronts. While Carew's language may at first convey a mocking irony in the very excess of the terms employed to characterize the trivial offenses defined by Honor—"Rivals, or . . . emulous Loves, that *dare* / Equall with thine, their Mistresse eyes, or haire"—the language builds in intensity, until the mocking tone of hyperbole disappears, leaving only the sense of actual enormity: "complaine of *wrong*," "*carve* out thy *revenge*," "fight and *kill*," "*brands* with marks of *infamie* my *coward* hands," "*religion* bids *from blood-shed flye*," and "*damns* me for the Act." This climactic series, building from wrong through revenge and infamy to damnation, prepares an intense emotional charge to be released, one would expect, by the final *quod erat demonstrandum*. And indeed, the poem's last two and a half lines have the impact of a blow in the face, but they certainly are not as simple as that. In them, the poet protests a double standard, but the terms of his last, bullying question present an unanswerable paradox about one of the central values or conventions of his class.

As argument, of course, the final strategy of the poem is to discredit Honor utterly as authorizing monstrous crimes: you wouldn't want to obey the dictates of someone like *that,* would you, Celia? There is a logical consistency in the argument—if you insist you will not do what I want because of Honor, and I show you that your criterion of behavior is so bad as to enjoin murder and atheism, then logically, consistently, shouldn't it make you a bad person, too? So the only way for a woman to be a morally consistent devotee of the Honor that makes her beau an atheist and murderer, is to become a whore. On the other hand, if Honor is *that* bad a guide, you wouldn't want to obey its dictates, anyway. (Heads, you lose, tails, I win.) But rhetorically, emotionally, a persuasion to love that ends by inviting the lady in so many words to be a whore, even if logically consistent, is a disastrous tactical mistake.

So that is not what the poem was about, in the first place. It is not a persuasion to love, or an Ovidian elegy, or a pastoral erotic epyllion, or a satiric take-off on *précieux* glorification of a religion of spiritualized love—or any of the conventional genres upon which it plays its virtuoso variations. The last lines of "The Rapture" raise questions that reverberate back through all the strategies and arguments of the poem, asking the reader to reexamine the effectiveness of each again. For example, Carew's reliance on the force of those two potent words, *atheist* and *whore,* undermines that denaturing of such terms argued for earlier (ll. 107–14), while the unreality of the lovers' pastoral Elysium is only heightened by the demonstrated continuing power of conventional usage. "Atheist" invokes the real religious standard and demands a revaluation of all the imagery depicting a religion of carnal love and a lovers' paradise and purgatory drawn so lusciously before (ll. 115–46).

It is instructive to note that in the spectacular cataloging of varieties of erotic poetry "The Rapture" indulges, it eschews direct invocation of the carpe diem argument. The poem makes little or nothing of

Time and the fading of youth and beauty as the lovers' foes. Carew concerns himself here with social and conventional barriers to love, not ultimate and universal ones.[20] Only to Carew's poem among the many imitations it inspired is "Adieu! the fancy cannot cheat so well / As she is fam'd to do, deceiving elf" one of the possible responses elicited—in fact, at the deepest level, the appropriate response. The courtly, illicit love with which the poem is concerned may be imagined as a private garden, or as a state with laws and exchequer. Such love may be conceived as a following of nature without restraint, or as a hieratic observance of "religious" rites and rituals. It may be fancied as a conventionally charming or seductive picture, but at last all of this comes down to an ugly word that we cannot exclude from our real vocabulary and associations, try as we may.

Observe that, in his concluding coup, Carew does not affirm the truth or endorse the correctness of conventional morality and religion; he merely demonstrates that we cannot easily ignore or discard them, or subvert them with emotional impunity in our social and literary games. His skeptical stance enables him to enter fully into the fictional alternatives he explores, without committing himself to any, for he sees through their relative status as well as their arbitrary power. Like Montaigne, seeking some sanction by which to conduct himself, he rests in nominal acquiescence to the custom of the country. He is either too intelligent, or too fastidious, to act on his ironic superiority to the fables and conventions his society embraces by trying to erase them all, and return to "Nature" and the dictates of interest and appetite, as Suckling does, for he sees that, too, as a pose, and a rather limited one at that.

In fact, "The Rapture" is a sport among Carew's poetic productions. The testing juxtaposition of discordant conventions and the violence of the ending uncover a dissatisfaction with the received order of things that is uncharacteristic. Carew rarely mixes modes and confounds generic expectations in his later verse as he did in "The Rapture." It is more convenient to play artfully by whatever set of rules

20. It is equally unlike closer relatives such as Randolph's "A Pastoral Courtship" and "Upon Love Fondly Refused for Conscience' Sake," John Hall's "To Chloris: A Rapture," or William Cartwright's "A Song of Dalliance," all of which lack the harshness and force of the conclusion of "The Rapture" and its complex, testing juxtaposition of viewpoints and moods borrowed from various kinds of literary erotic convention.

the kind he is working in affords, and the audience he writes for expects. Such a course has its rewards for a detached, uncommitted, highly intelligent, indolent man; as Suckling said, "his Grace / Consider'd he was well he had a Cup-bearers place" (71.39–40). In this accommodation, he assures that his art will remain, like Cavalier lyric in general, minor and decorative, a source of pleasure and even intellectual delight on occasion, but aspiring to no strenuous higher synthesis, no truly heroic motive or profound attempt to resolve the contradictions of the human condition.[21]

However, while capable of witty representation of libertine stances and never wholly *précieux* in constructing his accommodations to the tastes of his age and class, Carew in fact, unlike Suckling, approximates many of what Odette De Mourgues has defined as the positive traits of *précieux* literature:

> Precieux literature only reflects the literary tendencies of its age in so far as those tendencies are compatible with its essential aim: to form a polite society, in which the blessings of culture and civilization can be enjoyed without the intrusion of the most troublesome problems of the age. A precieux society does not fight for any creed, political, religious, or literary, but stands in firm opposition to everything that menaces the vested interests of civilizations.[22]

In writing his amatory verse, Thomas Carew was carefully constructing part of the persona of a worldly, sophisticated, courtly gentleman. In an age that was also becoming conscious of nature and human motives in terms that would be codified by Thomas Hobbes, Carew chose instead the terms of Castiglione. His works provide a constant illustration of his command of all the ameliorating graces, the right moves of his culture and their appropriate linguistic embellishments. Poetry was a minor enough, to be sure, but a still significant aspect of his role as courtier and gentleman-servant to his royal master. And because no part of any role escapes ideological implica-

---

21. The ground of A. J. Smith's frustration with these often graceful, gifted poets: see *The Metaphysics of Love,* 252. Just such an "accommodation" would seem to characterize Carew's whole relation to life and society, while at least the darker undertones of the poems by Suckling examined here suggest their author's incapacity for compromising his finally bleak vision of the little satisfaction "nature" affords.

22. *Metaphysical, Baroque, & Précieux Poetry,* 115–16.

tion, the amatory verse, with its invocation of various courtly or pastoral "paradises of wit and gallantry," was not without its political
significance, as well—again, in however minor a way. When he demurs
to Aurelian Townshend from writing to commemorate the death of
Gustavus Adolphus, the fallen protestant champion in Europe, Carew
does so by creating a generic counterweight to Gustavus's epic adventures and aspirations. The soft blandishments of love, the courtly
leisure that sports with Amaryllis in the shade, are a not wholly in-
significant part of the representation of *otium,* civilization, and culture that his careful, urbane art creates.[23] Carew had a firm grasp
on his place and metier: his superior, knowing participation in and
refinement of conventions affords him an accommodation he could
live with.

What I have been talking about as the obvious polarities of erotic
stance marked by the labels of *précieux* and *libertin* both turn out to
be curiously limiting and self-defeating: the one confined to the artful
elaboration of private grace notes in a merely arbitrary and nugatory
text; the other ultimately so disillusioning in its exposure of unaccommodated man as to prove self-destructive. What is left out of a
topography of literary eroticism arranged around such poles is best
illustrated by introducing into the unmarked territory the literary
representation of love in the works of John Milton. By the late 1630s,
most strongly marked in the revised *Masque presented at Ludlow
Castle,* an incandescent strain of Platonic idealism in Milton's work
spiritualizes the erotic impulse into a stable relation to an Other, even
an absent Other, like the classical doctrine of friendship. The love
relation here is felt neither as "role" nor as a given theme upon which
variations may be played according to the wit of the improviser, but
as a "true," "real," and categorically imperative relationship. Even at
this point, the difference between Milton's Platonizing and Henrietta
Maria's might be marked by the differing emphases: the one on the
substance of an idealist ethic, the other on external mannerisms and
gestures. Milton's prose of the 1640s uncovers more clearly the buried second source for his conception of love: the Christian doctrine of

23. For two contrasting readings of this poem, see Kevin Sharpe, "Cavalier Critic?"
142–44, and Michael P. Parker, "Carew's Politic Pastoral: Virgilian Pretexts in the
'Answer to Aurelian Townshend,'" *John Donne Journal* 1 (1982): 101–16.

incarnation redeeming the flesh while asserting the partnership (and priority) of the spiritual and intellective, as given expression particularly in the Protestant (and bourgeois) glorification of marriage. What was missing in either the *libertin* or the *précieux* stances is what both the true Platonic and the Protestant Christian impulses insist on: the seriousness and transcendent value of a personal commitment superior to external circumstance and change. Furthermore, the ideologies of the erotic in the Caroline court milieu, whether *libertin* or *précieux,* finally find the importunacy of passion and the physical facts of sex an embarrassment that must be mocked from a stance of pretended superiority, hidden away, or disguised and transformed in borrowed generic scenes or the hand-me-down conventional costumes of pastoral or romance. In contrast, the Protestant Christian mentality as exemplified in both the discursive polemics and the great epic of Milton's later work attempts to redeem the flesh and chasten and domesticate the passions to the end of rational participation in all delight. If the pitfall awaiting such developments was the next century's wallowing in self-gratulatory sentimentality, at least the revival and development of those neglected ideas and attitudes, and the insistence on something to be taken seriously that they entailed, opened a way to further cultural development that seemed utterly closed off in the elegant, brittle, finally idle and despairing play of mind embodied in both the *libertin* and *précieux* stances.

Roger B. Rollin

Robert Herrick and the Erotics of Criticism

Although three decades of modern scholarship have conclusively demonstrated the remarkable variety and complexity of his poetic achievement, to readers who know of him mainly from anthology collections, Robert Herrick's name is usually synonymous with love poetry, with graceful lyrics on more than a dozen mistresses. Such promiscuity, even if it was (as seems likely) more literary than literal, sets him apart from many other love poets of the period, who either (like Lovelace) drop the names of just a few mistresses, or (like Donne) seldom bother to give them names at all. Whether Herrick is construed to be celebrating many women under a variety of names (some of them actual) or a few women under many names, his discourses of desire have caught the attention of a number of critics. While some have been merely amused and entertained by the erotic verses of *Hesperides*, others have professed to be shocked, disgusted, even repelled. As a consequence, since the beginnings of substantive Herrick criticism in the later nineteenth century, as much ink has been spilled in condemning the poet's eroticism as in offering airy speculations about the possible reality and the supposed identities of his Corinnas, Antheas, and Julias.[1]

1. See especially John L. Kimmey, "Robert Herrick's Persona," *Studies in Philology* 67 (1970): 221–36, and "Order and Form in Herrick's *Hesperides*," *Journal of English and Germanic Philology* 70 (1971): 255–68; A. Leigh DeNeef, "*This Poetick Liturgy*": *Robert Herrick's Ceremonial Mode* (Durham: Duke University Press, 1974); Robert H. Deming, *Ceremony and Art: Robert Herrick's Poetry* (The Hague: Mouton, 1974); "*Trust to Good Verses*": *Herrick Tercentenary Essays*, ed. Roger B. Rollin and J. Max

Victorian critics not only deplored Herrick's sexually explicit lyrics but professed puzzlement as to his failure to suppress them, as did Canon Henry C. Beeching: "Every one must regret that he wrote such verses even in youth, and every one must wonder why he published them in mature years." The reason, the good reverend goes on to speculate, is probably that Herrick's interest in such poems was more "technical" than emotional. In *Hesperides*, Beeching claims, "There is passion of a sort, but the passion is not 'all air and fire.'" Critical tactics of this sort have been employed periodically in Herrick criticism up to the present: reader after reader defends against the discomfort aroused by Herrickean eroticism by attributing to the poet an infantile or even deviant sexuality. Thus, Herrick has been condemned as, at best, a voyeur in verse, one whose gratification is solely in perception—of a globed breast here, a white thigh there—"the Peeping Tom of English poetry" in the view of one critic. At worst he has been portrayed as a fetishist, more enamored of petticoats, silk gowns, and other female garments than of their wearers. "His sensuality is lukewarm," complains John Press, "and adulterated with a self-conscious roguishness. He is one of those who, in Meredith's phrase, 'fiddle harmonics on the strings of sensualism.'"[2] But Herrick has also been faulted for failing to portray actual sexual consummation in his amatory verse—as if that were unusual for published Renaissance love poetry.[3] And, in the unkindest cut of all, J. B. Broadbent, perceiving a Herrickean obsession with sexuality itself, judges the vicar of Dean Prior's poems to be derived "from a recognizable, if nasty, personality." Here Broadbent echoes the ornate disgust of the Victorian critic who deplored "Herrick's voluptuousness of temperament and not very cleanly ardor of imagination."[4]

Patrick (Pittsburgh: University of Pittsburgh Press, 1977), 65–75; Ann Baynes Coiro, *Robert Herrick's "Hesperides" and the Epigram Book Tradition* (Baltimore: Johns Hopkins University Press, 1988); and Roger B. Rollin, *Robert Herrick,* rev. ed. (New York: Twayne, 1992). *Poems of Herrick,* ed. Henry C. Beeching (Edinburgh: T. C. & E. C. Jack, 1905), xxxix-xl; xxvi.

2. "Peeping Tom," *Times Literary Supplement,* December 15, 1961, 898; J. B. Broadbent, *Poetic Love* (London: Chatto & Windus, 1964), 245: "These poems are crammed with fetichistic superfluities" [*sic*]; John Press, *Herrick,* Writers and Their Work no. 132 (London: Longmans, Green & Co., 1961), 9.

3. Gordon Braden, *The Classics and English Renaissance Poetry* (New Haven: Yale University Press, 1978), 222, 223, 225, 231.

4. Broadbent, *Poetic Love,* 246.

A consequence of such criticism is that Herrick is implied to be, finally, no true Cavalier poet and something less than a man: "People sense something wrong, a lack of genuine sexuality." For Cavalier gallantry and passion, it is alleged, he merely substitutes dirty-minded rhetoric because he is more in love with love (or lust) than with women—and more in love with art than either. In short, in today's parlance, he lacks machismo. "The sexual impulse in Herrick," charges one critic, "habitually expresses itself in decor," thus dismissing poetry that may present psychologically threatening erotic issues by projecting a deficient sexuality upon the poet.[5]

Such evaluations of Herrick's discourses of desire often appear to depend upon which of the *Hesperides*' scores of amatory verses critics have read or have chosen to single out. From a psychoanalytic standpoint such critics practice the defense of avoidance: it is as if they had never read "To Anthea" (H-74)—"Kissing and glancing, soothing, all make way / But to the acting of this private Play"—for example, or "Clothes do but cheat and cousen us" (H-402)—"Give me my Mistresse, as she is, / Drest in her nak't simplicities"—or even "Corinna's going a Maying" (H-178). It is also reasonable to suppose that a rage to make *judgments* about the sexual "quality" of erotic literature derives in part from the erotic personalities of such critics themselves. Northrop Frye has observed that when critics make qualitative judgments about literature they are revealing more about themselves than they are about texts. Moreover, as reader-response criticism indicates, when texts deal with such sensitive subjects as sex, critics' *evaluations* of erotic themes, tones, and moods—as distinct, largely, from their *explications* of them—are even more likely to reflect the critics' own unconscious wishes, anxieties, conflicts, and frustrations. For example, in a brief discussion of Herrick's erotic epigram, "Upon the Nipples of Julia's Breast" (H-440), Broadbent fantasizes an entire critical scenario: "Casual readers, not knowing the title, think at first it's a poem about the clitoris; but with a faint giggle they turn away." Broadbent's own readers may be forgiven if they wonder just who it is

---

5. W. Carew Hazlitt, ed., *Hesperides: The Poems and Other Remains of Robert Herrick*, 2 vols. (London: John Russell Smith, 1869), 1:viii; Broadbent, *Poetic Love*, 246; Braden, *Classics*, 156.

that defends against Herrick's epigram by giggling, that expresses defensive avoidance by turning away.[6]

All literary evaluation is, of course, subjective. All literary critics are, of course, erotic. There needs no Freud come from the grave to tell us that it is likely that those who feel compelled to evaluate literary eroticism may in their criticism be unconsciously working out subjective sexual issues. When, for example, one critic finds Herrick "faintly unpleasant" because "we" readers of *Hesperides* become "surfeited with poems about petticoats or about kissing paps and insteps," considerably more may be revealed about the psychical personality of the critic than about the texts in question.[7] There are, then, critical as well as literary discourses of desire.

Some critics, capable of handling traditional love poetry with relative equanimity, defend against the destabilizing influence of explicitly erotic verse by appearing to be unconscious of its existence. Despite its significance as a dimension of a poet's artistic sensibility they pass over it in silence. Alfred Pollard, on the other hand, in a famous instance, was so conscious of Herrick's bawdry that in his edition of *Hesperides* he consigned all of it to a special appendix (with its own set of notes), thereby not only destroying the poet's careful arrangement of his collection but doing a favor to specialists in the prurient by gathering all the poems of particular interest to them in one place.[8]

Textbook editors also exercise conscious choices: mindful of those who make a profession of finding smut in schoolbooks, they tend to exhibit considerable prudence when it comes to poetic prurience. Thus, that standard of the traditional sophomore literature survey, *The Norton Anthology of English Literature,* included none of the poet's erotica in its Herrick selection until the fifth edition (1986) when "The Vine" (H-41)—one of those poems exiled by Pollard— made its appearance. Given the fact that "The Miller's Tale" had been

6. All quotations from Herrick and the numberings of his poems are taken from *The Complete Poetry of Robert Herrick,* ed. J. Max Patrick (New York: New York University Press, 1963). Frye, "Contexts of Literary Evaluation," *Problems of Literary Evaluation,* ed. Joseph Strelka (University Park: Pennsylvania State University Press), 16; Broadbent, *Poetic Love,* 246.

7. Press, *Herrick,* 9.

8. See *Robert Herrick: The Hesperides and Noble Numbers,* ed. Alfred Pollard, 2 vols., rev. ed. (London: Lawrence & Bullen, 1898), 2:373–410.

a fixture of the Norton since its first edition (1962), the omission of this notable example of seventeenth-century bawdry must be attributed to the vagaries of editorial sensibility.[9]

That a clergyman would see fit to print a piece of comic but explicit erotica like "The Vine" appears to have been less remarkable in the seventeenth century—often condemned by Victorian critics as a franker age—than in our own (whose frankness may be overestimated). Indeed, in spite of the nervousness of some of his critics, modern as well as Victorian, Herrick himself exhibits as much poise about explicitly sexual matters as he does about romantic ones. Thus, "The Vine," far from being buried by him somewhere deep within *Hesperides,* appears on page 14 of the first edition—an early example of Herrickean "cleanly-*Wantonnesse.*"[10]

Gordon Braden, who calls attention to "The Vine" not once but twice in his monograph-length study of Herrick, announces that the eroticism of the poem almost constitutes "a polymorphous perversity, an act of prepubescent exploration, wide-eyed and for the time being innocent." It exemplifies what he judges to be an essentially unhealthy or unwholesome sexual quality of Herrick's book: "What is missing in the *Hesperides* is aggressive, genital, in other words, 'adult' sexuality." That indictment, however, raises more questions than it answers —such as why "adult" sexuality must be both aggressive and genital in order to be "healthy" (a Freudian notion no longer widely accepted in the psychoanalytic community), why such major poems as Herrick's epithalamia—to cite only two examples from *Hesperides*—with their celebrations of wedded love, cannot be construed as exhibiting "adult" eroticism, and indeed, whether most seventeenth-century amatory verse could be considered "adult" by the standards Braden sets forth. Space does not permit exploring all such questions, but the issue of the erotics of criticism can at least be highlighted in a brief consideration of his evaluation of "The Vine."[11]

9. *The Norton Anthology of English Literature,* gen. ed. M. H. Abrams, 5th ed., 2 vols. (New York: Norton, 1986), 1:1321–22. With the fifth edition, Barbara K. Lewalski replaced Robert M. Adams as editor for volume 1's seventeenth-century section.

10. "The Argument of his Book" (H-1), 6.

11. Braden, *Classics,* 223. Braden argues, "The major 'consummation poems'—the Epithalamia—dwell at extraordinary length on the psychology of delay" (223), but explicit descriptions of penetration and orgasm are not conventions of that genre. Moreover, as poems written for patrons, "An Epithalamie to Sir Thomas Southwell and his

It is important to note, as Braden does not, that "The Vine" is a dream-vision poem. Although today it would be viewed as more Freudian than medieval, in the seventeenth-century "The Vine" would have been perceived as a parody of a traditional genre. A comic exercise of this kind accomplishes at least two ends: it enhances the wit and humor of the poem and at the same time emphasizes its topic's surrealism:

> I Dream'd this mortal part of mine
> Was Metamorphoz'd to a Vine:
> Which crawling one and every way,
> Enthrall'd my dainty *Lucia.*
>
> (1–4)

Dreaming of one's penis appears to be, psychologically speaking, a regression to the phallic stage of infantile development, but all dreams have "a regressive character." The persona of this poem, however, is wide awake, recounting what psychoanalysis terms the "manifest dream," the remembered, "encoded" (and thus to an extent "creative") version of the true or "latent" dream.[12]

It is tempting to view that persona as the poet himself, in spite of the fact that he remains technically anonymous. In the order of *Hesperides,* however, "The Vine" almost immediately follows "Upon the losse of his Mistresses" (H-39), a poem in which Herrick gives prominence to his own name: "Onely *Herrick's* left alone, / For to number sorrow by / Their departures hence, and die" (12–14). Moreover, the second poem after "The Vine," "On himselfe" (H-43), is an Anacreontic imitation that alludes to its predecessor:

> Young I was, but now am old,
> But I am not yet growne cold;
> I can play, and I can twine
> 'Bout a Virgin like a Vine.
>
> (1–4)

Ladie" (H-149A), and "A Nuptiall Song, or Epithalamie, on Sir Clipseby Crew and his Lady" (H-283), could be expected to hail wedded love within the constraints of decorum.

12. Sigmund Freud, *The Interpretation of Dreams,* trans. and ed. James Strachey (New York: Avon Books, 1965), 581.

Part of "The Vine's" interest—and its humor—then, is its seemingly confessional nature: the poet is telling a joke on himself (and, as will be indicated later, upon us, his readers).

Initially it might be possible to interpret "this mortal part of mine" as a reference to the dreamer's body as a whole, his fleshly and transient self that, transformed into a plant, literally and figuratively captures the lady in an all-encompassing embrace. However, by the time the poem's punch line (23) has been reached, that more innocuous interpretation becomes untenable. The phrase is Herrick's uniquely witty euphemism for his penis, which may comically be inferred to be more "mortal" than the rest of him because it is so closely associated with "dying," experiencing sexual climax.

Like Eve in the Garden, "dainty *Lucia*" is "enthrall'd"—made captive of but also, perhaps, captivated by—the snakelike vine, sinuously "crawling one and every way." If these lines can be read as obliquely alluding to intercourse as a postlapsarian phenomenon (*contra* Milton), and as dimly reflecting Christian ambivalence concerning human sexuality, such serious considerations must soon be set aside by the poem's increasingly farcical tenor. Farce, and the fact that the lady is referred to as "my . . . *Lucia*"—Herrick's mistress or simply his dream girl— helps deflect attention from the possibility that what is being described here is a rape fantasy. There is evidence that, when they are sufficiently distanced from pathological realities (as they are in "The Vine"), such fantasies can be titillating to both males and females and, indeed, are common to both sexes.[13]

Like Milton, in his descriptions of Adam's and Eve's dreams in *Paradise Lost,* Herrick utilizes narratorial intrusion to keep the reader mindful that what is being recounted is just a dream: "Me thought," he continues, "her long small legs and thighs / I with my *Tendrils* did surprize" (5–6). Here the speaker shifts from the third person ("this mortal part of mine") to the first ("I"), in effect identifying with his penis ("my *Tendrils*"), confirming thereby the direst suspicions of womankind since time immemorial. Then, in a reversal of the traditional catalog-of-beauties, the penis-vine twines upward and around:

13. E. Barbara Hariton, "The Sexual Fantasies of Women," *Psychology Today* (March 1973): 43, and Nancy Friday, *My Secret Garden: Women's Sexual Fantasies* (New York: Pocket Books, 1975), 109.

"Her Belly, Buttock, and her Waste / By my soft *Nerv'lits* were embrac'd" (7–8). Like the almost dainty word, "*Tendrils,*" the delicate "soft *Nerv'lits*" has the effect of masking the phallic aggression of the poem's action and thus defusing it: Lucia is gently "embrac'd" rather than bound up.

In the subsequent triplet, with the dreamy rapidity of present-day time-lapse nature photography, Herrick's vine swiftly and inexorably grows upward: "About her head I writhing hung, / And with rich clusters (hid among / The leaves) her temples I behung" (9–11). The participial "writhing" does triple duty. Simultaneously, it suggests the coiling action of the vine and its becoming in effect a wreath around Lucia's head; in addition, as it connotes an emotionally charged contorting movement, "writhing" engenders a sexual intensity greater than any generated thus far in the poem. That intensity is further heightened by the possibility of fellatio hinted at here, as the vine's gyrations bring it in close proximity to Lucia's mouth. Moreover, we are now made aware that it is a grape vine, hung with testiculate "rich clusters," which with the pubic "leaves" that partially conceal them dangle over Lucia's forehead.

At this point the poem's comic-erotic excitement is bizarrely complicated by a kind of out-of-body experience: suddenly, the speaker exclaims, "my *Lucia* seemed to me / Young *Bacchus* ravisht by his tree" (13–14). Herrick the dreamer suddenly is able to view the action in which he is a participant, except that what he experiences is a hallucination: Lucia momentarily looks to him like a figure in a scene on a Roman urn, one in which the youthful god of wine is being "ravish'd" by the grape vine iconographically associated with him ("his tree"). The physical basis for the hallucination has already been established: with her "long small legs and thighs" and with the absence of any references to her breasts (somewhat unusual for Herrickean erotica), the narrator's "dainty" Lucia is vaguely androgynous: she could be mistaken for a beautiful young boy-god like Bacchus.[14]

The image of Bacchus being raped by a phallic vine fleetingly imposes a homoerotic fantasy upon a heterosexual one, creating a poetic moment fraught with ambivalence. Moreover, it is a psychologically authentic moment, for "many dreams . . . are bisexual, since they

14. Patrick, *Complete Poetry,* 26 n. 2.

unquestionably admit of an 'over-interpretation' in which the dreamer's homosexual impulses are realized—impulses . . . which are contrary to his normal sexual activities."[15] Thus here, contrary to his frequent practice of trying to direct his readers' responses, Herrick subtly contrives to distance himself from the dream-image, first by indicating that it is a hallucination, and second, by allowing it to last only the length of a couplet; in this way he places the burden for readers' reactions upon them. They may either embrace the homoeroticism of the image or defend against it in various ways: through avoidance failing to become conscious of the image's potentially threatening sexuality; through rationalization accepting it as a mere bawdy jeu d'esprit; or through projection attributing the image to the poet's possible bisexual tendencies.

Reader response to erotic images as psychologically complex and ambivalent as this one (and erotic images often are such) must finally be so intensely subjective and so heavily tied in with the individual reader's sexual identity that attempting to apply literary criticism to them comes to seem almost irrelevant and invoking aesthetic evaluation altogether absurd. Even assuming that the comic-erotic character of his poem was a conscious factor in Herrick's insertion of the Lucia-Bacchus couplet (surely a reasonable assumption), the role of his unconscious in that couplet's generation makes his "true" intentions finally unrecoverable. And so the critic is reduced in the end to mere reader, to a uniquely erotic psychical personality making an essentially private response.

In any case, the impending fellatio implicit in lines 9–13 is interruptus; the "vine" that had risen up to Lucia's head and hovered, "writhing" there, now twines downward:

> My curles about her neck did craule
> And armes and hands they did enthrall:
> So that she could not freely stir,
> (All parts there made one prisoner.)
> (14–17)

15. Freud, *Interpretation*, 432; Roger B. Rollin, "Sweet Numbers and Soure Readers: Trends and Perspectives in Herrick's Criticism," in *"Trust to Good Verses": Herrick Tercentenary Essays*, ed. Roger B. Rollin and J. Max Patrick (Pittsburgh: University of Pittsburgh Press, 1978), 6.

The bondage fantasy hinted at as early as line 4 of the poem at this point becomes more explicit with the repetition of the verb "enthrall'd." Here too Lucia's "parts," enumerated in the catalog of beauties, come together again in the image of the lady as "one prisoner." She is again the Lucia of the poem's opening and no longer merely an assemblage of erogenous zones. Nonetheless, she is also clearly a prisoner of lust, the helpless cynosure of the eroticism of domination. However, the lady does not protest and there is no marked strain of physical sadism present in the fantasy: the bondage is all.

In this vein, those who have been reading *Hesperides* in sequence may have their responses to "The Vine" complicated by the poem that is its immediate predecessor and possible companion piece, "The Dream" (H-40). The latter is a mildly masochistic fantasy in which Cupid whips Herrick to impress upon him the fact that "Love strikes, but 'tis with gentle crueltie" (4)—possibly a reference to "The Dream's" own predecessor in which Herrick laments "the losse of his Mistresses" (H-39). But "The Dream" continues, Cupid then "stroak'd the stripes, and I was whole again" (6), in effect freeing both poet and reader to enjoy the subsequent eroticism of "The Vine."

The omission of any response on Lucia's part to all of Herrick's phallic groping—what Gordon Braden wittily calls "viticultural fore-play"—is another indication of the fantastical nature of the poem's experience, of its dreamy surrealism. Like dreams, as psychoanalysis reminds us, all literature is, in subtle and various ways, a form of wish-fulfillment fantasy.[16] This is especially the case with erotica, which is at once highly overdetermined fantasy, eliciting a wide range of individual responses, and a genre tailor-made for its general audience: it is as characteristic of erotic poetry like "The Vine" to concentrate upon the responses of the male (a mainly male audience being assumed) as it is typical of modern "adult" movies, where the visual heavily outweighs the verbal in importance, to concentrate upon the image of the female, the depiction of whose face and form presumably gratifies the mainly male heterosexual audience.

Another difference between contemporary erotic films and Herrick's "The Vine" is the former's seriousness about, indeed obsession

16. Braden, *Classics,* 222. See Sigmund Freud, "Creative Writers and Day-Dreaming," *The Freud Reader,* ed. Peter Gay (New York: Norton, 1989), 436–43.

with, orgasm, leading typically to strenuous overacting and finally to ejaculation, presented in clinical closeup. The climax of Herrick's poem, however, is consistent with "The Vine's" comic central conceit:

> But when I crept with leaves to hide
> Those parts, which maids keep unespy'd,
> Such fleeting pleasures there I took,
> That with the fancie I awook;
> And found (Ah me!) this flesh of mine
> More like a *Stock,* then like a Vine.
>
> (18–23)

Gordon Braden, who tends to take the poem relatively seriously, makes a good deal of the fact that in its conclusion it "swerves away from actual consummation."[17] But this misses the joke and, indeed, the whole point of the poem. That joke, of course, is on us as well as on Herrick: by this stage of "The Vine" readers familiar with seventeenth-century discourses of desire are anticipating the naughty climax of the catalog-of-beauties convention—a titillating allusion to the female genitalia. It matters not whether such an allusion be veiled or explicit, for it is talking dirty that counts. Pretending moral purpose (a common technique for enhancing sexual excitement), the dreamer-penis creeps among Lucia's privates, purportedly to conceal them, but finds that even the briefest of forays into that terra incognita becomes an uplifting experience.

Braden also calls attention to the fact that this experience is "fleeting," but not to the fact that it is pleasurable. Moreover, he claims that—in contrast to the "obvious joke" in the wakening conclusion of a similar poem by Sir John Suckling—the "Such . . . That" syntactical construction in "The Vine" (21–22) implies "real causality." But the only "reality" Herrick creates in the main body of his poem is the illusory reality of an erotic dream. And even if that dream itself is taken seriously—a sizeable "if"—such a mood must give way to the comedy of the framing act of awakening, where, with the traditional hyperbole of male bonding humor, soft becomes not merely hard, but rigid, and vines become not merely bushes, but trees.[18]

17. *Classics,* 222.
18. Ibid.

"Prepubescent," Braden calls all this, "a child suddenly scaring himself awake when he touches upon adult mysteries." Earlier (as noted above) he characterized the eroticism of the poem as close to being polymorphous perverse. But psychoanalysis is quite clear on this point: "polymorphous perversity" is a function of infantile sexuality that lacks "centering and organization," and in which sexual pleasure may be derived from many parts of the body in addition to the sexual organs. Such is not the case in "The Vine," where the sexual functions of the penis are plainly indicated and where that organ is, quite literally, the centering and organizing principle of the poetic experience.[19]

Finally, awakening from an erotic dream just as consummation is about to take place is, psychoanalytically speaking, not necessarily infantile. In fact, a defensive avoidance of this kind on the part of a sexually mature individual would be quite understandable in the case of so literalistic an erotic dream, one whose "manifest content" and "latent content" are so close together—that is, whose wish is not as heavily "encoded" or disguised as wishes usually are in dreams. In such dreams nothing is more likely in individuals with mature super-egos than that the violation of the taboo, the achievement of the forbidden, will be "censored" or unconsciously defended against by terminating the dream through an abrupt awakening.[20] Indeed, it would be the more regressive, less "adult," dream that would be more likely to include sexual consummation, along with the consequent nocturnal emission that typifies the sleep of adolescents. For all its humor, then, the conclusion to Herrick's poem is also psychologically authentic and adult—scarcely "wide-eyed and . . . innocent."[21] All the evidence, including his siting of "The Vine" within the order of *Hesperides*,[22] indicates that the poet is about as aware of what he is revealing with

19. *Classics*, 222, 159; Sigmund Freud, *Introductory Lectures on Psychoanalysis*, trans. and ed. James Strachey (New York: Norton, 1977), 325, 209.

20. Thus, in *Interpretation*, 611, Freud notes that there are individuals who can exercise some control over their dreams, even to the extent of terminating them prior to emission.

21. Braden, *Classics*, 159.

22. "The Vine" is situated in the midst of a sequence of nine poems on the vagaries of love, from "To his Mistresse objecting to him neither Toying or Talking" (H-38) through "Upon Cupid" (H-46).

regard to the human sexual imagination and/or his sexual imagination as he is aware of what he is attempting artistically.

In sum, if dreams are keys to the unconscious, so must be our responses to erotica like "The Vine" that, more so than most dreams, are manifestly wish-fulfillment material. Such responses will be, as they have been in the case of Herrick's poem, positive, negative, or mixed, but never emotionally neutral. However consciously such responses are converted into literary criticism, so long as critics, as they must, unconsciously employ an array of defense mechanisms in the process of composing such literary criticism, the hermeneutics of erotica will inevitably become, to a greater or lesser extent, erotic hermeneutics. This especially must be the case when critics, as some critics of Herrick have done, insist upon evaluating not merely the literary quality of the erotic poetry itself—an emotive, hence fundamentally anti-intellectual, process at best—but the "quality" of the eroticism *displayed* in the poetry. Such criticism may be of use to critics' friends and lovers and psychoanalysts, but hardly to gentle readers.[23]

23. See Roger B. Rollin, "Against Evaluation: The Role of the Critic of Popular Culture," *Journal of Popular Culture* 9 (1975): 355–65.

Joseph Cady

Renaissance Awareness and Language for Heterosexuality
"Love" and "Feminine Love"

The greater critical emphasis on sexuality in literature in recent years has naturally prompted increased attention to the discourses of individual Renaissance writers about their experiences of desire. But at the same time recent discussions in the history of sexuality have implicitly raised broader questions about the discourse of desire in the period as a whole. So far those discussions have focused on homosexuality, and their prevailing view is that homosexuality is a new historical "invention," one that did not "come into existence" until the early eighteenth or late nineteenth centuries, depending on the commentator. This claim has become so widely accepted that it is, at least in tone, the vanguard position in discussions of homosexual history now, and in a previous study I labeled it "new-inventionism."[1] This argument portrays the Renaissance as a period that, at a minimum, had no conception of nor language for homosexuality as distinct, categorical, sexual orientation. Relying primarily on the terminology of earlier law codes, which literally proscribe only a generalized "sod-

1. Joseph Cady, "'Masculine Love,' Renaissance Writing, and the 'New Invention' of Homosexuality," in *Homosexuality in Renaissance and Enlightenment England: Literary Representations in Historical Context,* ed. Claude J. Summers (New York: Haworth Press/Harrington Park Press, 1992), 9–40; published simultaneously as a special issue of *Journal of Homosexuality* 23 (1992). See this article for a fuller explanation of new-inventionism and of what I see as its flaws, and for a fuller discussion of my point below about "masculine love" as a language for a male homosexual orientation in the Renaissance.

omy" and where sexuality is only referred to as a species of "act" or "behavior," new-inventionism implies that if homosexuality existed at all in the Renaissance, it did so only as one such kind of "act" or "behavior" that anyone could perform and not, for instance, as the expression of any inner inclination or directionality. A claim like Alan Bray's that "homosexuality . . . was not a sexuality in its own right" in the age, from his influential 1982 book *Homosexuality in Renaissance England,* suggests such a view, and that point is also reflected in such various remarks as Michel Foucault's comment that "the sensuality of those who did not like the opposite sex [was] hardly noticed in the past," and Jonathan Goldberg's assertion that "there were no discrete terms for homosexual behavior" in the Renaissance.[2]

Prominent as this outlook has become in academic discussions of the history of sexuality, it also has two clear corollaries that have so far gone unnoticed or undiscussed in explicit terms. The first is that heterosexuality, too, must be a new historical "invention." The other is the linked but broader implication that the Renaissance lacked any understanding of and language for the phenomenon of sexual orientation as a whole. These points follow inevitably from new-inventionism's more fundamental view that before the "invention" of homosexuality, humans were, or were understood to be, erotically bisexual (although without any such label of course being applied then). New-inventionists differ about the form of bisexuality that prevailed in what they might call the "pre-homosexuality" era. Some, like Alan Bray and Jeffrey Weeks, see an "undivided sexuality," or a generalized "flux of sexualities," in which a person's erotic attractedness followed no predominating or predictable pattern, including direction toward one sex or the other. Others, like Randolph Trumbach, see a more regularized and differentiated bisexuality, whose homosexual component was always age-asymmetrical, an "older pattern [in which] the debauchee or libertine who denied the relegation of sexuality to mar-

2. *Homosexuality in Renaissance England* (London: Gay Men's Press, 1982), 25. For representative praise of Bray by other new-inventionists, see Eve K. Sedgwick, *Between Men: English Literature and Male Homosocial Desire* (New York: Columbia University Press, 1985), 221, 225; and Jonathan Goldberg, "Renaissance Hom[m]osexuality," omnibus review, *Gay Studies Newsletter* 13.2 (July 1986): 9–12. Foucault, *The History of Sexuality. Volume I: An Introduction* (New York: Pantheon, 1978), 38–39; Goldberg, "Sodomy and Society: The Case of Christopher Marlowe," *Southwest Review* 69 (1984): 371.

riage [could] find . . . women and boys with whom he might indifferently . . . enact his desires." But whichever kind of bisexuality new-inventionists see in earlier times, a clear corollary of their argument is that heterosexuality, like homosexuality, is a new historical "invention," with both at some point splitting off simultaneously from an earlier, undivided, "orientation-less," bisexual eroticism. According to this perspective, the Renaissance envisioned, or actually practiced, that kind of eroticism as its norm of sexuality, differentiating neither homosexuality *nor* heterosexuality and, in the broadest sense, having no conception of nor language for the phenomenon of sexual orientation in itself. Again, Alan Bray implies this view clearly in his further remark that "the barrier between heterosexual and homosexual behavior . . . was . . . vague and imprecise" in the age.[3]

My previous study focused on the Renaissance's awareness of homosexuality and implicitly disputed this view by proposing that the phrase "masculine love" was a particularly notable language in the age for male homosexual orientation, at least among those who were willing to face and discuss the subject frankly. In this essay I want to question this picture of the Renaissance further and in fuller terms by proposing that the era also had an awareness and language for heterosexuality and thus, more broadly, had a sense of different sexual orientations that is continuous with our popular one today, though of course not literally phrased in the same way. My main point here is that the Renaissance not only had a definite comprehension of the phenomenon of heterosexuality but held so strongly to other-sex attraction as the norm of sexuality that what under other circumstances might be thought of as the general vocabulary of desire—that is, "love" and related erotic terms—was, in effect, the age's language for heterosexuality. I do not of course mean by this that every appearance of the word *love* in the Renaissance must be understood heterosexually or even sexually. For instance, when used in a romantic context in the

3. "Before Homosexuality" is the title David F. Greenberg gives to part 1 of his two-part *The Construction of Homosexuality* (Chicago: University of Chicago Press, 1988). Bray, *Homosexuality in Renaissance England,* 25. Weeks, "Havelock Ellis: Sexuality as Knowledge," review of *Havelock Ellis: A Biography,* by Phyllis Grosskurth, *Body Politic,* October 1980, 33. Trumbach, "Sodomitical Subcultures, Sodomitical Roles, and the Gender Revolution of the Eighteenth Century: The Recent Historiography," *Eighteenth-Century Life* 9 (May 1985): 118. Bray, *Homosexuality in Renaissance England,* 69.

period, the verb *love* clearly denoted passionate desire in the fundamental sense, with no restriction as to sexual orientation—as when
speakers in Renaissance homosexual literature (for example, Barn-
field's and Shakespeare's sonnets) tell other males that they love them.
Furthermore, the terms *love* and *lover* were sometimes used nonsex-
ually in the age, to mean something like "intimate friend" or "best
friend," as in Menenius's reference to Coriolanus as his "lover" and
Brutus's addressing the crowd as "Romans, countrymen, lovers."[4]
But when the dominant culture of the Renaissance used the term *love*
as a noun indicating and classifying desire (as in Robert Burton's
remark about what "is . . . called love," which I shall discuss below),
it was referring to other-sex attraction exclusively, in that way establishing "love" and its associated terminology as the period's de facto
language for heterosexuality.

Among the strongest supports for this point is the related period
phrase "masculine love." This prominent Renaissance term for male
homosexual orientation carries information about the age's language
for heterosexuality as well. In clearly implying that the word *masculine* must be added to the word *love* to establish the term's homosexual meaning, the structure of "masculine love" suggests that to the
Renaissance audience the noun "love" by itself, when used in an erotic
context, denoted male-female attraction only—that is, a qualifying
term like "masculine" was needed to revise that basic heterosexual
meaning and to denote male-male attraction instead. (Because of the
contemporary misconception that could easily arise about the phrase, I
should stress here that for the Renaissance the qualifier "masculine"
in "masculine love" had no connotation of male-supremacy. Rather
than intended to imply that there is something "more manly" or "better" about this love than about male attraction to women, "masculine"

4. *Coriolanus* (5.2.14), *Julius Caesar* (3.2.13). All quotations from Shakespeare are
from *The Complete Works of Shakespeare,* ed. George Lyman Kittredge (Boston: Ginn,
1936). Homophobic critics commonly use these nonsexual instances of "love" and
"lover" to promote the view that the terms *never* had erotic meaning when used between
men in the Renaissance, but instead always meant "friendship" and "friend" in such
cases. For a classic example, see Edward Hubler, *The Sense of Shakespeare's Sonnets*
(Princeton: Princeton University Press, 1952), 153. A trenchant critique of Hubler, with
convincing opposing evidence from the period, appears in Joseph Pequigney, *Such Is My
Love: A Study of Shakespeare's Sonnets* (Chicago: University of Chicago Press, 1985),
75–76.

in "masculine love" is simply a neutral, descriptive term to denote the male-male content of that love.)[5]

The same point about Renaissance "love" is supported by other references to homosexuality in Renaissance writing that echo "masculine love" in their content and structure. The most familiar of these is probably Thersites' characterization of Patroclus as Achilles' "masculine whore" in *Troilus and Cressida* (1601–1602), a phrase that is pertinent here both in itself and for the interchange in which it occurs.[6] First, "masculine whore" has the same design and carries the same larger cultural information as "masculine love." For some later readers, the word *whore* in itself would presumably have been enough to make Thersites' point about the reputed sexuality between Patroclus and Achilles. But Shakespeare's method seems to say that had he used that word alone his audience would have been confused, because in its mind the term belonged exclusively to the realm of male-female sexuality—the adjective "masculine" was necessary to make the homosexuality of the situation clear. Here again the general language of eroticism (in this case the language of officially disreputable eroticism, "whore") concerns heterosexuality only and thus serves ipso facto as its identifying language.

Furthermore, the interchange in which "masculine whore" occurs actually begins with Thersites' calling Patroclus Achilles' "male varlet." But Patroclus replies, "What's that?", and it is then that Thersites explains, "Why, his masculine whore." Shakespeare's use of "varlet" in what is clearly a sexual sense here has perennially puzzled scholars, since there is no precedent for it; some have suggested that he may have meant "harlot" instead. However, the only basis they have found for a possible synonymy between "varlet" and "harlot" is admittedly tenuous. In "The Image of Hypocrisy," a lengthy diatribe of around 1550 attributed to Skelton, the two terms are rhymed, when a character is attacked for being, among other things, "The helper of harlettes, / And captayne of verlettes." Another confusion here, not previously noted by the commentators, is the fact that "harlot" has not always had the exclusive meaning of "unchaste woman" or of female prostitute it eventually assumed, so the term might not have been a Renaissance writer's inevitable choice for a sexual reference in the first place. The OED indicates that in the Middle Ages and the Renaissance "harlot" also had several masculine, nonsexual, meanings—for instance, "rogue, rascal, villain, low fellow, knave" (a meaning very close, of course, to one of the usual senses of "varlet"), a male servant or attendant, and, in the playful sense, a "fellow" or "good fellow." Whatever may have determined Shakespeare's opening use of "male varlet" here, for our purposes the more important feature of the expression is that Patroclus (like the Shakespearean scholars to follow) does not understand it and only grasps the term's meaning when Thersites translates it as "masculine whore." This substitution of course suggests how familiar Shakespeare's audience was with the second phrase. It should also be noted that *if* "varlet" meant "harlot" to Shakespeare here, and *if* "harlot" had only a sexual meaning for him, then "male varlet" still mirrors "masculine love" and "masculine whore" in its design and still suggests the same larger cultural practice—that is, the reserving of the general language of eroticism for heterosexuality only, a language that must be revised by the word *male* to denote male homosexuality.[7]

A further example of the same point is the phrase "male stews" (or, sometimes, "malekind stews"), a Renaissance erotic term that has gone unexplicated until now but that apparently was the accepted English designation for a male-male brothel in the period. For instance, in the third satire of his 1598 *The Scourge of Villainy,* a Juvenalian protest against what he sees as the age's widespread corruption, Marston includes an attack on the "monstrous filth" of "male stews" where, "Nero-like," men engage in "Sodom villainy." Similarly, in his 1627 *The Moon-Calf,* a long poem detailing the adventures of the male and female halves of a monstrous "androgynous" set

7. For a summary of the scholarly perplexity about "male varlet," see the *Variorum Troilus and Cressida,* ed. Harold N. Hillebrand (Philadelphia: Lippincott, 1953), 254–55, n. 16. The possible varlet-harlot connection is made by Kenneth Palmer in his edition of *Troilus and Cressida* (London: Methuen, 1982), 262, n. 14, when he points out the attributed Skelton lines, as cited by the OED in its entry on "varlet." For the originals, see *The Poetical Works of John Skelton,* ed. Rev. Alexander Dyce, 2 vols. (Boston: Little, Brown, 1864), 2:406.

of siamese twins after they are separated, Drayton has the "feminine man" twin exemplify "Sodom," whose "sin again [is] / Embraced by beastly and outrageous men," calling him "one for . . . malekind stews [whom] nought doth . . . so delight, / As . . . his . . . catamite."[8] Again we have what would seem to be a generalized erotic term—the OED lists "stew" as a common word for a brothel dating from the late Middle Ages—that a Renaissance author cannot let stand alone in depicting a homosexual situation. As with "love" and "whore" above, the author's technique seems to say that such language signaled only male-female sexuality to his audience and had to be qualified by the word *male* to convey a homosexual meaning.

In the "third partition" of his *Anatomy of Melancholy,* Robert Burton remarks that the "comeliness and beauty which proceeds from women . . . is more eminent above the rest, and properly called love." Burton is moving here from a discussion of the other kinds of love males can feel (for example, for "virtue, wisdom, eloquence, profit, wealth, money, fame, honour") to a consideration of the romantic love that causes "love-melancholy."[9] However, from the perspective of the evidence I have just cited, Burton's comment emerges not just as a signaling of a new subject but as an act of cultural lexicography. It effectively expresses the official Renaissance definition of erotic "love" as heterosexuality only and demonstrates how the term thus functioned de facto as heterosexuality's identifying language in the age. Of course, the Renaissance did not, like the modern period, coin a new word for other-sex attraction—clearly, when a Renaissance eye sighted male-female passion it did not literally say to itself something like "that is the separate sexual category of heterosexuality"; rather, as my materials imply, in that situation it simply said to itself "love."

8. Marston, Satire III in *The Scourge of Villainy,* in *The Poems of John Marston,* ed. Arnold Davenport (Liverpool: Liverpool University Press, 1961), 112. *The Moon-Calf,* in *The Works of Michael Drayton,* ed. J. William Hebel, 5 vols. (1932; repr., Oxford: Basil Blackwell, 1961), 3:170, 171, 174. I was led to these extremely interesting references by Alan Bray's mention of them in *Homosexuality in Renaissance England;* Bray does not, however, examine them as I do.

9. *The Anatomy of Melancholy,* 3 vols. (New York: Sheldon, 1862), 3:3; 2:439. The first, small, edition of the *Anatomy* appeared in 1621, the second and third, to which many additions were made, in 1624 and 1628. I am grateful to Winfried Schleiner's essay on the *Anatomy,* "Burton's Use of *Praeteritio* in Discussing Same-Sex Relationships" (below), for directing me to the major relevance Burton's work has in this context.

But this fact should not be misconstrued to mean that there was a significant discontinuity between Renaissance and modern understandings of sexual orientation. In the first place, the Renaissance, like the modern period, perceived other-sex attraction as a definite "thing," as my examples here clearly suggest. The Renaissance's recognition and denotation of homosexuality imply its prior recognition of heterosexuality—that is, the age recognized heterosexuality well enough to know that homosexuality was definitely *not* it and accordingly needed a different language to depict it, such as the addition of "masculine" to "love" to denote male-male desire.

Secondly, the cultural prizing of other-sex attraction implicit in the Renaissance use of the word *love* has continued into the present, despite the potential for change contained in our different modern terminology. For example, the Renaissance classification of "love" and "masculine love" recognizes both heterosexuality and homosexuality as real categories of experience, but with different worths and statuses within it—here heterosexuality is implied to be so primary and normative that the general language of desire is sufficient to denote it, while homosexuality is presumed to be so secondary and eccentric that an identifying language for it must be derived from the language for heterosexuality. In contrast, our modern terms *heterosexuality* and *homosexuality,* when taken literally, suggest a more egalitarian vision, one with the potential to dethrone male-female attraction as a culture's endorsed form of desire. That is, the addition of the prefixes hetero- or homo- to the core term *sexuality* could imply an equivalence between the two directions of desire, with no judgments about the normativeness or desirability of one or the other.

However, this implied egalitarianism was certainly not the understanding or intention of the sexologists who helped propound the new literal heterosexual-homosexual distinction from the late nineteenth century on, nor is it yet the prevailing conception in our popular culture. In the imaginations of those sexologists, heterosexuality was quite literally synonymous with normalcy—as illustrated baldly by Krafft-Ebing's evocation of "the normal heterosexual love" ("der normalen heterosexualen Liebe") in *Psychopathia Sexualis*—and, despite the subversive potential the new terminology might have had, for them the heterosexuality-homosexuality distinction became just another, more "scientistic," way of saying normal-abnormal or natural-unnatural.[10] Though these features could change under continuing pressure from gay liberation, the same tacit understanding still dominates in our general society, as does the unstated belief that heterosexuality actually needs no special language. For example, heterosexuality is still presumed to be so normative today that the word itself is rarely used to denote it, while the identifying term *homosexual* is almost always applied in situations of same-sex desire. Contemporary adolescents who realize that they are predominantly attracted to the other sex do not usually then say reflexively to themselves "I must be a heterosexual," while a parallel identifying moment is still a fundamental part of most gay people's development. Similarly, in discussing matters where they deem sexual orientation to be relevant, seen most obviously in cases of sexual scandal, the popular media still customarily use generic terms when referring to the heterosexual situation but the word *homosexual* to refer to the same-sex one. Common instances are "rape" and "prostitute" in heterosexual cases but "homosexual rape" and "homosexual prostitute" in homosexual ones. In their remarkable parallel to the "stews"/"male stews" and "whore"/ "masculine whore" that I discussed above, these usages suggest how continuous the Renaissance's understanding of sexual orientation is with our popular one today, despite the literal differences between the age's terminologies for the subject.

There was at least one other categorical term in the Renaissance that evoked heterosexuality. This was the phrase "feminine love," a piece of earlier sexual terminology that, to my knowledge, has never been commented on before. The usage I am familiar with appears in book 3 of Sidney's *Old Arcadia* (completed 1581), in a scene between Musidorus and Pyrocles. Musidorus has finally succeeded in his pursuit of Pamela but hesitates in telling Pyrocles his happy news. When, overcome by emotion, Musidorus finally does so, the narrator attributes his outpouring to the conquering force of "feminine love," proclaiming, "But, O feminine love, what power thou holdest in men's hearts!" "Feminine love" is clearly invoked as a definite "thing" here, designating the kind of attraction Musidorus feels toward Pamela,

10. *Psychopathia Sexualis,* 6th ed. (Stuttgart: Ferdinand Enke, 1891), 143. See my "'Masculine Love'" for a fuller discussion of the rise of the word *heterosexuality* and of Krafft-Ebing's use of it.

and in the situation seems strongly to suggest what we would now call "male heterosexuality."[11]

For readers limited to our traditional notions of sex-role behavior, where the correlation between heterosexuality and "real manhood" is airtight, this use of the language of femininity in connection with male heterosexuality would seem puzzling. Grounds for the same reaction existed at least in part in the Renaissance, too. The now-familiar stereotype for homosexuality of what I would call "gender transference"—the notion that homosexuality represents some sort of "shift over into" the identity of the other sex—did already exist by the Renaissance, and the language of effeminacy was correspondingly used to denote male homosexuals then. For example, an anonymous 1576 broadside poem against Henri III's mignons/lovers that the court official Pierre de L'Estoile included in his private scrapbook refers to them as "these effeminates, . . . these wretched effeminates, . . . who wear more make-up than women" ("ces efféminés, . . . ces vilains efféminés, . . . le fard / Leur est plus commun qu'à a la femme").[12]

But, as scholars of the period know, at times the Renaissance also applied the terminology of effeminacy to male heterosexuality, a practice that of course now no longer exists. For example, in his epigram "The Jughler" (1587?–1596?) Donne mockingly protests against being called "effeminat" because he "love[s] womens joyes." In addition, Nicholas Breton's portrait of "An Effeminate Fool" in his 1616 collection of character sketches, *The Good and the Bad,* is what we would now call entirely heterosexual: "An Effeminate Fool . . . loves nothing but . . . to keep among wenches and . . . to be his mistress' servant and . . . to send his page of an idle message to his mistress. . . . In sum, he is . . . a woman's man." The best-known examples of this usage to Renaissance scholars would of course be from Milton,

11. In "Nobody's Perfect," *South Atlantic Quarterly* 88 (Winter 1989): 14–15, Stephen Orgel discusses several uses of the word *effeminate* in a male heterosexual context in Renaissance writing. But he interprets the term in the usual sense of "effeminizing," that is, making weak or "woman-like," and does not address it as a possible categorical language for male heterosexuality. Sidney, *The Countess of Pembroke's Arcadia (The Old Arcadia),* ed. Jean Robertson (Oxford: Clarendon Press, 1973), 174. All further references are to this edition and are given parenthetically in the text. I am grateful to Peter Lindenbaum for pointing out this important passage to me.

12. *Mémoires-Journaux,* ed. G. Brunet et al. 12 vols. (Paris: Alphonse Lemerre, 1888), 1:149, 148, 146.

who employs it in both *Paradise Lost* and *Samson Agonistes.* In book 11 of *Paradise Lost,* for instance, when Adam says "man's woe . . . from woman [began]," Michael counters, "From man's effeminate slackness it begins," in a juxtaposition that clearly associates "effeminacy" with male sexual susceptibility to women (632–34). Samson's description of himself as "Effeminately vanquished" by Dalila (562) and his lament that "foul effeminacy held me yoked / Her bondslave" (408–11) seem part of the same tradition, although, in a work so concerned with the theme of strength, they may also carry here the more familiar, sexist, meaning of weak or "woman-like" with no particular connotation of sexual orientation.[13]

Sidney's phrase "feminine love" seems clearly to belong to this common Renaissance convention, but, next to the evidence I presented earlier, it does not seem tenable as an equivalent term for the entire category of male heterosexuality. In fact, if "feminine love" followed the same structural logic that I proposed was inherent in "masculine love"—a possibility that the strong literal echo between the two terms certainly encourages us to consider—it would make sense only as a term for female homosexuality instead (that is, "feminine love" as female-female love paralleling "masculine love" as male-male love). Of course, one way to give "feminine love" the meaning of categorical "male heterosexuality" would be to argue, contrary to my main point here, that "love" in the Renaissance denoted generalized male eroticism only and that the adjectives "masculine" or "feminine" were then added to that term to indicate the orientations male sexuality could take, "masculine" toward other men and "feminine" toward women. While official Renaissance sexual discourse does seem to have been formulated entirely from a male point of view, denying or suppressing any independent sexuality in women, for the latter point to hold it would seem that all generalized Renaissance sexual terminology would have to be thus "orientation-less" (if still male-centered) and in regular need of these qualifying adjectives to indicate

13. *The Complete Poetry of John Donne,* ed. John T. Shawcross (New York: New York University Press, 1968), 165; I am grateful to Claude J. Summers for pointing out this poem's importance in this context to me. Breton, *The Good and the Bad, or Descriptions of the Worthies and Unworthies of this Age,* in *The Works in Verse and Prose of Nicholas Breton,* ed. Alexander B. Grosart, 2 vols. (Edinburgh: Edinburgh University Press, 1879), 2:12–13. All quotations from Milton are from *The Complete Poetical Works of John Milton,* ed. Douglas Bush (Boston: Houghton Mifflin, 1965).

gender direction or erotic "population." That is, to adapt the examples from my earlier discussion, we could expect to find in common use in Renaissance sexual discourse not only "feminine love" and "masculine love" but "feminine whore" and "masculine whore" and "female stews" and "male stews," and that is clearly not the case.

Rather, the evidence so far suggests that to its Renaissance users "feminine love" signified not the entire category of "male heterosexuality" but rather one particular kind of that sexuality, a particularly obsessive or otherwise out-of-control form of male attraction to women. The details of Breton's portrait above could certainly support this understanding, with their emphasis on the dominating and seemingly humiliating nature of the "effeminate fool['s]" passion (for example, "loves nothing but . . . to be his mistress's servant"). The same problem seems to be the issue in Milton—he does not seem to be saying that Adam and Samson were, so to speak, undone by their heterosexuality per se, but by their "slack" form of it that propelled them into an erotic thralldom or bondslavery to women. And a similar situation is in fact the larger context for the narrator's use of "feminine love" in the *Old Arcadia*. Musidorus's news is not only that Pamela has returned his love, but that the two are planning to elope. Pyrocles has not yet had the same success in his own pursuit of Philoclea, and Musidorus is anguished at the thought of leaving Pyrocles alone and miserable, which he sees as a breaking of his vow of "true friendship" with him. "I do herein violate that holy band of true friendship wherein I . . . am knit unto you," he says, but his reason is helpless and he cannot do otherwise. Using some of the same language Milton gives to Samson, although of course not in a situation of similarly grave consequences, Musidorus declares: "This enchantment of my restless desire hath such authority in myself above myself that I am become a slave unto it. I have no more freedom in mine own determinations" (173).

While "feminine love" is thus a significant piece of Renaissance sexual terminology that needs to be noted in any study of the subject, it does not seem to have had the same status in the period as "love" and related general erotic terms. As I documented earlier, those basic terms instead served in effect as the age's accepted language for heterosexuality, indicating that the Renaissance not only had a clear awareness of a definite male-female eroticism but regarded that eroticism as the norm of sexuality. In closing, I want to mention two other pieces of evidence that in different ways provide further telling support for this point. The first, from outside the Renaissance, echoes the terminological pattern I have described here. In his 1764 *Philosophical Dictionary,* Voltaire has two entries about love. The first, which he simply titles "Amour," contains only male-female examples. He then titles the entry that follows, which concerns male-male eroticism, "Amour Nommé Socratique," or "Socratic Love." Here Voltaire is following the spirit, if not the exact letter, of the basic Renaissance practice I have just described, implicitly defining "love" as heterosexuality only and needing a qualifying term to that basic vocabulary when discussing homosexuality; in this case, he takes that term from the traditional association of male homosexuality with ancient Greece because his examples are mostly of age-asymmetrical homosexuality. This marked echo suggests how established the assumptions and languages about love I illustrated earlier may have been in Renaissance culture, strong enough there to persist into the era immediately following.[14]

The other evidence, from within the Renaissance, concerns simple historical fact rather than terminology in literature and is most significant here ultimately for that reason. Michelangelo's romantic poems to other males and the preponderantly homosexual poems in Shakespeare's *Sonnets* (126 out of 154 refer to the young man) could be considered the most extended bodies of Renaissance homosexual writing, and what I am referring to here is the bowdlerizing of those works later in the period by the editors who prepared the first collected editions of the authors' poems for publication, Michelangelo the Younger in 1623 and John Benson in 1640. Both editors aimed to make the poems appear to have been written to women, and their falsifying chiefly took the form of changing pronouns from masculine to feminine, although Michelangelo the Younger was also not above simply omitting seriously "incriminating" texts—for example, he reduced from fifty to five the set of passionate memorial poems Michelangelo wrote about Checchino Bracci in 1544.[15] Clearly, the

---

14. *Philosophical Dictionary,* ed. and trans. Theodore Besterman (London: Penguin, 1971), 29–34. Besterman translates "Amour Nommé Socratique" as "So-called Socratic Love."

15. For an account of the publication and bowdlerization of Michelangelo's poems, see Robert J. Clements, *The Poetry of Michelangelo* (New York: New York University

mere fact that these expurgations happened implies the larger Renaissance situation I have been discussing here—why else would the editors have reversed the original erotic content of the poems, except for their knowledge that their dominant culture recognized both a distinct heterosexuality, which was its sanctioned sexuality, and a distinct and different homosexuality, which it viewed with much alarm?[16] Furthermore, evidence like this pointedly questions new-inventionism's "language-determinism," its implication that conclusions about the "existence" or awareness of sexual orientation in a culture must rest on the discovery of differentiating language for the subject there.[17] In the cases of Michelangelo the Younger's and John Benson's tamperings, we need not locate explicit language for their awareness at all; the mere act of their censoring implies it. (Since these expurgations are common knowledge in the scholarship on both authors, it is puzzling that new-inventionism does not discuss them.)

The indications I have discussed here of a Renaissance awareness and language for heterosexuality have implications both for Renaissance literary study and for students of the history of sexuality. For the latter, they would further question new-inventionism's claims about earlier sexual understanding, offering yet more evidence that the Re-

---

Press, 1965), especially chaps. 1, 6, and 10. Benson's altering of the *Sonnets* is well known; for a recent discussion, see Pequigney, *Such Is My Love*, 2–3. In their first publication, in the 1609 "Q" (quarto) edition, the *Sonnets'* homosexual content was intact. Given the universal abhorrence of "masculine love" in Renaissance official culture, it is puzzling how this frankness could have occurred, and, as far as we know now, there was a mysterious contemporary silence about the book. In *The Book Known as Q: A Consideration of Shakespeare's Sonnets* (New York: Atheneum, 1982), Robert Giroux argues that Q was probably unauthorized by Shakespeare and quickly suppressed after publication; Hyder Rollins also argues for suppression in his *Variorum* edition of *The Sonnets*, 2 vols. (Philadelphia and London: Lippincott, 1944), 2:237.

16. The same cultural situation is reflected by the related, though not identical, censoring that Robert Burton does of his discussion of homosexuality in the "Love-Melancholy" section of *The Anatomy of Melancholy*. As documented in Winfried Schleiner's essay below, Burton renders his discussion of same-sex eroticism totally in Latin, while he leaves his surrounding discussion of heterosexual "brutish passion" in English (for example, the "burning lust [of] Troy," 3:15–19).

17. See, for example, Jonathan Goldberg's claim that "there were no discrete terms for homosexual behavior" in the Renaissance, cited in n. 1; Alan Bray's contention that homosexuality in the Renaissance remained "largely unrecognized and unformed" because of "means" that were "largely nominal—a question of giving or withholding a name" (*Homosexuality in Renaissance England*, 79–80); and, most broadly, Jeffrey Weeks' assertion, "Nothing is sexual . . . but naming makes it so" (*Sexuality* [Chichester: Ellis Horwood, 1986], 25).

naissance was not at all a fluidly bisexual age but had a sense of different sexual orientations continuous with our popular one today. My materials also suggest that heterosexuality is as crucial a topic to the historical study of sexuality as is homosexuality and call for bringing that subject to the forefront of inquiry in the field now. For example, since new-inventionism implies that all eroticism was bisexual, either in fact or in concept, before the "invention" of homosexuality, new-inventionism's outlook cannot be ultimately valid until it shows that heterosexuality is just as recent an "invention"—until, for instance, it documents *The Construction of Heterosexuality* or *One Hundred Years of Heterosexuality* (to adapt the titles of two recent and much-discussed new-inventionist books).[18]

For Renaissance literary scholars, the most immediate relevance of my evidence here is the forbidding picture it paints of the options for open sexual discourse in Renaissance writing. Generalizing from their belief that the era did not comprehend the phenomenon of different sexual orientations, some new-inventionist critics have gone on to suggest that the Renaissance was largely unconcerned about the direction of gender attraction or at least offered a relatively open field to authors for the representation of sexual difference.[19] In contrast, my materials here reveal a sexually constricting and hazardous Renaissance whose official sexual boundaries resembled the most repressive that still exist today, an age not only possessing a definite awareness and language for heterosexuality but so officially heterocentric that the general language of desire was sufficient to denote that sexuality. The mentions of "love" I have discussed here strongly suggest that individual Renaissance writers produced their particular discourses

---

18. David F. Greenberg, *The Construction of Homosexuality,* cited in n. 3; David M. Halperin, *One Hundred Years of Homosexuality* (New York & London: Routledge, 1990).

19. Some new-inventionists have even gone beyond this point to imply that the Renaissance was much less concerned about homosexuality than about the potential social and psychic disruptiveness of heterosexuality. For example, in "Nobody's Perfect" Stephen Orgel suggests that Renaissance culture had "surprisingly little anxiety" about homosexuality, which "appears to have been less threatening [to it] than heterosexuality. . . . [The] real fear [was of the power] of women's sexuality . . . to evoke men's sexuality" (22, 26; see also 19–20). Eve K. Sedgwick's reading of Shakespeare's *Sonnets* in *Between Men,* which presents the sequence's heterosexual situation as much more destabilizing than its homosexual one, seems based on a similar view (see especially 45).

of desire in an atmosphere of marked cultural constraint and jeopardy, knowing, on some level of their beings, that their society sanctioned only one discourse about the gender direction of desire, a
discourse that those who were inclined to depart from did so only at
their own risk.

Winfried Schleiner

Burton's Use of *praeteritio*
in Discussing Same-Sex Relationships

Discourse of same-sex desire is forbidden discourse in early seventeenth-century England; in some sense it could not and, therefore, does not exist. In another sense this discourse exists, although in highly coded forms that call attention to its illicit status. I am not at present concerned with the language of persons whom we might, possibly anachronistically, call homosexuals but with the language then used to write and publish about them. To make this vast topic manageable, I will focus on Robert Burton's disquisition on same-sex relationships, a passage brief but chock full of the kind of matter that seems to have suggested itself to northern European, that is, Protestant, writers whenever they thought about such relationships. Since the special coding of the passage seems to warrant this, I will first go through it to clarify Burton's tactics of drawing on numerous and varied sources, his ways of highlighting and of omitting or, more specifically, of highlighting by omitting. Then I will tackle the more complex problem whether in a case like this, where the author seems to conform to official discourse, we may use certain elements of his coding to look through it and behind it.

My subject is a passage of about one and a half folio pages in the third edition of the *Anatomy of Melancholy* (1628), a passage to which Burton was subsequently to add only three words.[1] In the 1628 edi-

1. I am grateful to Nicolas K. Kiessling and J. B. Bamborough for reading early versions of this essay and making useful suggestions. The textual editors of the new Oxford

tion, it is clearly circumscribed or set off from the rest of the subsection, for it is written in Latin. Of course, Burton quotes much Latin in the *Anatomy,* but this passage on the subject of what used to be called "unnatural acts" is one of the longest in which his own sentences are in that language. The sixth edition takes note of this change of language by rendering Burton's sentences in italics, while printing his Latin quotations in Roman type, which is an exact reversal of the usual distribution of typeface elsewhere in the *Anatomy.* Thus framed by the text in Burton's usual idiom and type practice, the segment represents what in computer language could be called a "window," although modern readers without Latin might quibble and prefer to call it "hidden text." At the end of my reading I will suggest some ways in which this window functions.

The passage is introduced by a long sentence linking two topics that for Renaissance Protestant churchmen had more than a merely associative proximity, bestiality and same-sex love, and ends in a quotation from Romans 1:17: Depraved men "will commit folly with beasts, men *leaving the natural use of women,* as *Paul* saith, *burned in lust one towards another, and man with man wrought filthinesse.*" Then Burton switches to Latin and reports cases of bestiality starting with the proverbial ones: "Semiramis had intercourse with a horse, Pasiphae with a bull, Aristo of Ephesus with a female donkey, Fulvius with a mare, others with dogs, goats, etc., of whom sometimes monsters are born, centaurs, satyrs, and creatures for the fright of people." With *Nec cum brutis, sed ipsis hominibus rem habent, quod peccatum Sodomiae vulgo dicitur,*[2] Burton then turns to same-sex relationships and will in the main stay with them until almost the end of the paragraph when he returns to bestiality. Although my sense is that in his comments on sodomy Burton is very close to the center of the Protestant tradition—another way of saying this is to call his paragraph essentially a string of commonplaces—I detect in his presentation some interesting nuances (including his transition *nec cum*

University Press edition of the *Anatomy,* Thomas Faulkner, Nicolas K. Kiessling, and Rhonda L. Blair, kindly supplied me with a pre-publication copy of their text (3:49–51). The segment under consideration is of partition 3, section 2, number 1, subsection 2 (the subsection is entitled: "How love tyrannizeth over men. Love or Heroical melancholy, his definition, part affected").

2. "They have intercourse not only with animals, but even with men, which is familiarly called the sin of sodomy."

brutis, sed ipsis hominibus), which I will attend to after first elucidating his text and use of sources.

The "vice" is next located chronologically (*olim:* then; in the past) and geographically with the Orientals, with the Greeks "all too much" (*nimirum*), and (possibly with a fading of the time reference *olim*) with Italians, Africans, and Asians. Burton's first example, Hercules' amorous exploits with boys (that he abducted Hylas for love, that he loved Polycletus, Dion, Perithous, Abderus, Phriga, and according to some authors Eurystheus), represents academic learning, far from commonplace, to be found at the source he indicates: Lilius Gregorius Giraldus's *Vita Herculis,* and it is presented (since Burton omits the abduction mentioned in his source) without apparent bias.[3]

With Socrates, who according to several dialogues was attracted to the gymnasium, where he fed his eyes (as Burton puts it) "on the shameful spectacle" (no doubt of adolescents contending naked in their matches), Burton then proceeds to an image of Socrates different from the one presented by the Florentine explicators because it is ambiguous: "However, what Alcibiades says about the same Socrates, I feel free to keep silent about, but I also detest it—such an incitement it is to lust. And Theodoretus touches on that in *lib. de curat. graec. affect. cap. ultimo.*" The passage refers of course to Alcibiades' attempts to seduce Socrates (which, according to Plato's *Symposium,* failed) and could be interpreted as indicating Burton's responsiveness to the kind of temptation Alcibiades represents or at least his fear of the reader's being seduced—unless one were to insist that the sentence expressing reticence is merely borrowed from Theodoretus, namely from the passage that Burton adduces seemingly only for confirmation. While reporting Socrates' warnings against lust and against excess in food and drink, Theodoretus had said he was unimpressed because he did not see these warnings supported by facts; that Socrates frequented the gymnasium "and fed his eyes on shameful spectacles" for him is proof of the opposite. And in any case, for Theodoretus, what Alcibiades says about Socrates in the *Symposium* (that Socrates remained chaste) "is only written by Plato; but I should rather touch only lightly on Socrates and be silent, so much the dialogues bespeak Socrates' folly and wantonness, and so much incite-

3. *Vita Herculis* (Basel, 1539), 23–24.

ment to sin they offer uncertain people." Theodoretus adds that
Socrates was given to anger and drink and that he had two wives at
the same time (Xanthippe and Myrtona).[4]

With his references to Pseudo-Lucian, whom he summarizes in the
margin as reserving pederasty as a privilege to philosophers, and to
Achilles Tatius, Burton then extensively cites non-Neoplatonic traditions of love, of course only in order to dismiss them, for as they
discuss the respective advantages of same-sex versus heterosexual
love, both Pseudo-Lucian and Achilles Tatius decide in favor of the
former. We may adduce a little more context from both sources to
elucidate Burton's minimal reference: In Lucian, Lycinus gives the
following verdict (to which Burton refers): "Marriage is a boon and a
blessing to men when it meets with good fortune, while the love of
boys, that pays court to the hallowed dues of friendship, I consider to
be the privilege only of philosophy. Therefore all men should marry,
but let only the wise be permitted to love boys, for perfect virtue
grows least of all among women. And you must not be angry, Chari-
cles, if Corinth yields to Athens." Theomnestus, one of the partici-
pants in the debate, then confirms this verdict and gives an account of
Socrates' relationship with Alcibiades that differs markedly from
Plato's account: "For Socrates was as devoted to love as anyone, and
Alcibiades, once he had lain down beneath the same mantle with
him, did not rise unassailed." Achilles Tatius's debate on the relative
merits of love of women and of boys (the latest possible date for the
work is assumed to be 300 A.D.) belongs to the same genre. Very
distinctly this is a praise of the love of boys in the ancient tradition
and not the love of men, since its central notion is that the fleetingness
of the boys' beauty (here compared to the rose and contrasted with
the longer lasting beauty of women) is presented as the main stimulus
to love. According to Burton, Lucian and Tatius stand at the beginning of an apologetic tradition continued in his time (so he claims,
with little evidence, as we shall see) by "volumes written" or voluminous writings (*scriptis voluminibus*) by Italians. The remaining
examples of male-male admiration or infatuation, which conclude
Burton's section on the ancients—Plato for Agathon, Xenophon for

---

4. Theodoretus, *Opera omnia quae ad hunc diem Latine versa* (Basel, 1608), 1140–41
(PG 83, col. 1139–42).

Clinias, Virgil (that is, the persona speaking the *Eclogues*) for Alexis, Anacreon for Bathyllus, and Nero for Sporus—are largely commonplace. Burton's transition from the ancients to the moderns is marked by a version of the rhetorical figure *praeteritio,* a passing over: naming what is being left out and sometimes inversely calling attention to it. "But what is recorded about Nero, Claudius, and the monstrous lust of others, I would rather you seek from Petronius, Suetonius, and others, since it exceeds all credence that you can expect it of me."[5]

With Asians, Turks, and "Romans," Burton then moves to the topic of sodomy in his own time, a subsection in which he is comparatively even less original. In locating the phenomenon primarily with religious opponents, he reflects the preoccupations of his time, so evident in relation to the same subject at a more popular level in Thomas Beard's *Theatre of Gods Judgements,* at the more learned level of the historian writing in Latin in Christian Matthias's *Theatrum historicum theoretico-practicum,* and at the learned level of the Protestant collector of universal knowledge in Theodor Zwinger's *Theatrum humanae vitae.* This is to say that Burton's narrowing from *Itali* to *Romani* (in the sentence "The Diana of the Romans is sodomy," a sentence that is one of very few substantive additions to this paragraph after the 1628 edition) is not an innocent *pars pro toto* but gathers its strength from all that *Rome* connotes to the Protestant, implying a modern aberration equivalent to the cult and idolatry of Diana, which Paul observed in Ephesus. In a similar vein, the Protestant historian Matthias quotes a saying in somewhat "low" Latin: *Romanizare est Sodomizare.*[6] At the same time the cult of Diana (metaphorically invoked and, for a reader of Paul's letters, associated with Ephesus) provides a link with the modern Turks, on whose

5. Lucian, "Affairs of the Heart," ch. 51, Loeb Classical Library, 8 vols. (Cambridge: Harvard University Press, 1967), 8:229. Some of examples of male-male infatuation can be found in the largest commonplace book ever printed, Theodor Zwinger's *Theatrum humanae vitae* (Basel, 1576) under the heading *libido mascula,* including Plato (col. 2302), Anacreon (2304), Nero (2303 and 2304). It is worth noting that Zwinger rejects the view of Plato as an ordinary lover as incredible: "Verum tantam turpitudinem in tam excelsum animum cadere potuisse, incredibile videtur. Amavit ille Socratico more, non corpus sed animum" (2302). On *praeteritio,* see Heinrich Lausberg, *Handbuch der literarischen Rhetorik,* 2d ed. (Munich: Hueber, 1970), 436–37 (§882–86).

6. Beard, *Theatre of Gods Judgements* (London, 1597), bk. 3, chap. 32; and "Cambysis," in Matthias's *Theatrum historicum theoretico-practicum,* cap. 2, sect. 6 "Incestus," 2d ed. (Amsterdam, 1656), 171.

habits the imperial ambassador Augerius Gislenius Busbequius is Burton's informant.

In letters dating from the 1550s and later that describe the mores of the Turks, Busbequius, the first observer to Turkey after the Turkish expansion into central Europe, had commented several times on the Turks' inclination toward same-sex love (both male and female). To illustrate his point, he reported that for decorum Turkish wives use a special code when they appear before a magistrate to make it known that their husbands had turned to boys.[7] Burton used some of Busbequius's words when he presented this code, which was one of *not* saying. As he made explicit the implied cause of the women's appearance, namely that their husbands had turned to sleeping with men, he clarified the sense of his reference that ceases to be an exact quotation. From the modern Turks he then turned to the modern Italians, who, he claimed with little supportive evidence, defend same-sex love at length following such apologists as Pseudo-Lucian and Achilles Tatius *scriptis voluminibus*. His only example was Giovanni della Casa, bishop of Benevento, who (according to Burton) "called it divine work, a sweet crime, and even brags not to have used any other kind of love." Burton did not document his statement, perhaps feeling that he did not need to since della Casa in this context was one of the most often rehearsed commonplaces of Protestant propaganda. Thus, John Jewel, one of the most influential apologists of the English church, was able to ask: "Who hath not herde . . . what Jhon Casus Archbyshop of Benevento the Popes legate of Venice, wrote of that horrible filthinesse whereas even that thing which ought not to be heard of, out of any man's mouthe, he dothe commend with most filthy wordes and eloquence?"[8] Burton's implication was, of course, what other

7. *Iudice causam quaerente nihil respondent, sed excutum pede calceum invertunt. id iudici abominandae veneris indicium est.* "They do not reply to the question of the judge, but remove a shoe and turn it upside down. This is for the judge a sign of perverted love" (*Legationis Turcicae epistolae quatuor* [Frankfurt, 1595], 145). See also (on the same subject) p. 81 and (on lesbian relationships) p. 146. Burton owned this edition. See Nicolas K. Kiessling, *The Library of Robert Burton* (Oxford: The Oxford Bibliographical Society, 1988), no. 268.
8. See my essay "'That matter which ought not to be heard of': Homophobic Slurs in Renaissance Cultural Politics," *Journal of Homosexuality,* forthcoming. Also Gilles Ménage, *Anti-Baillet ou critique du livre de Mr. Baillet intitulé Judgemens des savants,* 2 vols. (La Haye, 1690), 2:88–153. Jewel, *An Apologie, or Aunswer in Defence of the Church of England* (London, 1562), fol. 24v.

Protestants stated explicitly, namely that della Casa wrote a book *De laudibus sodomiae*.

To the passages from French, German, and English Protestants that I collected elsewhere, I would like to add just two more: Charles Du Moulin, who in an oration before the senate of the University of Tübingen said in 1554 that della Casa "composed and edited a book in praise of sodomy"; and Melchior Goldast, who wrote that della Casa deserved being burned at the stake for publishing a book whose title he gives as *De laudibus sodomiae*. But there is no such book. The references are to a poem "Capitolo del Forno" that della Casa published in 1538, long before he became archbishop. I quote the lines from the poem in which the speaker appears to present himself somewhat ironically (if irony implies *meiosis,* making oneself small) and refers to what is probably anal sex (but not necessarily homosexual) as *mestier divino* (divine craft or work). The poem is long, and my translation of its indirect and coded language is tentative:

> Tennero il forno gia le donne sole:
> Hoggi mi par, che certi garzonacci
> L'habbin mandato poco men, ch'al sole.
>
> S'pazinlo à posta lor, nessun non vacci.
> Dican pur ch'egli è humido e mal netto,
> Et sonne ben cagion questi fratacci.
>
> Io per me rade volte altrove il metto
> Con tutto che 'l mio pan sia pur piccino,
> E'l forno delle donne un po grandetto.
>
> Benche chi fa questo mestier divino
> Sa ben trovar dove l'hanno nascosto
> Cola dirieto un certo fornellino.[9]

9. Du Moulin, *Omnia quae exstant opera,* 5 vols. (Paris, 1681), 5:ix (col. 1); Goldast, "In S. Valeriani . . . sermonem de bono disciplinae colectanea," in Valerianus, *De bono disciplinae sermo,* ed. M. Goldast ([Geneva], 1601), 71. It would seem that David F. Greenberg walked into the same trap as did generations of Renaissance Protestants when he credits della Casa with a work written in 1550, *De laudibus sodomia sev pederastiae* (*The Construction of Homosexuality* [Chicago: University of Chicago Press, 1988], 323). Della Casa, *Le terze rime de Messer Giovanni dalla Casa, di Messer [Gianfrancesco] Bino et d' Altri,* in Berni, *Tutte le opere del Bernia in terza rima,* per Curtio Navo et Fratelli (n.p., 1538): 2-2ᵛ (22–33). There are editions with the same title of 1540 and 1542; I am quoting from the 1538 edition. Of the later editions, I noted that the one of

At one time women alone kept the oven. Today it seems to me that some nasty
fellows have sent them to little less than to the sun. Let them [the women]
sweep it instead of the fellows; no one goes there [to the women's oven]. It
should indeed be said that it is humid and less than clean, and the reason is
those nasty friars. I for myself only rarely put it elsewhere, even though my
bread is a little one and the oven of the ladies a bit large, although he who
practices this divine craft knows well how to find where they have hidden it,
back down there, a certain little oven.

Although the lines may well have referred, as the embattled church-
man later claimed, to a heterosexual act rather than a homosexual
one, della Casa's poem is important for a history of homophobia.
Readers fought over the poem's elusive meaning for centuries.[10]
   The context in which Burton refers to the *opus divinum* indicates
that like other Protestants of his time, he takes della Casa to refer
unambiguously to same-sex love. The poem, of which Burton, like so
many of his Protestant contemporaries, does not seem to have had
more than a hearsay knowledge, remains his only example of the
volumines scripta of modern Italian defenses of same-sex love (Burton does not even mention Aretino, named in one breath with della
Casa by Melchior Goldast). His next example is of a different kind:
Angelo Politiano "laying violent hands on himself" for the love of a
boy. Incidentally, the contemporary biographer Iovio's report of the

London (Giovanni Pickard, 1721) replaces *piccino* (29) by *piccolino,* that Gilles Ménage
in the segment he quotes (p. 105) from the poem (see my n. 8) has *quelle sue stracci* for
questi fratacci (27)—I do not know on what authority—and that the edition of "Usecht
al Reno, 1760" replaces the adjective in the notorious phrase *mestier divino* (31) by dots.
   10. After Ménage (see my n. 8), Nicolaus Hieronymus Gundling once more published
della Casa's (prose) letter of defense against Vergerio; see Casa, *Latina Monumenta*
(Hallae Magdeb., 1709): 179–93. Here della Casa charges that his religious opponent
Vergerio maliciously misreads the poem of his youth. He admits that the verses are licentious, but claims that they praise relationships with women, not men. Gundling reviewed
the whole issue in his "Observatio VI: Joannes Casa an paederastiae crimen defenderit,"
Observationum selectarum ad rem litterariam spectantium, 2d ed. (Halle, 1737), 2:
120–36, agreeing with Ménage and adding little of substance. Adolphus Clarmundus
[i.e., Johann Christoph Rüdiger] argued what seems to be the opposite (Protestant) view
in *Vorrede zur Lebens-Beschreibung des weltberühmten Polyhistoris, Konrad Samuel
Schurtzfleischens* (Dresden & Leipzig, 1710) and *Vitae clarissimorum in re literaria virorum,* part 9 (Wittenberg, 1713), 8–9 ("Vorrede: Geneigter Leser"). Finally there is a
rebuttal of Gundling (in style almost a return to the contentiousness of the age of the
Reformation) by Johann Georg Schelhorn, *Apologia pro Petro Vergerio adversus Joan-
nem Casam, accedunt monumenta quaedam inedita* (Ulm & Meiningen, 1774).

famous humanist's end (to which Burton refers in the margin) is considerably more sympathetic and ambiguous. Iovio has Politiano, "stung by the mad love for a noble [or delicate?] adolescent," first slip into mortal illness and rave in violent fever, suggesting it seems that at his end he was not *compos mentis*.[11]

Burton's transition from sodomy in contemporary Italy to his next topic, sexual license (and particularly same-sex relationships) in monasteries during the time of Henry VIII, is conventional in polemical Protestant writings, for both were used as ammunition in English rejection of celibacy and in defense of the dissolution of the monasteries and of the attendant secularization of church property. Burton writes, "And it is truly shameful to say how much with us within memory of our parents this detestable wickedness raged!" Then follows a sentence excerpted from the important and polemical John Bale (in the title of the most recent book about him called *Mythmaker of the English Reformation*), which praises the "most prudent" Henry VIII for sending a team of doctors of law to monasteries and similar institutions to record the vast numbers of whoremongers and sodomites. Burton expressly imitates Bale's Rabelaisian plethora of words by giving six near synonyms of the word *sodomitae* (*cinaedi, ganeones, paedicones, puerarii, paederastae, ganymedes*). By filling his sentences with such strings of words, Bale, the master ideologue of the sixteenth century, had iconically suggested their content: "In each [of these institutions] you might have thought a new Gomorrah"—together with the list of synonyms for *sodomitae*, Burton also quotes this phrase from Bale. The "catalogues" or lists of sexual transgressors for which Burton sends the reader to Bale had a considerable fortune in the arguments of Renaissance Protestants and are found on the same page of Bale's preface: here Bale cites samples of the visitors' findings in the monasteries, separating *sodomitae* from other *incontinentes* and giving name and number of each. Burton's two references to Bale, who played on homophobia as on an instrument,

---

11. *Elogia virorum literis illustrium* (Basel, 1577), 711: "Ferunt eum ingenui adolescentis insano amore percitum, facile in lethalem morbum incidisse. Correpta enim cithara, quum eo incendio, & rapida febre torretur, supremi furoris carmina decantavit ita, ut mox delirantem, vox ipsa, et digitorum nervi, et vitalis denique spiritus, in verecunda urgente morte deserreent quum maturando indicio integrae, stataeque aetatis anni, non sine gravi Musarum iniuria, doloreque seculi, festinante fato eriperentur."

may not tell the extent of Burton's imaginative "debt" to him, for Burton might have taken all his information about della Casa and even the notion that the Diana of the Romans is sodomy from the master ideologue.[12]

Sandwiched between Burton's reference to Bale and Burton's comment (introduced with another *praeteritio* or figure of passing over: *sileo*) on masturbating monks are two rhetorical questions of considerable importance because they are on a subject area that is not commonplace. For, after saying with Bale that in those recent times girls could not sleep securely for the activities of necromantic friars, Burton asks: "If this was so with the religious, with holy men or rather manequins, what would you suspect to have been done in the marketplace or at court? Among the nobility or in the houses of prostitution what else but abomination and filthiness?" Because of Burton's cautious imprecision, we do not learn what he knew or thought about King James's court in general or specifically about his favorites. Instead, with an insincere "I pass them over," he mentions the "mastrupations of monks, masturbators," a slur belonging to Bale's mode of polemical discourse but misleadingly footnoted. Burton's first reference here is to the medical doctor Mercuriale's discussion of "priapismus," a pathological condition in which a patient experiences erection without erotic stimulation. Among the causes of priapismus (frequently discussed in Renaissance medicine), Mercuriale mentions "long abstinence from coition, for which reason monks often suffer from this illness," but also "excessive coitions" and "manstrupatio" without ejection of semen. Contrary to what Burton implies, Mercuriale does not say that monks masturbate, but they tend to suffer from priapism because they abstain—the word *manstrupatio* belongs to a different clause altogether. (The etymology of *masturbor* is possibly *manus stuprare,* to defile one's hands.)[13] The reference to Ro-

---

12. *Scriptores duo Anglici: De vitis Pontificum Romanorum,* "Praefatio Joannis Balei ad Lectorem" (Lugd. Bat., 1615), 3 (2d count), 569–70; Bale, *Scriptorum Catalogus* (Basel, 1555–1559), 1:682.

13. Mercuriale, *Medica practica seu de cognoscendis et curandis omnibus humani corporis affectionibus* (Frankfurt, 1601), lib. 3, chap. 38 "De priapismo," lists among the causes of priapism: "cogitationes frequentes rerum venererum, sermones, aspectus, abstinentia longa a coitu, propter hoc monachi solent saepe haec aegritudine tentari, nimias etiam coitus, strictura lumborum, manstrupatio sine seminis eiaculatione" (Frequent mulling over libidinous matters, words as well as images, long abstinence from

derigo à Castro's medical book on women forms a link for Burton between his discussion of masturbation and that of lesbianism (a link not syntactically obvious). Castro uses the word *masturbatores* (Mercurialis does not) and in a long scholion discusses medical implications of masturbation; he also serves as Burton's main authority on lesbians (whom Castro calls *tribades*).[14]

Burton lumps together in one sentence sado-masochists using whips for erotic stimulation, male prostitutes (*sp[h]intricae,* possibly one of the most distasteful terms), female prostitutes (*Ambubeiae,* deriving from a Syrian word and denoting Syrian dancing girls in Rome), lesbians exciting one another, and women using eunuchs and artificial private parts. "It is even more strange," he adds, "that one woman some time ago ruined another in Constantinople," and then summarizes the story of a woman of high birth (*mulier magno natu* in the source, Busbequius's account) who cross-dressed so that she could marry the girl she had fallen in love with at the public bath. Burton, following his source, would hardly have called the woman's daring behavior "clearly incredible" had he known the very similar case of a sixteenth-century French woman from the Touraine, which H. Estienne recounts.[15]

With another *omitto* ("I am passing over"), Burton's characteristic transition to a further aspect of his tabooed subject and, of course, another instance of the rhetorical figure *praeteritio,* he touches on the topic of necrophilia (drawing on Aegyptian uses and abuses told by

intercourse—that is why monks are often tried by this illness—also excessive intercourse, constriction of the loins, and masturbation without ejaculation of semen). The passage in Galen (at the very end of *De locis affectis,* 6), to which Burton refers in the margin, is also on priapism. Galen here counsels a friend suffering from that condition to emit semen and distinguishes that action from a reprehensible use of the same activity.

14. Castro, *De universa muliebrium morborum medicina,* 2d ed. (Hamburg, 1617). For masturbation, see pars 2, lib. 1, chap. 15 "De gonorrhaea," particularly p. 100 and (for the scholion) pp. 108–9. For *tribades, fricatrices, subigatrices,* and *mutuus coitus incubus succubus,* see pars 1, lib. 1, chap. 3 (p. 10) and pars 1, lib. 3, chap. 3 (p. 108). For the Caelius passage (about masturbation among the Lydians) which Burton cites (as does Castro), see Ludovicus Caelius Richerius [or Rhodiginus], *Lectionum antiquarum libri xxx* (Frankfurt, 1599), lib. 20, chap. 14 (cols. 939–40). Burton's reference (1.2 c. 14) seems faulty.

15. The story of the Turkish lady's elaborate scheme of wooing the daughter of a mean citizen is told in considerable detail by Busbequius, *Epistolae* (Frankfurt, 1595), 146. For H. Estienne, see *L'introduction au traité de la conformitié des merveilles anciennes avec les modernes, ou Traité préparatif à l'apologie pour Hérodote,* chap. 13 (Lyon, 1592), 97–98. See also my essay mentioned in n. 8.

Herodotus) and then moves to cases of making love with pictures and statues, for which he relies on Ovid, Hegesippus, and Pliny. But the light touch suggested by the *praeteritio* is only rhetorical effect, for if one combines his sentence about certain lascivious Aegyptian embalmers' habits of sleeping with the dead bodies of beautiful women with his detailed summary in the margin, very little is in fact omitted of Herodotus's brief paragraph about the origin of the custom of a delay in turning bodies over for embalming (presumably the stench was to discourage abuse).[16]

The story of Pygmalion's falling in love with a statue of his own making (Ovid *Metam.* 10.243) is proverbial. It and almost all of Burton's additional examples of men loving pictures and statues are contained in Zwinger's collection (2300–2301), which Burton does not mention as his source. The one exception is Burton's reference to Hegesippus's story of Mundus and Paulina (*Paulini* is an error in all early editions of the *Anatomy*), and indeed this account of Mundus falling in love with a chaste married woman (Paulina) and of tricking her (with the connivance of priests of the temple) into believing that the god Anubis desired to have intercourse with her does not fit perfectly into Burton's context, since it has little to do with the preceding case of loving a statue or the following (from Pliny) of loving a picture.[17] Just as curiously, Burton then does not refer to Pliny's cases of statues inciting males to lust (a statue of Venus and one of Cupid, each left with a *macula* or *amoris vestigium*), but he chooses to highlight Pliny's story of a man falling so madly in love with the pictures of Atalanta and Helen that he wanted to steal them. Burton does so possibly because he is intrigued by his identification of the libidinous thief with an almost archetypal religious opponent, Pontius Pilate, who had Christ crucified. The version Zwinger quotes in his handbook calls the would-be thief indeed "P. Pilatus, legatus Caii principis," and the 1599 edition of Pliny by Jacobus Dalecampius reads "Pontius Legatus Caii principis." Unfortunately for Burton's identification, modern editions of Pliny have a different wording.[18]

16. See Herodotus, 2.89.

17. As Burton says, the story is told by Hegesippus (or Aegesippus), *De bello Iudaico,* lib. 2, chap. 4 (Cologne, 1559), 218–20.

18. *Theatrum humanae vitae,* 2301; Plinius, *Historia mundi* [i.e., Nat. hist.], ed. Jacobus Dalecampius (Frankfurt, 1599): 830 and Nat. hist. 35.3 (Meihoff ed., 5:234):

The word *lust* or *libido* serves Burton as a transition: first to the proverbially debauched emperor Heliogabalus who, as Burton says, "experienced lust through all orifices of his body,"[19] then to Seneca's memorable exemplum of depravity, to finally, in a long quotation from Plutarch, the two subjects with which he started—bestiality and same-sex love—except now in reverse order so that he gives the impression of coming full circle. From Heliogabalus, who for Lampridius represented the *non plus ultra* of perversion by his diet (the choice of food and the location of the elaborate feasts described), by his government (creating a senate for women and making his cook his minister) and, of course, by his sexual habits, it is an easy step for Burton to Hostius Quadra, Seneca's ultimate in the sophistication of sexual debauchery, elements of which Burton summarizes: "Hostius had mirrors made and placed them so that he would see all motions as he submitted to his male partner. He also delighted in false magnification of his friend's member while acting man and woman at the same time, a most shameful thing to say."[20] His moral indignation leads Burton to agree with the satirical speaker Gryllus (whose name suggests that he is a pig) in Plutarch's dialogue *Bruta animalia ratione uti*. At Ulysses' question whether there are any Greeks on her island, Circe had referred him to Gryllus who, to Ulysses' surprise, rebuffs him, opting to remain beast rather than be liberated. Burton quotes (with some omissions) from the Latin version of Wilhelm Xylander. The Loeb translation of the equivalent sentences is this:

> Whence it comes about that to this very day the desires of beasts have encompassed no homosexual mating. But you have a fair amount of such traficking among your high and mighty nobility, to say nothing of the baser sort. . . . Just so Heracles pursuing a beardless lad, lagged behind the other heroes and

---

"Gaius princeps tollere eas conatus est libidine accensus, si tectorii natura permisisset." The difference shows strikingly the importance of using Renaissance editions when elucidating Burton's text. Burton's reference to Aelianus in the same sentence is to the unnamed Athenian youth who fell in love with the statue of good fortune and embraced it; see Aelianus, *Variae historiae libri xiv*, lib. 9, chap. 39 (Lyon, 1604), 259.

19. For Lampridius's account of Heliogabalus, see, e.g., *Historiae augustae scriptores sex*, ed. I. Casaubon (Paris, 1603), 169D: "Libidinum genera quaedam invenit, ut sphinthrias veterum malorum vinceret: & omnes apparatus Tiberii et Caligulae et Neronis norat."

20. The reference is to Seneca Nat. quaest. 1.16.

deserted the expedition. . . . Not even Nature, with law for her ally, can keep within bounds the unchastened vice of your hearts; but as though swept by the current of their lusts beyond the barrier at many points, men do such deeds as wantonly outrage Nature, upset her order, and confuse her distinctions. For men have, in fact, attempted to consort with goats and sows and mares, and women have gone mad with lust for male beasts. From such unions your Minotaurs and Aegipans ["goat Pans"], and, I suppose, Sphinxes and Centaurs have arisen.[21]

As I mentioned above, the words of the sober beast Gryllus (who was so well known in the Renaissance that Spenser could refer to him in the *Faerie Queene* with little explanation ("Let Gryll be Gryll, and have his hoggish minde" [2.12.87]) allows Burton to retrace his survey of acts "against nature" in reverse order, ending where he started, with bestiality, and thus give the impression of closure or completeness.

Burton's last sentence fulfills paratextual functions (in Gérard Genette's sense), since in it Burton names his addressees and attempts to clarify his intentions by saying what he does *not* want to achieve: "But that I do not teach by confuting, or that I make public what is not fitting for all to know (for not unlike Roderigo à Castro, I would like to have written this only for the learned) so that I would not give ideas about abominable crimes to light and depraved minds, I do not want to defile myself with these filthy matters any longer." The sentence frames Burton's window, and he returns to English.

Rhetorically the sentence functions as another and ultimate figure of *praeteritio*—after it, Burton falls silent on the subject. Indeed, we have seen that *praeteritio* is the dominant rhetorical figure of this passage (expressed by *conticesco, sileo, omitto*). It should be noted that figures of "passing over" do not actually leave out—in one instance we found in fact that after saying *omitto*, Burton gives about as much information as he found in his source (Herodotus). From another point of view instances of *praeteritio*, characteristic of the discourse of and about same-sex desire, are signals marking and calling attention to the special status of what is foreshortened and seemingly omitted.

The switch from English to Latin makes a similar statement. It

21. Plutarch, *Moralia,* trans. H. Cherniss and W. C. Helmbold, Loeb Classical Library (Cambridge: Harvard University Press, 1967), 12:519–23; Plutarch, *Quae exstant omnia,* Lat. trans. Xylander (Frankfurt, 1599), 2:990D.

may be questionable whether actually, even from Burton's perspective, anyone who had progressed through the *Anatomy of Melancholy* to the third partition would or should be excluded from reading this passage. Would not a twelve-year-old grammar school student in the early seventeenth century have enough Latin to read this page? Perhaps. But my rhetorical question is deliberately gendered. Indeed, few women of the period would have had the Latin to read it—if we believe Retha M. Warnicke; even fewer would have been able to do so in the previous century.[22] When, in the third edition of the *Anatomy,* Burton fleshed out slightly this paragraph on what he calls "brutish passion" by adding references to Roderigo à Castro's work *De universa mulierum morborum medicina* (the reference to Castro's account of masturbation and the middle clauses of the final sentence with the reference to Castro are among the few substantial additions he ever made to the entire passage), he used Castro's example to clarify the addressees he had in mind for his paragraph: the learned (*docti*)—perhaps it is an accident of Latin grammar that the dative he uses (*doctis*) obliterates gender. In the third edition, he expressly stated that it does not behoove just anyone to know the subject of his disquisition. Perhaps it should be noted that Castro, as he writes on women, has views about their faculties that are not only easily recognized as sexist now, but were attacked as such by another physician in the seventeenth century.[23]

Thus, while there is no question that the paragraph excludes some readers, its language and style keep telling those who are able to read it that this is unusual material. But to claim that by changing certain formal features Burton wanted to add a special spice for his learned readers (in addition to giving them the satisfaction of recognizing themselves as *cognoscenti*) would probably be anachronistic. If one were to write a speech act theory of the seventeenth century, one would have to recognize (as Austin and Searle do in modern English for the speech acts of swearing, promising, proclaiming a couple man and wife, etc.) that language relating to sex (including so-called unnatural acts) has a special status: it not only denotes but suggests,

22. *Women of the English Renaissance and Reformation* (Westport: Greenwood Press, 1983), 194–96.
23. Johann Peter Lotichius, *Gynaicologia* (Rinteln, 1630), 18–19. As far as I can tell, Lotichius's praise of women is serious and not *declamatio*.

conjures up, calls to mind, or in Burton's terms, calls to the imagination. To counteract this suggestiveness, authors writing on such matters will, as Burton does here, weave into their discourse a string of morally loaded terms, such as monstrous, abhorrent, and abominable. Because of this implicit assumption of how language works, I am tempted to take Burton's comment on Heliogabalus's amorous habits literally rather than idiomatically: *quod dictu foedum et abominandum*. In other words, if the supinum is given full force, not only Heliogabalus's practice, but to *say* it, is shameful and abominable. Since language thus is taken to infect the speaker Burton, it is possible that Burton may mean what he says when he finally refuses "to defile" himself with these matters any longer.[24]

If some of the topics strung together in Burton's paragraph (necrophilia and the lust stimulated by statues and paintings) seem arcane, a glance into Renaissance compendia of learning will show the imaginative interest of these phenomena for minds of that period. The difference between such handbooks of *loci communes* and later alphabetical encyclopedias is crucial, since only the onomasiological principle of organization of the older reference works can prove my point, namely that the topics here pulled together by Burton were conventionally so conjoined—irrespective of the question whether Burton used such handbooks. Thus, for instance, in Zwinger's *Theatrum humanae vitae,* a section on necrophilia (entitled *libido cum mortuis*) is followed by a section on love of statues and images (aptly called *libido mechanica, cum statuis et simulacris*)—the latter with eight entries, which include all of Burton's exempla. These sections are followed by a very detailed collection of examples under the heading *libido mascula* (more than three folio pages), followed in turn by exempla under the title *tribades* (lesbians). The overarching title of the section, which also includes entries on *libido bruta*, is *impudicia venerea.*[25]

With his remarks about Turks, Italians, and sworn celibates, and

24. For a more strident version of a sentence in similar position, i.e., at the end of a clearly Protestant disquisition on *sodomia* (which also mentions della Casa), see Heinrich Salmuth: "I will say no more, since its mere name may somehow infect my pages" (Nihil dicam amplius: cum vel solum ipsius nomen chartas quodammodo inficiat); Guido Pancirolli, *Rerum memorabilium libri duo* cum commentariis ab H. Salmuth (Frankfurt, 1646), pars 1, tit. 43 (p. 222).

25. *Theatrum humanae vitae,* 2301–302.

his association of same-sex love with them, Burton is at the center of the preoccupations and prejudices of Protestant churchmen of his time. Perhaps one might expect a scholar and librarian, who had access to some of the best repositories of learning, not to assume lightly and without proof the existence of a broad Italian apologetic tradition of pederasty in the wake of Tatius and Pseudo-Lucian. But as I have shown elsewhere, the condemnation of the Archbishop della Casa by his Protestant opponents on the basis of what may be called hearsay evidence was so general, before and after Burton, that it may be called a mainstay and commonplace of Protestant accounts of this topic; thus, it perhaps never even occurred to Burton to check on it. Since he is familiar with the polemical antipapal tradition in which John Bale was notable and notorious, it is perhaps worth noting that Burton does not include popes among his noted *sodomitae,* a fact all the more remarkable considering that even the usually measured Richard Hooker had presented the popes as giving themselves "unto acts diabolical."[26] But, as we noted, if his reference to the physician Mercuriale to support his comment on the "masturbations of monks" is an error and not deliberate deception, the error is not accidental or random: it is a result of what he wanted to see and prove, the result of prejudice.

Therefore, while Burton's account is very much "middle of the road" in terms of Protestant discourse on this subject, it is not altogether commonplace. It is my impression that the references to Busbequius's observations on Turkish habits, and particularly those of Turkish women, were not yet part of the handbooks available: they would have had to come from Burton's own reading.[27] Although he seems to have used the learned compendium by Richerius or Rhodeginus (Caelius), to whom Burton refers on the topics of masturbation and lesbianism, he curiously does not seem to refer to the same author's detailed discussion of *venus mascula.*[28] Of course, Burton may have taken his phrase *qui saxa mandant semina* (who send their seed onto stones), which he applies to the Turks, from lib. 20, c. 10. The agricultural metaphor with which Burton continues (*arare,* also

---

26. *Of the Laws of Ecclesiastical Polity,* bk. 3, chap. 1, 13 (Oxford, 1890), 286.
27. He annotated his copy extensively; see Kiessling, *The Library of Robert Burton,* no. 268.
28. *Lectionum antiquarum libri XXX,* lib. 15, c. 9 and 10 (1599 ed., cols. 676–80).

in Rhodeginus) makes this quite possible but not certain, since the phrase he uses is almost proverbial in this context.[29] The fact remains that he did not refer to the same author's physical account of what used to be called *coitus praeposterus* in the same chapter (lib. 20, c. 10 [col. 680]). Probably his sense of decorum forbade him to do so, for even in the language of the *docti,* some matters are not sayable, except in metaphor.

Finally, in spite of Burton's touching on so many commonplaces of Protestant homophobia, I sense what may be an important nuance, although here I am moving toward the realm of imponderables where proof is difficult if not impossible. As we saw, Burton switches from the topic of bestiality to that of *sodomia* with the sentence *Nec cum brutis, sed ipsis hominibus rem habent, quod peccatum Sodomiae vulgo dicitur.* If I am not overreading the logical link in *nec cum brutis, sed ipsis hominibus,* Burton is suggesting that on his scale of shame or abomination acts of *sodomia* are worse than acts of bestiality. Now it is true that all his examples of intercourse with (female) brute beasts implied a difference of sex, thus at least mechanical compatibility of organs, and the *ipsis*—"even" with men—refers to this change of topic. But if I sense a shrillness to Burton's voice at this point, this is so because I do not find his hierarchy credible: I suspect that such a ranking is not shared in the period even by the loudest Protestant railers against presumably "Roman" *sodomia,* and, more importantly, it seems to be refuted by Burton's own survey of "unnatural acts."

When the arch-Protestant Henri Estienne writes a book to defend Herodotus against the charge of wild exaggeration, he collects some of the most outrageous deeds of modern times to suggest that the ancient historian deserves trust. In the course of demonstrating how the moderns outdo the ancients in monstrosities, he surveys the range of "acts against nature" in chapter 13 that touches on some of the topics we have been discussing. Toward the end of the chapter, Estienne recounts the case of a woman "who prostituted herself to a dog" and then of a woman from the Touraine who pretended to be a

29. Rhodeginus, *Lectionum,* col. 679: "Cognata iis sunt, quae Maximus scribit Tyrius: Cum masculo, inquit, corpore iniqua fit permixtio, sterilisque congressus. Quid saxis mandas semina? Sabulum quid aras?" As we saw, Burton's printer may have misread the Roman numerals, mistaking book XX for book II.

man in order to marry another woman—a case very similar, we noted, to the Turkish story Burton summarizes out of Busbequius and calls *res plane incredibilis*. This is how Estienne ranks the two cases on his own hierarchy of shame: "I have just told an extraordinarily strange misdeed: but I am going to cite another one that is even more so (although not so shameful) which also happened in our time some thirty years ago."[30]

Of course this would only be one man's personal scale against another's (and a Frenchman's against an Englishman's), if we did not have the evidence of Burton's own paragraph. When he claims that della Casa calls same-sex love "divine work" (*divinum opus*), he paraphrases this as "sweet crime" (*suave scelus*), and I cannot find della Casa nor any of the Protestants who chastised him using these terms. Encoding contradictory feelings of attraction and moral stricture, the oxymoron perhaps does not so much describe della Casa's attitude to his subject as Burton's own. As we have seen, his most insistent and expressive *praeteritio* in the entire paragraph is: "However, what Alcibiades says about the same Socrates, I feel free to keep silent about, but I also detest it—such an incitement it is to lust. And Theodoretus touches on that in, etc." Burton presents the *praeteritio* as his own and not as Socrates' as Floyd Dell and Paul Jordan-Smith make it appear in their translation.[31] Considering Burton's way of working with sources, of speaking with them and through them, the fact that his wording about the strength of the lure is borrowed from Theodoretus does not take away from his seriousness. The opposite is true: Burton expresses his opinion using Theodoretus's words without indicating this specific dependence and then refers to Theodoretus as having touched on that subject. This is as clearly as this bookish man, with thousands of views and opinions of others at his fingertips, ever expresses his own opinion on this subject. If, then,

30. Estienne, *L'introduction au traitté de la conformité des merveilles anciennes avec les modernes: ou Traitté préparatif à l'Apologie pour Hérodote,* chap. 13 (Lyon, 1592), 97: "Ie vien de reciter un forfait merveilleusement estrange: mais i'en vay reciter un autre qui l'est encore d'avantage, (non pas toutefois si vilain) advenu aussi de nostre temps, il y a environ trente ans." After telling the story, Estienne says that the modern cross-dresser is more detestable than the ancient *tribades* (lesbians).

31. "And in truth it was this very Socrates who said of Alcibiades: gladly would I keep silent, and I am averse, he offers too much incentive to wantonness." Burton, *Anatomy of Melancholy,* ed. F. Dell and P. Jordan-Smith (New York: Tudor, 1955), 652.

Alcibiades' words to Socrates as he slips under the teacher's mantle
are such a seductive incitement, how can same-sex love outrank bestiality in shamefulness? To all instances of *praeteritio* in this section
we may apply the ancient adage *cum tacent clamant.*[32] The figures
of "passing over," and particularly this one about Alcibiades' seductive words, indicate that Burton, following the fashion of homophobia
of his time, overstated his sentiments; in other words, that his tone
was a little strident. At the same time, the views and scales he expressed
bear on claims made in recent discussions of Renaissance same-sex
relationships that the Renaissance had no concept of homosexuality
and therefore, strictly speaking, knew no homophobia.

32. My argument here owes much to Stephen Orgel's essay "Nobody's Perfect: Or
Why Did the English Stage Take Boys for Women?" *South Atlantic Quarterly* 88 (1989):
7–29. Other important works on the subject include Alan Bray, *Homosexuality in Renais-
sance England* (London: Gay Men's Press, 1982); James M. Saslow, *Ganymede in the Re-
naissance: Homosexuality in Art and Society* (New Haven: Yale University Press, 1986);
G. Ruggiero, *The Boundaries of Eros: Sex, Crime, and Sexuality in Renaissance Venice*
(New York: Oxford University Press, 1985); Eve K. Sedgwick, *Between Men: English
Literature and Male Homosocial Desire* (New York: Columbia University Press, 1985);
Bruce R. Smith, *Homosexual Desire in Shakespeare's England: A Cultural Poetics* (Chicago: University of Chicago Press, 1991); and Claude J. Summers, "Homosexality and Re-
naissance Literature, or, the Anxieties of Anachronism," *South Central Review* 9 (1992):
2–23.

Eugene R. Cunnar

Fantasizing a Sexual Golden Age in Seventeenth-Century Poetry

When the speaker in Donne's elegy "Variety" laments the difficulties of maintaining multiple relationships, he complains,

> I love her well, and would, if need were, dye
> To doe her service. But followes it that I
> Must serve her onely, when I may have choice?
> (21–22)[1]

To justify his previous argument that nature intends sexual variety instead of monogamous relationships, he resorts to a comparison between the present and the Golden Age, exclaiming,

> How happy were our Syres in ancient times,
> Who held plurality of loves no crime!
> With them it was accounted charity
> To stirre up race of all indifferently;
> Kindreds were not exempted from bands:
> Which with the Persian still in usage stands.

1. John Donne, *The Complete Poetry,* ed. John T. Shawcross (Garden City: Doubleday, 1967), 74. Further references to Donne are to this edition and will be cited in the text by poem title and line numbers. Although Helen Gardner in her edition of *The Elegies and the Songs and Sonnets* (Oxford: Clarendon Press, 1965), xliii-xlv, denies Donne's authorship of this poem, I follow convention in attributing it to him.

> Women were then no sooner ask'd then won,
> And what they did was honest and well done.
>   (37–44)

From his male and Ovidian perspective, Donne's speaker protests certain social conventions governing gender and sexual relationships that he believes have extinguished male-dominated love that existed in the Golden Age. The speaker continues his lament, stating,

> But since this title honour hath been us'd
> Our weake credulity hath been abus'd;
> The golden laws of nature are repealed,
> Which our first fathers in such reverence held;
> Our liberty revers'd and Charter's gone,
> And we made servants to opinion
> A monster in no certain shape attir'd,
> And whose originall is much desir'd,
> Formelesse at first, but growing on it fashions,
> And doth prescribe manners and laws to nations.
>   (45–54)

In looking backward to a Golden Age in which uninhibited and ever-potent male desire and sexuality supposedly prevailed, free from shame, guilt, responsibility, and social custom, Donne's speaker articulates a male *desideratum* that reached back to classical literature.

The Elizabethan revival of Golden Age mythology for political, social, and religious purposes is well known. Less emphasized is the fact that the myth also contained within it a subtheme that reflected directly on facets of male desire and male poets' attempts to retain power over the representation of the female for that desire. As an important subtext or discourse of desire within the traditions of pastoral and Golden Age literature and art, the myth achieved popularity in seventeenth-century literature, appearing in Donne, Carew, Herrick, Cowley, Randolph, Cartwright, Milton, and Lovelace, among others. The widespread employment of the myth reveals that it provided one example of a traditional discourse of desire that males appropriated and reworked in order to create sexual fantasies in which there is a perfect love dominated and controlled by the male for male pleasure and desire.[2]

While some seventeenth-century poets were satisfied with literary fame as a substitute for winning the lady, others engaged in a witty debate between the virtues of fruition or nonfruition in love. Within the revival of Ovidian love modes, these attacks on idealized love frequently signified a poet's rebellion against the frustrations in love explicit in Petrarchan and Neoplatonic love. Moreover, these attacks reflected on the male poet's underlying concern about the paradox of desire. On the one hand the poet is driven by desire; on the other the experience often fails to meet the expectations of desire and appetite. Subsequently, the appeal to a sexual Golden Age provided one alternative to the sufferings and anxieties of the scorned male that are inscribed within Petrarchan unrequited love. However, the myth of a sexual Golden Age as a male discourse of desire also contained an explicit attempt on the part of male poets to regain control of male-female relationships. On the surface, the appeal might sound attractive in that it advocated a return to a seeming innocent, natural form of love that would allow both male and female the opportunity to express reciprocally their passions. However, as I argue in this study, the appeal to a male myth of a sexual Golden Age does not represent an appeal to mutual freedom but instead embodies a male power play—a discourse of desire—supporting patriarchal assumptions about and control over the nature of women.[3]

On one level, poets employ the myth as a means of seducing the reluctant mistress by promising that their love will be mutual and free from inhibiting social conventions, that is, innocent just as it was in

2. For standard accounts of the Golden Age myth see Harry Levin, *The Myth of the Golden Age in the Renaissance* (Bloomington: Indiana University Press, 1969); A. Bartlett Giamatti, *The Earthly Paradise and the Renaissance Epic* (Princeton: Princeton University Press, 1966); Gustavo Costa, *La leggenda dei secoli d'oro nell letteratura italiana* (Bari: Editori Laterza, 1972), 1–155; and Thomas G. Rosenmeyer, *The Green Cabinet: Theocritus and the European Pastoral Lyric* (Berkeley: University of California Press, 1973). James Grantham Turner, *One Flesh: Paradisal Marriage and Sexual Relations in the Age of Milton* (Oxford: Clarendon Press, 1987), 230–309, provides an excellent approach to the topic, but one that differs from mine.

3. On the topic of fruition versus antifruition and Petrarchism see Gordon Braden, "Beyond Frustration: Petrarchan Laurels in the Seventeenth Century," *Studies in English Literature* 26 (1986): 5–23; and William Kerrigan and Gordon Braden, "Milton's Coy Eve: *Paradise Lost* and Renaissance Love Poetry," *ELH* 53 (1986): 27–51.

the Golden Age. At this level, the myth masks its quest for domination by appealing to the natural world of pastoral and, thus, bears out Renato Poggioli's astute observation that "pastoral is a private, masculine world, where woman is not a person but a sexual archetype." In this context, the relationship between the sexes in the myth becomes a site for the conflict between the genders while also mirroring gender and political conflicts in the larger society. In the dialectic contained within the myth, the male complains that chastity, possessiveness, jealousy, prudery, hypocrisy, and shame poison love and that a return to nature will liberate love from such destructive restraints. However, underlying this attractive appeal for mutual and reciprocated love are the dynamics and anxieties of male desire coming in conflict with the sexual tensions generated by sexual difference and the hierarchical relationships between genders. As numerous critics have recently shown, male sexual fears and anxieties about the feminine other and the loss of potency were prevalent in numerous male writers during the Renaissance. One way in which male poets displaced these fears was by employing the myth of a sexual Golden Age that promised reciprocal love but actually engaged in phallogocentrism, that is, recreating the myth as a form of male dominance. Within the sexual economy inscribed by the myth, male desire and the underlying anxieties that accompany that desire are displaced into a fantasy time where women pose no threat to masculine identity or sexual prowess.[4]

In order to show how seventeenth-century male poets manipulated this monological myth of male fantasy toward dominance and the cultural significance of that manipulation for male identity, I need to briefly examine representative examples within the historical evolution of the myth from the classical through the Renaissance period.

4. *The Oaten Flute: Essays on Pastoral Poetry and the Pastoral Ideal* (Cambridge: Harvard University Press, 1975), 16. For the now voluminous literature on the topic of male sexual fears about women, see Nancy Cotton, "Castrating (W)itches: Impotence and Magic in *The Merry Wives of Windsor,*" *Shakespeare Quarterly* 38 (1987): 321–26; Madelon Gohlke, "'I wooed thee with my sword': Shakespeare's Tragic Paradigms," in *Representing Shakespeare: New Psychoanalytic Essays,* ed. Murray M. Schwartz and Coppelia Kahn (Baltimore: Johns Hopkins University Press, 1980), 150–70. For this use of the term *phallogocentrism,* see Janel M. Mueller, "'This Dialogue of One': A Feminist Reading of Donne's 'Exstasie,'" *ADE Bulletin* 81 (1985): 41.

I

The myth of a sexual Golden Age originates in the early legends of the Golden Age in Homer, Hesiod, and the Greek pastoral tradition. In addition to invoking a place—Elysium or another Edenic garden—where life is peaceful, harmonious, and ideal, these early writers associated the Golden Age as a place and time when there was no conflict in love or when lovers who have been separated will be reunited. For example, Homer suggests that Helen and Menelaus will be reunited in Elysium. However, even in this early stage the myth reveals an underlying expression of patriarchy. In Hesiod's *Works and Days* a golden race of men live like gods in a world without women. For Theocritus, the Golden Age was a time of mutual and reciprocal homoerotic love, free from jealousy and unhappiness. In *Idyll* 12 he imagines a pastoral landscape where

> Each lov'd each, even-peise:
> O other golden days,
> Whenas love-I love you
> All men did hold for true.
>
> (15–18)

The idea of the Golden Age as a time of mutual and reciprocated love was soon reimagined as a time of sexual freedom.[5]

The Roman poets Tibullus and Propertius reconceived the popular Augustan theme of a Golden Age as set in a pastoral paradise and as a time of sexual freedom in which there was neither conflict in love nor any restraints on male desire.[6] Tibullus contrasts the frustrations of

---

5. *The Odyssey,* trans. Albert Cook (New York: Norton, 1974), 57. See also H. C. Baldry, "Who Invented the Golden Age?" *Classical Quarterly* 2 (1952): 83–92, for useful background. *Hesiod, the Homeric Hymns and Homeriea,* trans. H. G. Evelyn-White (Cambridge: Harvard University Press, 1936), 11, 15. The Theocritus extract is from *The Greek Bucolic Poets,* trans. J. M. Edmonds (Cambridge: Harvard University Press, 1912), 151.

6. These poets were reacting to Augustus's moral reforms, especially those dealing with sexual relations, marriage, and adultery. See Leo Radista, "Augustus' Legislation concerning Marriage, Procreation, Love Affairs, and Adultery," in *Aufstieg und Niedergang der romanischen Welt,* ed. Hildegard Temporini and Wolfgang Haase, 27 vols. (Berlin: W. de Gruyter, 1972-1987), 2:278–339; W. Ralph Johnson, "The Emotions of Patriotism: Propertius 4.6," *California Studies in Classical Antiquity* 6 (1973): 151–80.

love within the world of elegiac poetry with its absence in the Golden Age. Hoping that his Delia will be chaste and faithful, Tibullus imagines Elysium as a lover's paradise:

> But since I've never scorned the power Love wields,
> Venus shall lead me to the Elysian fields;
> There songs and dance reign, and through the sky
> Birds with sweet voices chirrup as they fly.
> The earth untilled bears cassia; all around
> Sweet roses flourish in the generous ground.
> There ranks of boys mingling with young girls play.
>
> (1.3.59–65)[7]

The creation of Elysian love depends upon more than not scorning love's power. It depends upon the poet wresting control of the love relationship. The desire for mastery is seen in 2.3, where the poet is worried that Delia, who is in the country, may be unfaithful. Promising to be her slave, he compares his Iron Age with its difficulties in courtship to a Golden Age, when "Happy the days when gods could openly, / Without shame, own to Venus' mastery" (33–34) and where,

> Our sire ate acorns—Love was theirs at Will;
> What loss to have no furrows to fill.
> To those Love breathed on Venus openly
> Gave joy in valley's cool opacity.
> There were no guards, no doors to exclude in pain
> Sad lovers; days of old, return again!
>
> (73–78)

By invoking a time when there were neither rules nor inhibitions governing male desire, Tibullus sublimates his frustrated desire through a fantasized vision of male desire being satisfied at will. For Tibullus, the Golden Age is an age of male sovereignty in which the woman has neither the will nor voice to deny him.

In his elegies to Cynthia, Propertius laments her unfaithfulness and the pain and suffering she causes him. Nevertheless in 1.9 he pro-

---

7. Tibullus, *The Poems,* trans. Philip Dunlop (Baltimore: Penguin Books, 1972), 70.

fesses his eternal devotion or enslavement to her while fearing she will find yet another lover. The male pose of being enslaved by passion to the woman and engaged in love's warfare reflects the dilemma of desire, but it also becomes a subterfuge masking the actual social status of Roman women, who were expected to be monogamous and chaste while the male was free to take on mistresses. In several poems (2.9, 2.22, 2.24, 2.32), he advocates libertinism as a recompense for the inconstancy and turmoil in love that results from his perception of the innate changeableness of women. From this misogynistic and patriarchal perspective Propertius begins to project a sexual Golden Age where "to see / A naked goddess brought no penalty" (3.13.37–38), that is, uninhibited male gazing or the desire to possess the female without suffering castration is the rule.[8]

Although a sexual Golden Age is Propertius's wish, he also knows that it is only a wish. In 4.7 Cynthia's ghost comes to him in a dream and berates him for not performing her funeral rites properly, complaining that he depicted her in his verses as unfaithful when it was he and not she who was untrue. She tells him that although now other women will have him, after death they will be reunited in Elysium: "Soon I alone shall hold you; / with me you will be, and bone mixed with bone, I shall wear you down" (99–100). Through this witty reversal Propertius highlights both the male desire for domination in love in a Golden Age and the possibility of its failure even in Elysium.[9]

During the middle ages the concept of a Golden Age was Christianized as a time before the Fall. Nevertheless, the sexual myth receives ironic treatment in *The Romance of the Rose,* providing a contrast with courtly love that created frustrated desire. Explaining that the Golden Age was lost when Jupiter cut off Saturn's testicles giving birth to Venus, De Meun articulates the underlying fear of castration

8. Propertius, *The Poems,* trans. A. E. Watts (Baltimore: Penguin, 1966), 49–50. For a succinct statement on the status of Roman women in contrast to their representation in poetry and bibliography see Phyllis Culham, "Ten Years After Pomeroy: Studies of the Image and Reality of Women in Antiquity," *Helios* 13 (1987): 9–30; and J. P. Hallett, "The Role of Women in Roman Elegy: Counter-Cultural Feminism," *Arrethusa* 6 (1973): 103–24.

9. For other classical writers employing the myth see Lucretius, *On the Nature of the Universe,* trans. R. E. Latham (Baltimore: Penguin, 1951), 200–201, 214, who also criticizes the concept. Seneca, *Tragedies,* trans. Frank Justus Miller, 2 vols. (Cambridge: Harvard University Press, 1917), 1:203; 2:265. For Ovid, Vergil, and Horace see Levin, *Myth,* 3–32; and Giamatti, *Earthly Paradise,* 11–47.

or the loss of male identity and power that drives the myth. In the satirical and misogynist world of *The Romance of the Rose,* the quest to satisfy desire in the face of jealousy, betrayal, and deceit is contrasted with a Golden Age where the rule was "all females want all males. All women willingly receive them" (241). In this Golden Age there was no marriage, greed, or covetousness for those who follow Nature's urge to procreate (154–55).[10]

The male myth of a sexual Golden Age moved from the realm of literary trope to that of reality during the Renaissance. During the period from 1493 through 1560 or so, numerous accounts of the New World, especially America, as a Golden Age were published. Not only did these accounts emphasize the material riches such as gold to be found in the New World, but they also discussed the lives of the inhabitants as if they lived in a sexual Golden Age. Grounded in accounts by Mandeville, Peter Martyr, and others, writers as different as Amerigo Vespucci, Richard Eden, Richard Hakylut, and Sir Walter Ralegh furthered the perception of the New World as a Golden Age in which no laws governed male sexual appetite and nudity and sexual license prevailed. Typical of this literature is Vespucci's description of America: "Having no laws and no religious faith, the Indians live according to nature. . . . Here is no possession of private property among them, for everything is held in common. . . . Each one is his own master. . . . Their marriages are not with one woman only, but they mate with whomever they desire, and without much ceremony." Accounts such as Vespucci's make it clear that what had been considered a myth or literary trope of a sexual Golden Age might now be considered a reality. This and other accounts lie behind the further literary and artistic evolution of the myth, especially in the increased awareness by male poets that what had been fantasized could now be considered real.[11]

---

10. Guillaume de Lorris and Jean de Meun, *The Romance of the Rose,* trans. Charles Dahlberg (Princeton: Princeton University Press, 1971), 113, 154–56. Further citations to deMeun are to this edition and are made in the text. For discussion of Dante's use of the myth see Charles S. Singleton, *Dante Studies 2: Journey to Beatrice* (Cambridge: Harvard University Press, 1958), 184–203. For Chaucer's use of the myth see Geoffrey Chaucer, *The Works,* ed. F. N. Robinson, 2d. ed. (Boston: Houghton Mifflin, 1957), 859–60.

11. For these writers and discussion see Sir John Mandeville, *The Travels,* trans. C. W. R. D. Mosley (Baltimore: Penguin, 1983), 127; Peter Martyr, *De Orbe Novo: The*

Renaissance poets were quick to adapt the geographical and thematic conventions of a sexual Golden Age—an eternal spring with pearling streams and flower laden banks, timelessness, leisure, full nakedness, carefree dancing and singing, mutual gazing, and unhindered sex. Supported by the accounts of discovery, the myth is invoked as a narrative of male desire by Sannazaro, Sperone, Joannes Secundus, Marino, and others, but it is Tasso's use of it in the Chorus of *Aminta* that becomes the textual touchstone for later poets. Written for a courtly audience, the pastoral play contrasts Aminta's naturalistic love for Silvia with the more hypocritical and deceitful courtly love that was part of the poet's culture. Aminta, whose love is natural, instinctive, passionate, and uninhibited in terms of the prevailing moral codes, is ultimately rejected by Silvia, whose pride in her chastity prevents her from reciprocating his love. Subsequently, Tasso invests the myth with an explicit libertine naturalism that posits hedonistic nature against the traditional restraints in Christian and Neoplatonic ethical values. He imagines a Golden Age in which male desire rules in a pastoral Elysium where the golden law ("legge aurea") is "If it is pleasing, it is permitted" ("S'ei piace, ei lice"). Here, nature and its law is defined by the male for male pleasure.[12]

In its praise of this sexual Golden Age, the Chorus of *Aminta*

Eight Decades of Peter Martyr D'Anghera, trans. Francis Augustus McNutt, 2 vols. (New York: George Putnam and Sons, 1912), 2:78–83, 237; Richard Eden, *The Decades of the Newe Worlde or West India* (1550; repr. *The First Three English Books on America,* ed. Edward Arber [Birmingham, 1885]); Richard Hakylut, *The Voyages* (Baltimore: Penguin, 1972), 273–74; Sir Walter Ralegh, *The discoverie of the Large, Rich, and Bewtiful Empyre of Gviana* (London, 1596); Hugh Honour, *The New Golden Land: European Images of America from the Discoveries to the Present Time* (New York: Pantheon, 1975); Amerigo Vespucci as quoted in Frederick J. Pohl, *Amerigo Vespucci, Pilot Major* (New York: Columbia University Press, 1945), 131–33.

12. For Sannazaro and Sperone see Levin, *Myth,* 43–48. Joannes Secundus, *The Love Poems,* trans. F. A. Wright (New York: E. P. Dutton, 1930), 41–43, 117. Giambattista Marino, *Adonis: Selections from L'Adone,* trans. Harold Martin Priest (Ithaca: Cornell University Press, 1967), 29–38. For a more detailed study see Costa, *La leggenda dei secoli d'oro,* who also provides an excellent discussion of classical sources and bibliography. Torquato Tasso, *Aminta,* ed. C. E. J. Griffiths (Manchester: Manchester University Press, 1972), 42. For useful commentary see C. P. Brand, *Torquato Tasso: A Study of the Poet and of His Contribution to English Literature* (Cambridge: Cambridge University Press, 1965); and Richard Cody, *The Landscape of the Mind: Pastoralism and Platonic Theory in Tasso's Aminta and Shakespeare's Early Comedies* (Oxford: Clarendon Press, 1969), 23–78.

condemns female chastity and wishes for the overthrow of "honour" and the return of eternal, male potency:

> O Happy Age of Gould; happy houres;
>
> . . . .
> But therefore only happy Days.
> Because that vaine and ydle name,
> That couz'ning Idoll of unrest,
> (Whom the madd vulgar first did raize,
> And call it Honour, whence it came,
> To tyrannize or'e ev'ry brest),
>   Was then suffred to molest
> Poure lovers hearts with new debate;
> More happy they, by these his hard
> And cruell lawes, were not debar'd
> Their innate freedome; happy fate;
> The goulden lawes of Nature, they
> Found in their brests; and thus they did obey.
>   (1.2.1,14–26)[13]

Male desire explicitly subordinates the female through the guise of appealing to sexual freedom.

Having condemned "honour" or female chastity, Tasso follows the classical writers in describing the *locus amoenus* where male-dominated love exists:

> Amidd the silver streames and flowers,
> The winged Genii then would daunce,
> Without their bowe, without their brande;
>
> . . . .
> Whispering love-sports, and dalliance,
> And ioyning lips, and hand to hand;
>   The fairest Virgin in the land.
>   (1.2.27–29, 31–33)

In this pleasant setting it is eternal spring where flowers, trees, and love constantly blossom. Indeed, the fecundity of nature parallels

---

13. I cite Torquato Tasso, *Aminta,* trans. Henry Reynolds (London, 1628).

Aminta's passion and the wished for eternal potency of the male. However, this wished for state in which there is mutual gazing and love making is destroyed by the laws and customs of society:

> Thou Honour, thou didst first devize
> To maske the face of Pleasure thus;
> Barr water to the thirst of Love,
> And lewdly be nyce, and scrupulous,
> And from the gazing would remoove
>   Their beauties.
>   (1.2.40–45)

Tasso's vision of uninhibited male love thwarted by the artificial trappings of society troped as female chastity ends in disillusionment when Silvia refuses Aminta's love. In effect, Tasso, like Petrarch before him, can only find consolation by displacing frustrated male desire with a fantasized vision of male dominance. Nevertheless, Tasso's invocation of a male sexual Golden Age proved a popular source for naturalistic libertine concepts as he was imitated or translated by Giovanni Guarini, Abraham Fraunce, Samuel Daniels, John Reynolds, and Richard Fanshawe and alluded to by Spenser, William Browne, Thomas Watson, Donne, Jonson, Drummond, and Cowley, among others.[14]

Underlying the male call to return to a sexual Golden Age are male sexual frustrations, fears, and anxieties that become explicit in Montaigne's essay, "On Some Verses by Virgil." Montaigne overtly ties his masculine identity and sense of power to his penis: "And no other [part] makes me more properly a man than this one." Accordingly, he states, "In most parts of the world this part of our body was deified" (653). To reify this sense of phallic power he urges in this essay and in

---

14. For the English imitators of Tasso see Brand, *Tasso,* 277–308. See also Battista Guarini, *Il Pastor Fido, The Faithfull Shepherd,* trans. Sir Richard Fanshawe and ed. J. H. Whitfield (Austin: University of Texas Press, 1976), 321–25, where Guarini refutes the sexuality in Tasso, arguing instead for a Christianized Golden Age where sexuality follows true honor and ennobles the soul. Guarini attempts to reverse the uninhibited male sexuality in Tasso by stating "Piaccia, se lice" ("It is pleasing, if it is lawful" [322]). See also Edmund Spenser, *Poetical Works,* ed. J. C. Smith and E. De Selincourt (London: Oxford University Press, 1912), who in *FQ* 4.30.8 states that "each vnto his lust did make a lawe" (252).

"Of Cannibals" (150–59) that one should follow nature or primitivism instead of the rules of civilization. However, as in so many invocations of a return to a Golden Age by a male writer, nature is defined and characterized from a male perspective.[15]

Montaigne's desire for unrestrained, male sexual freedom derives from his own anxiety over sexual performance. He consistently worries about the comparative sexual prowess of men and women, arguing that because women are insatiable creatures of lust they pose an imminent threat to male sexual identity and the power of the phallus as the cultural sign of male domination. He explains that,

> The Gods says Plato, have furnished us with a disobedient and tyrannical member, which, like a furious animal, undertakes by the violence of its appetite to subject everything to itself. To women likewise they have given a gluttonous and voracious animal, which, if denied its food in due season, goes mad impatient of delay, and, breathing its rage into their bodies stops up the passages, arrests the breathing, causing a thousand kinds of ills, until it has sucked in the fruit of the common thirst and therewith plentifully irrigated and fertilized the depth of the womb. (654)

Subsequently, Montaigne denies women desire, claiming that according to

> the law that Nature gives them, it is not properly for them to will and desire; their role is to suffer, obey, consent. That is why Nature has given them a perpetual capacity, to us a rare and uncertain one. They have their hour always, so that they may be ready for ours: *born to be passive* [Seneca]. And whereas Nature has willed that our [male] appetites should show and declare themselves prominently, she has made theirs occult and internal, and has furnished them with parts unsuitable for show and simply for the defensive. (674–75)

15. Montaigne, *The Complete Works,* trans. Donald M. Frame (Stanford: Stanford University Press, 1958), 677. Further references to Montaigne are to this edition and will be cited in the text. For useful commentary on Montaigne's sexual anxieties see Lee R. Entin-Bates, "Montaigne's Remarks on Impotence," *Modern Language Notes* 91 (1976): 640–54. For the dissolution of sexuality into textuality see Robert D. Cottrell, *Sexuality/Textuality: A Study of the Fabric of Montaigne's Essais* (Columbus: Ohio State University Press, 1981). For useful background on Montaigne's libertinism see Hiram Hayden, *The Counter-Renaissance* (New York: Harcourt, Brace and World, 1950), 505–24.

This misogynistic attitude informs Montaigne's definition of female nature, which, in turn, shapes his sexual performance anxiety, his fear that he can not satisfy the woman and, thus, will lose not only face, but power.

Montaigne cites from several classical texts examples of male sexual inadequacy that reflect his own anxiety that male sexual performance "involves more effort than submission; and that consequently they [women] are always able to satisfy our needs, whereas it may be otherwise when it is up to us to satisfy theirs" (675–76). In this context he quotes one of the Priapea poems: "But if the penis be not too long or stout enough . . . / Even the matrons—all too well they know— / Look dimly on a man whose member's small" (677). Fear of the sexually insatiable women and male sexual inadequacy leading to the experience of *post coitum triste* underlie Montaigne's advocacy of a return to the Golden Age or primitivism in which men may enjoy sexual freedom and prowess.

II

Renaissance artists, such as Bertoja, Titian, Rubens, and Poussin also treated the theme, but a cycle of paintings known as *Gli Amori de' Carracci,* grounded in Ovid's account of the ages of man, became a touchstone for poets to imitate.[16] Like Montaigne's, these works encode the empowering myth of male sexual domination while they paradoxically reveal its subversion via male sexual anxieties. The first work, *Love in the Golden Age,* depicts fully naked lovers in the garden of love engaged in mutual eye gazing as a sign of the desire for unrestrained, mutual or reciprocated, love. In the background are naked dancers taken from the classical tradition. The inscription at the bottom of the work, "From reciprocal love, which is born and comes from the pious cause of virtuous affection, in sincere souls there is born a form of delight, bringing joy to mankind and taking away grief from it," makes it clear that the narrative celebrates the male desire for uninhibited, mutual or reciprocal love between men and women.[17] Moreover, Carracci also depicts in the middle ground

16. See Otto Kurz, "'Gli Amori De' Carracci': Four Forgotten Paintings by Agostino Carracci," *Journal of the Warburg and Courtauld Institute* 14 (1951): 221–33.
17. Cited by Kurz, "'Gli Amori,'" 227. My translation.

the figures of Eros and Anteros, the two sons of Venus who struggle for the palm branch. In the legend, Venus was unhappy with Cupid's perpetual immaturity and gave him a brother, Anteros, to cure his ailment. The struggle between the two represented the conflict between excessive love or lust (Eros) and reciprocal love (Anteros). This popular myth received various interpretations ranging from the conflict between lust and chaste love, sensual love and virtue, and earthly and heavenly love. Anteros was, moreover, often interpreted as the punisher of those who did not reciprocate love.[18] In many ways the myth of Eros and Anteros reflects the paradox of male desire simultaneously to want both domination and reciprocal love. This myth was extremely popular in the Renaissance, appearing in paintings such as Annibale Carracci's frescoes in the Farnese Gallery, in emblem books such as Alciati's, Van Veen's, and Wither's, and in numerous poems such as Jonson's and Shakespeare's.[19] The print depicts then the struggle between the desire for reciprocal love and male desire to possess the female without guilt or responsibility and without fearing sexual impotence.

The second painting, *The Golden Age,* has the following inscription: "Just as the palm is the sign of victory, so the fruit suits Cupid-love. This sweetness, from whence the seed is produced, which is nature that heaven glories in." Here the sense of male victory or dom-

18. For commentary on Eros and Anteros see Kurz, "'Gli Amori,'" 226–27; Robert V. Merrill, "Eros and Anteros," *Speculum* 19 (1944): 265–84; Guy de Tervarent, "Reciprocal Love in Ancient and Renaissance Art," *Journal of the Warburg and Courtauld Institute* 28 (1965): 205–8; and Erwin Panofsky, *Studies in Iconology* (New York: Harper and Row, 1962), 122, 126, 166.

19. For the theme in the Farnese Gallery and other Renaissance artists see John Rupert Martin, *The Farnese Gallery* (Princeton: Princeton University Press, 1965), 86–89; Charles Dempsey, "'Et Nos Cedamus Amori': Observations on the Farnese Gallery," *Art Bulletin* 50 (1968): 363–74; Kenneth Clark, *The Nude* (Garden City: Doubleday, 1956), 179; Elise Goodman, "Rubens's *Conversatie à la Mode:* Garden of Leisure, Fashion, and Gallantry," *Art Bulletin* 64 (1982): 247–59; Shelia McTighe, "Nicolas Poussin's representations of storms and *Libertinage* in the mid-seventeenth century," *Word & Image* 5 (1989): 333–61. For emblem books see Dempsey, "Observations on the Farnese Gallery," 364, 367; Barbara K. Lewalski, *Protestant Poetics and the Seventeenth-Century Religious Lyric* (Princeton: Princeton University Press, 1979), 184, 190–96. See also Otto van Veen, *Amorum emblemata, or Emblemes of Love* (Antwerp, 1608), 10. See William Shakespeare, *Shakespeare's Sonnets,* ed. William Booth (New Haven: Yale University Press, 1977), 131–32. *Ben Jonson,* ed. C. H. Herford, Percy Simpson, and Evelyn Simpson, 11 vols. (Oxford: Clarendon Press, 1925–1952), 7:394–95.

inance is codified via sexual consummation. The figures of Eros and Anteros are no longer present, having been replaced by scenes of almost violent sexual possession reminiscent of Giulio Romano's illustrations of Aretino.[20]

The third work depicts the extinction of love and male dominance that prevailed in the Golden Age. The inscription explains its major theme: "Happy the one who from the river to the bank ascends, his torch extinguishing unlawful Love and impious with surfeit and every honor, strips himself of his own vain pleasure."[21] As Eros extinguishes his burning torch in the river Seleno, the statue of "Amore Letheo" is brought to life, according to Cartari.[22] In other versions of the Venus myth, her birth caused the loss of the Golden Age through the introduction of strife and frustration in love.[23] Now the male lover must experience deceit, jealousy, violence, and sexual weakness as the concept of honor and other social customs regulating sexual relationships replace the male fantasy of sexual freedom and dominance.

The fourth work is entitled *Il Castigo d'Amor* and depicts the expulsion from the sexual Elysium. The inscription echoes Ovid's account of the Iron Age when Astrea, the Virgin of Justice, leaves the earth: "From love's chastisement is aimed the example of that love which does a great wrong to upright [action], which, hasty, makes affliction remain, guides it, so that it continues unjust and impious."[24] As the couple leave their sexual paradise several figures are seen committing suicide as the result of unrequited or unreciprocated love. Whereas in the Golden Age uninhibited love prevailed, Iron Age lovers must suffer through deceit, jealousy, violence, and sexual weakness brought about by the introduction of morality, honor, chastity, and other social customs regulating sexual relationships. Agostino's cycle derives from a long literary tradition that laments the loss of the male fantasy for sexual freedom and dominance in the Golden Age. These

20. Cited by Kurz, "'Gli Amori,'" 228. My translation. See Pietro Aretino, *The Letters*, trans. Thomas C. Chubb (Hamden: Shoe String Press, 1967), 124; and for recent commentary on the Aretino illustrations see Lynne Lawner, *I Modi: The Sixteen Pleasures* (Evanston: Northwestern University Press, 1988), xi-xxi.

21. Cited by Kurz, "'Gli Amori,'" 229. My translation.

22. Kurz, "'Gli Amori,'" 226, cites Cartari, *Le imagini de i dei gli antichi* (1580), 501. Tervarent, "Eros and Anteros," 205, provides a translation.

23. For this myth see *Romance of the Rose,* ed. Dahlberg, 379.

24. Cited by Kurz, "'Gli Amori,'" 229. My translation.

paintings and works derived from them became very popular during the Renaissance and provided poets with visual equivalents in discussing their own variations on the male myth of a sexual Golden Age.

III

The male myth of a sexual Golden Age appears throughout seventeenth-century poetry, generally in the context of libertine, Ovidian, or anti-Petrarchan verse. Although much of this new libertine verse served male coterie poets with a means of challenging Petrarchan codes within the contexts of patronage and politics, it also became the site of contest or conflict between genders.[25] Within the conflict generated between law, custom, and morality and male desire, the male poet could project a time when, as does Donne's speaker in "Variety," in the absence of law all desires were innocent and could be fulfilled at will without pain, loss, or guilt. However, the surface fantasy of man's limitless power to enjoy the female also articulates the underlying dynamics and anxieties of male desire in the face of sexual tension surrounding the Renaissance's understanding of the hierarchical relationship between genders and gender difference, especially as male poets contemplated their own sexual inadequacies.

In seducing the mistress and satisfying desire the male poet frequently experienced *post coitum triste,* which is, as one of Donne's speakers says, "A kinde of sorrowing dulnesse to the minde" ("Farewell to love," 20), or, as Shakespeare states, "Enjoyed no sooner but despised straight, / Past reason hunted, and no sooner had, / Past reason hated as swallowed bait" (Sonnet 129, 5–7). The relationship between sexual orgasm, death, and the threat to masculinity as expressed through desire was not taken lightly by many poets. On the one hand, satisfying sexual desire produced disappointment and revulsion, while on the other it paradoxically increased desire. Ben Jonson summarizes this dilemma by paraphrasing Petronius: "Doing, a filthy pleasure is, and short; / And done, we straight repent us of the sport" (Underwood 90, 1–2), while Donne expresses the paradox

25. For important aspects of this topic see Arthur F. Marotti, "'Love Is Not Love': Elizabethan Sonnet Sequences and the Social Order," *ELH* 49 (1982): 396–428; and *John Donne, Coterie Poet* (Madison: University of Wisconsin Press, 1986).

as "Our desires give them fashion, and so / As they waxe lesser, fall, as they sise, grow" ("Farewell to love," 8–9). Numerous poems written on antifruition articulate other responses to the dilemma and are summed up in Suckling's "Against Fruition": "Fruition adds no new wealth, but destroyes, / And while it pleaseth much the palate, cloyes" (7–8). To alleviate the dilemma male poets projected a sexual Golden Age where desire was satisfied without loss; where as Donne wishes, "Ah cannot we, / As well as Cocks and Lyons jocund be, / After such pleasures" ("Farewell to love," 21–23). Subsequently, William Browne of Tavistock projects a Golden Age in which

> None had a body then so weak and thin,
> Bankrupt of nature's store, to feed the sin
> Of an insatiate female, in whose womb
> Could nature all hers past, and all to come
> Infuse, with virtue of all drugs beside,
> She might be tir'd, but never satisfied.
> To please which work her husband's weakened piece
> Must have his cullis mixed with ambergris.
> (*Britannia's Pastorals,* Bk2, "Third Song," 343–50)

Browne fantasizes a Golden Age in which male sexual prowess was more than the woman's and no aphrodisiacs were needed to stimulate desire.[26]

Perhaps one of the wittiest uses of the appeal to a sexual Golden Age occurs in Donne's "The Extasie." This problematical poem has

---

26. This quotation highlights the paradox of male desire in that the male's identity is tied up with his ability to fulfill desire. For useful discussion see Christopher Ricks, "Donne After Love," in *Literature and the Body: Essays on Populations and Persons,* ed. Elaine Scarry (Baltimore: Johns Hopkins University Press, 1988), 33–69; and Malcolm Evans, "'In Love with Curious Words': Signification and Sexuality in English Petrarchism," in *Jacobean Poetry and Prose: Rhetoric, Representation and the Popular Imagination,* ed. Clive Bloom (New York: St. Martin's Press, 1988), 119–50; Jonson, *The Complete Poetry,* ed. William B. Hunter, Jr. (New York: Norton, 1963), 269. For a classical expression of male sexual revulsion see Ovid, *The Art of Love,* trans. Rolfe Humphries (Bloomington: Indiana University Press, 1957), 193–94; Suckling, *The Works of Sir John Suckling: The Poems,* ed. Thomas Clayton (Oxford: Clarendon Press, 1971), 37; Browne, *Britannia's pastorals. Two Books* (London, 1613?), 58. Donne wittily engages this idea when he exclaims, "If all faile, / 'Tis but applying worme-seed to the Taile" (152).

been variously interpreted as one of Donne's attacks on Neoplatonic and Petrarchan love as well as a clever seduction poem.[27] More recently, critics have debated whether the poem reflects a statement of mutual or reciprocal love or remains a "dialogue of one" (74), that is, a poem serving the male speaker's own selfish interests.[28] Part of the interpretative dilemma arises from the difficulty in reconciling the appeal for an equal, mutual love with the presence of a third party, a male onlooker who engages in an act of voyeurism at the end of the poem and to whom the poem may be addressed. When we examine how Donne employs the myth of a sexual Golden Age in the poem, then I think it becomes clear that the speaker uses his argument for mutuality as another, clever valorization of male desire and dominance.

Donne's speaker opens his argument by appealing to the mythical setting of a sexual Golden Age. The sexual imagery in the initial horticultural and optical metaphors—"pillow," "bed," "Pregnant," "swel'd," "entergraft" (1, 2, 9)—establishes the setting for a Golden Age where "soules language" later "interinanimates two soules" (22, 42). However, just as Donne reverses the traditional Neoplatonic ascent in the poem, so too he reverses or inverts the traditional male appeal to a sexual Golden Age. This ironic reversal becomes apparent in the first stanza setting the scene for the lover's ecstasy in a paradisiacal garden in which there is a stream and "a Pregnant banke swel'd up" (2), filled with flowers. Donne's poem engages in an ekphrastic form of *ut pictura poesis* in that his speaker clearly establishes the visual equiv-

27. From the debate over this poem see as representative Helen Gardner, "The Argument about 'The Ecstasy,'" in *Elizabethan and Jacobean Studies presented to F. P. Wilson,* ed. Herbert Davis and Helen Gardner (Oxford: Clarendon Press, 1959), 279–306; A. J. Smith, "The Metaphysic of Love," *Review of English Studies* 9 (1958): 362–75; A. J. Smith, "The Dismissal of Love: Or, Was Donne a Neoplatonic Lover," in *John Donne: Essays in Celebration,* ed. A. J. Smith (London: Methuen, 1972), 89–131; and A. J. Smith, "No Man Is a Contradiction," *John Donne Journal* 1 (1982): 21–38; Arthur F. Marotti, "Donne and 'The Extasie,'" in *The Rhetoric of Renaissance Poetry: From Wyatt to Milton,* ed. Thomas O. Sloan and Raymond B. Waddington (Berkeley: University of California Press, 1974), 140–73; and T. Katherine Thomason, "Plotinian Metaphysics and Donne's 'Extasie,'" *Studies in English Literature* 22 (1982): 91–105. For background on the libertine tradition see Louis I. Bredvold, "The Naturalism of Donne in Relation to Some Renaissance Traditions," *JEGP* 22 (1923): 471–502; and Robert Ornstein, "Donne, Montaigne, and Natural Law," *JEGP* 55 (1956): 213–29.

28. On these two positions see Helen B. Brooks, "'Soules Language': Reading Donne's 'The Extasie,'" *John Donne Journal* 7 (1988): 47–63; Mueller, "'This Dialogue of One,'" 42. See also Janel M. Mueller, "Women among the Metaphysicals: A Case, Mostly, of Being Donne For," *Modern Philology* 87 (1989): 142–58.

alent of Agostino Carracci's *Golden Age of Love*.[29] When the speaker says,"Our eye-beames twisted, and did thread / Our eyes, upon one double string" (7–8), he echoes the lovers engaged in mutual gazing as a sign of uninhibited, reciprocated love depicted in Agostino's first painting.[30] Also like Agostino's cycle, this poem reflects the struggle between Eros and Anteros as the speaker tries to reconcile his desire for reciprocal love with his desire for erotic mastery. However, what is immediately apparent is that this Golden Age scene initially is not one in which bodies sexually unite, but instead one in which the lovers' souls stand apart from their bodies in a mutual and idealized ecstasy of reciprocal understanding. At the same time that the witty play on Golden Age motifs satirizes Neoplatonic love, it also masks a clever argument for seduction and male dominance.

The speaker's argument that their souls freely and uninhibitedly unite in ecstasy just as they did in the Golden Age or Elysium is designed to convince the lady of the speaker's "honorable" intentions. This pose is short-lived because the speaker quickly shifts his position, now arguing that having become one, new "abler soule," "pure lovers soules descend / T'affections, and to faculties, / Which sense may reach and apprehend" (43, 65–67). The shift in the argument indicates the speaker's "masculine perswasive force" ("Elegie: On his Mistris," 4), his ultimate intent to seduce the lady, thereby reasserting erotic power over her.

Within the Golden Age setting the speaker can next argue that their physical love will be such that "Weake men on love reveal'd may looke" ("The Extasie," 70). This invitation to the male onlooker to engage in voyeurism follows from the Golden Age setting where there is no shame, honor, or clothes to inhibit love. Placing the reader in a position to observe their lovemaking, the speaker recreates Agostino's painting that similarly situates the viewer as a voyeur. However, instead of just being a clever seduction argument, the speaker's audacious and ironic appeal to a sexual Golden Age turns out after all to

29. I am not claiming that Donne was directly influenced by these particular paintings, but instead I am suggesting that he might have known the many engravings or copies of them or similar works.

30. See Lance K. Donaldson-Evans, *Love's Fatal Glance: A Study of Eye Imagery in the Poets of The Ecole Lyonnaise* (University, MS: Romance Monographs, 1980), for this use of eye imagery.

be his proof for the necessity of physical lovemaking dominated by the male. The shift from the initial appeal to reciprocal gazing to uninhibited voyeurism signifies the speaker's ultimate treatment of the lady as a sexual object in the service of male desire. Whereas Donne's speaker may wish for mutual love, his employment of the male myth of a sexual Golden Age suggests that he actually wants to fulfill desire and dominate, or, as he says, "Small change, when we'are to bodies gone" (76). In effect, the speaker advocates the social and sexual appropriation of the woman, who is rendered passive and exposed to view and, thus, silent and available. Therefore, the invitation to engage in Golden Age love becomes one more way in which the speaker can eliminate the threat of female sexuality while satisfying male desire. For all of its metaphorical twistings and turnings, the speaker's argument ultimately turns on the control and fulfillment of his desire, which, in turn, marginalizes the woman.

Thomas Carew's "Rapture" follows Donne while echoing Montaigne, Tasso, Aretino, and other expressions of the myth when the speaker assails the concept of "Honour" as hindering the fulfillment of male desire:

> The Gyant, Honour, that keepes cowards out,
> Is but a Masquer, and the servile rout
> Of baser subjects onley, bend in vaine
> To the vast Idoll.
>
> (3–6)[31]

In the speaker's fantasized sexual Elysium, he tells Celia,

> We seek no midnight Arbor, no darke groves
> To hide our kisses, there, the hated name
> Of husband, wife, lust, modest, chaste, or shame,

---

31. *The Poems of Thomas Carew,* ed. Rhodes Dunlap (Oxford: Clarendon Press, 1970), 49. For useful discussion of the poem see Paula Johnson, "Carew's 'A Rapture': The Dynamics of Fantasy," *Studies in English Literature* 16 (1976): 145–55; and Ada Long and Hugh MacLean, "'Deare *Ben,*' 'Great DONNE,' and 'my *Celia*': The Wit of Carew's Poetry," *Studies in English Literature* 18 (1978): 75–94. Although these readers perceive the element of male sexual fantasy in the poem, they do not relate the poem to the male myth of a sexual Golden Age.

> Are vaine and empty words, whose very sound
> Was never heard in the Elizian Ground.
>
> (106–10)

From the speaker's perspective, concealment, deceit, and hypocrisy, possessiveness, jealousy, and revenge result from society's sexual customs and should be banished in love's Elysium because

> All things are lawfull there, that may delight
> Nature, or unrestrained Appetite;
> Like, and enjoy, to will, and act, is one,
> We only sinne when Loves rites are not done.
>
> (111–14)

The speaker's argument that the artificial inhibitions and prohibitions of civilization thwart sexual pleasure is designed to appeal to Celia.

However, for all the speaker's libertine bravado and promise to Celia of the mutual pleasures of Golden Age sex, she becomes only an object of nonthreatening desire, who relieves the speaker of his own anxieties. The speaker's patriarchal attitude is reflected in the word *rapture,* which can mean either an exalted mental state or a seizure or rape. Consequently, the speaker begins by stating his wish for fulfilling his own desire: "I will enjoy thee now my *Celia,* come / And flye with me to Loves Elizium" (1–2). As Renee Hannaford points out, the speaker is not really interested in Celia as a person with whom to engage in social interaction, but only as an object through whom he may indict social conventions. Whereas Hannaford perceives Carew's poem as exploring attitudes antithetical to social norms, I see Carew as employing the myth of a male sexual Golden Age as the means of seduction and as the means of gratifying male desire without the anxieties that threaten masculine identity or power. In effect, the appeal to this myth does not liberate love or assure mutual love; instead it becomes one more example of how the male poet attempts to construct and socially control sexuality.[32]

32. "'My Unwashed Muse': Sexual Play and Sociability in Carew's 'A Rapture,'" *English Language Notes* 27 (1989): 34–36; and "Self-Presentation in Carew's 'To A. L. Perswasions to Love,'" *Studies in English Literature* 26 (1986): 97–99.

The speaker's wish for sexual dominance becomes clear when the speaker turns Celia's body into an Elysian garden in which he is free to explore and exploit.[33] Celia's body becomes the landscape upon which the speaker's desire enacts and proves itself—"to will, and act, is one" (113). Carew's manipulation of this sexual Golden Age *topos* reflects another variation within the myth, namely the trope of exploration as exploitation in which the exploration of new lands was often perceived as the discovery of a new Golden Age. In turn, this trope became homologous with the exploration and exploitation of the woman's body. Perhaps the most explicit use of this theme is found in Donne's "Elegie: Going to Bed," where the speaker compares his discovery of his mistress's body with the discovery of America: "Licence my roving hands, and let them go, / Behind, before, above, between below. / O my America! my new-found-land, / My kingdome" (25–28).[34] In this context, Carew's speaker is giving license to his own desire in an imagined sexual Golden Age without regard for Celia's will, desire, or being.

In fact, her only personality traits are her sexual attributes. In denying agency to the woman, the speaker paradoxically thwarts the reciprocity necessary to satisfy completely his desire. Consequently, the speaker does not express love but lust, as seen in his imagining Aretino's sexual postures carved on the tree trunks:

> The Roman *Lucrece* there, reades the divine
> Lectures of Loves great master, *Aretine,*
> And knowes as well as *Lais,* how to move
> Her plyant body in the act of love.
> To quench the burning Ravisher, she hurles
> Her limbs into a thousand winding curles,

33. Hannaford, "'My Unwashed Muse,'" 35–36.

34. As representative of the literature on this trope see Paul Brown, "'This thing of darkness I acknowledge mine': *The Tempest* and the Discourse of Colonialism," in *Political Shakespeare: New Essays in Cultural Materialism,* ed. Jonathan Dollimore and Alan Sinfield (Ithaca: Cornell University Press, 1985), 48–71. For applications of this interpretation to Donne see, R. V. Young, "'O my America, my new-found-land': Pornography and Imperial Politics in Donne's *Elegies,*" *South Central Review* 4 (1987): 35–48; and M. Thomas Hester, "Donne's (Re)Annunciation of the Virgin(ia Colony) in *Elegy XIX,*" *South Central Review* 4 (1987): 49–64.

> And studies artfull postures, such as be
> Caru'd on the bark of every neighbouring tree.[35]
> ("A Rapture," 115–22)

As in the Roman elegiac tradition, Celia is taught the arts of love as those are pleasing to men. The speaker subordinates female nature to male desire, thereby creating a male sexual paradise. At best, Celia is but a passive reflection of the speaker's own desires. Put most simply, Carew envisions a Golden Age in which male desire under the "cancell'd lawes" of morality has free reign to repeatedly enjoy Celia without loss or guilt.

Other writers echoed various aspects of the myth. For example, Thomas Stanley's invocation of the myth leaves no room for the experience of *post coitum triste* when he states, "A while, our senses stoln away, / Lost in this Extasie we lay. / Till both together rais'd to Life, / We reingage in this kind strife" ("The Enjoyment," 81–84). Similarly, Thomas Randolph employs the vision of a sexual Golden Age in which sexual freedom in a *locus amoenus* is used to convince a mistress who has rejected him. He tells her, "Nature, Creations law, is judg'd by sense, / Not by the Tyrant conscience" ("Upon Love fondly refus'd for conscience sake," 1–2). He then argues for the free sexual use of women—variety—because "I'th' golden age no action could be found / For trespasse on my neighbours ground" (15–16). Echoing Carew's "Rapture" and Donne's "The Extasie," John Hall imagines a heavenly Elysium in which he and his mistress's souls make perpetual love:

> yet will thou and I
> Divested of all flesh so folded lie,
> That ne'er a bodied nothing shall perceive
> How we unite, how we together cleave.
> ("A Rapture," 31–34)

35. For the *topos* of carving the mistress's name on a tree and its sexual implications see my "Names on Trees, the Hermaphrodite, and 'The Garden,'" in *On the Celebrated and Neglected Poems of Andrew Marvell,* ed. Claude J. Summers and Ted-Larry Pebworth (Columbia: University of Missouri Press, 1991), 121–38.

Also echoing Carew and Donne, William Cartwright in "A Song of
Dalliance" underscores male sexual dominance masking as liberated
female sexuality when the speaker states, "Let me use my force to-
night, / The next conquest shall be thine" (31–32).[36]

In many ways Robert Herrick's *Hesperides* is a mythic invocation
of a Golden Age in which males rule by constructing and controlling sexuality for male desire.[37] However, within Herrick's invocation
of a male sexual Golden Age the seeds of disillusionment begin to
appear. In "The Apparition of His Mistress calling him to Elizium"
(H–575) Herrick returns to Propertius and Tibullus, the poets who
first made the myth explicitly sexual. Following Propertius, Herrick
has his mistress invite him to Elysium, "Where ev'ry tree a wealthy issue beares / Of fragrant Apples, blushing Plums, or Peares" (9–10).[38]
As in other Herrick poems, such as "The Vine" (H–41), the natural
and floral imagery takes on sexual connotations. Here, the ever-bear-
ing fruit trees imply the perpetual potency of the male. After describing the blissful paradise, the speaker's mistress says,

> Here, naked Younglings, handsome Striplings run
> Their Goales for Virgin kisses; which when done,
> Then unto dancing forth the learned Round
> Commixt they meet, with endlesse Roses crown'd.
> (17–20)

However, there is no unrestrained sexual consummation here. Instead, the mistress invites Herrick to hear the fabled poets recite of

36. Stanley, *The Poems and Translations,* ed. Galbraith Miller Crump (Oxford: Clarendon Press, 1962), 25. Richard S. Sylvester, ed., *The Anchor Anthology of Seventeenth-
Century Verse* (Garden City: Doubleday, 1969), 419–21. See also Michael Drayton's
"The Muses Elizium," in *The Anchor Anthology,* 22–26; Hall, *Poems,* in *Minor Poets of
the Caroline Period,* ed. George Sainstbury, 3 vols. (Oxford: Clarendon Press, 1906),
2:200; Cartwright, *The Plays and Poems of William Cartwright,* ed. G. Blakemore
Evans (Madison: University of Wisconsin Press, 1951), 468.

37. On sexuality in Herrick see Achsah Guibbory, "'No lust theres like to Poetry':
Herrick's Passion for Poetry," in *"Trust to Good Verses": Herrick Tercentenary Essays,*
ed. Roger B. Rollin and J. Max Patrick (Pittsburgh: University of Pittsburgh Press,
1978), 79–87; Gordon Braden, *The Classics and English Renaissance Poetry* (New
Haven: Yale University Press, 1978), 154–254; and Sarah Gilead, "Ungathering 'Gather
ye Rosebuds': Herrick's Misreading of Carpe Diem," *Criticism* 27 (1985): 133–53, who
offers an insightful reading of Herrick's substitution of textuality for sexuality.

38. Robert Herrick, *The Complete Poetry,* ed. J. Max Patrick (New York: Norton,
1968), 273.

love with the added irony: "and that done, / Ile bring thee *Herrick* to *Anacreon,* / Quaffing his full-crown'd bowles of burning Wine, / And in his raptures speaking Lines of Thine" (31–34). As in Propertius, the wish for a male sexual Golden Age is revealed as a dream. This disillusionment is foreshadowed by the poem's epigraph: "*Desunt nonulla,*" "Some things are lacking." The dream of a sexual Elysium is just that insofar as the male myth functions as a wishful vision of erotic mastery.

In "A Dream of Elysium," Abraham Cowley projects a Golden Age garden in which "All Loves / Faithful perseverers, with amorous kisses, / And soft imbraces taste their greediest wishes" (76–78). The speaker sees "every couple alwayes dancing, sing / Eternall Ditties to *Elysiums* King" (85–86). However, the vision is short-lived:

> But see how soone these pleasures fade away,
> How neere to Evening is delights short Day
> . . . .
> and all these vanisht from my sight.
> (87–88, 90)

Like Herrick's speaker, Cowley's speaker is left only with the dream of male dominance: "that I may Dreame for ever so. / With that my flyting *Muse* I thought to claspe / Within my armes, but did a shadow graspe" (94–96).[39]

The nature of that "shadow" or false dream of a sexual Golden Age is given a witty turn in Richard Lovelace, who also looks back to a sexual Golden Age in his attempt to seduce Chloris:

> In the Nativity of time,
> *Chloris*! it was not thought a Crime
>   In direct *Hebrew* for to woe.
> Now wee make Love, as all on fire,
> Ring retrograde our lowd Desire,
>   And Court in *English* Backward too.
> ("Love made in the first Age: To Chloris," 1–6)

39. *The Complete Works,* ed. Alexander Grosart, 2 vols. (1881; repr. New York: AMS Press, 1967), 1:18. See also Sir William Davenant's "Elizium. To the Duchess of Buckingham," in *The Shorter Poems and Songs from the Plays and Masques,* ed. A. M. Gibbs (Oxford: Clarendon Press, 1972), 350–51.

As the speaker tries to seduce Chloris, he paints a picture of a sexual Golden Age embodying male wishful thinking of total female compliance:

> Thrice happy was that golden Age,
> When complement was constru'd Rage,
>   And fine words in the Center hid;
> When cursed *No* stain'd no Maids Blisse,
> And all discourse was summ'd in *Yes,*
>   And Nought forbad, but to forbid.
>   (7–12)

In this Golden Age the speaker tells his mistress, "Lads, indifferently did crop / A Flower, and a Maiden-head" (17–18). Lovers enjoyed "A Fragrant Bank of Strawberries, / Diaper'd with Violet Eyes, / Was Table, table-cloth, and Fare" (25–27). The result is that "Their Troth seal'd with a Clasp and Kisse, / Lasted untill that extreem day" because "no fault, there was no tear" (33–34, 37). However, the speaker's plea is rejected, causing cynical bitterness: "I must deny, / Whilst ravish'd with these Noble Dreams, / And crowned with mine own soft Beams, / Injoying of my selfe I lye" (57–60). The speaker's retreat into autoeroticism demolishes the fantasy of a sexual Golden Age controlled by the male while revealing his underlying sexual fears and anxieties the myth was meant to alleviate.[40]

The male myth of a sexual Golden Age provided seventeenth-century poets with a means to construct fantasies designed to secure their power over women as it alleviated male sexual anxieties. In this imagined Golden Age male desire and sexuality were not subjected to any laws or inhibitions. As part of the anti-Petrarchan and anti-Neoplatonic movement the myth allowed male poets a new means of seducing the woman through the evocation of mutual love. For most poets, the myth became a way to displace or sublimate their own sexual fears and anxieties while controlling the woman for male desire. Typically, the male poet promised the woman mutuality and freedom from social inhibitions regarding sexuality. However, most male poets used the myth as a subterfuge in that they really did not promise the woman

---

40. *The Poems,* ed. C. H. Wilkinson (Oxford: Clarendon Press, 1953), 146.

equality nor did they voice any real concerns about woman's desire. Instead, the woman employed in the myth becomes a means of defining and satisfying male desire. This exercise in male wish-fulfillment was wittily exposed late in the century by Aphra Behn, who also projected a sexual Golden Age but from a feminine viewpoint. Moreover, Behn makes clear why women also desire a sexual Golden Age in her poem, "The Disappointment," where young Lysander, after winning Cloris, loses his "Vigor" because an "envying God conspires / To snatch his Power, yet leave him the Desire!" (86, 79–80). The result is that "The Insensible fell weeping in his Hand" (90). Thus, for Behn the generation of male power and authority and the alleviation of sexual fears and anxieties that the myth embodies does not match up with the realities perceived by the woman. Such was the triumphant female riposte to the overplayed, male fantasy of a sexual Golden Age.[41]

41. Aphra Behn, *The Works,* ed. Montague Summers, 6 vols. (1915; repr. New York: Benjamin Blom, 1967), 6:180. See also her long poem, "The Golden Age" (6:138–44). I want to thank my colleague, John F. Moffitt, for advice, criticism, and help with translations.

Achsah Guibbory

Sexual Politics / Political Sex
Seventeenth-Century Love Poetry

Sex and politics often intertwine in seventeenth-century poetry. In Donne's elegies, for example, the public world of politics intersects the private world of love as Donne explores the dynamics of male-female relations. These poems in various ways reject Petrarchan love, with its worship of the mistress, and attempt through wit to reestablish male sovereignty. But love is not kept separate from politics, for the attack on female dominance in love repeatedly spills over into an attack on female rule in the public world. Donne's analogy between love and politics had special point during the reign of Queen Elizabeth, who favored the coded language of Petrarchan conventions as a way of representing political relations. But the sense of a connection between the discourses of love and politics did not end with Elizabeth's reign. The analogy appeared with some regularity in Cavalier poetry, which was, significantly, indebted to Donne's treatment of love. Carew complains in "A deposition from Love" that a man who's been jilted in love "feeles a woe, / Onely deposed Kings can know." In poems such as "Song. To Lucasta, Going to the Warres" or "To Lucasta. From Prison. An Epode," Lovelace moves easily from speaking about his love for Lucasta to declaring his loyalty to Charles. Suckling, in "Sonnet I," explains the fickleness of male desire with the observation that a beautiful woman can no more hope to remain attractive to her lover than "empires" can expect their power to last forever. The politics and the poetry of Charles I's reign was obviously quite different from that of Elizabeth's, but the analogy between heterosexual love and politics continued to have considerable political and poetical importance.[1]

I do not want to argue that the "real" subject of seventeenth-century love poetry is politics, but rather that the intimacies of the private world and the social orders of the public world are complexly intertwined in this period in ways that have yet to be fully understood.[2] As a step toward understanding this interrelation, this essay will examine three poems about what love would be like in the best of all possible worlds: Carew's "Rapture," Lovelace's "Love made in the first Age: To *Chloris*," and Aphra Behn's "The Golden Age." All three poems have a comic, playful element, but there is a serious dimension as well that should not be ignored. As idealizations of what sex should be like, these poems construct models of human sexuality and of private male-female relations that involve analogous models of political order.[3] In all three poems, "good sex" is defined in opposition to the existing order—both social and political. Carew's and Lovelace's libertinism is essentially conservative, for their poems present models of female obedience and submission, which I under-

1. See my article "'Oh, let mee not serve so': The Politics of Love in Donne's *Elegies*," *ELH* 57 (1990): 811–33. See *The Poems of Thomas Carew*, ed. Rhodes Dunlap (Oxford: Clarendon Press, 1949); *The Poems of Richard Lovelace*, ed. C. H. Wilkinson (Oxford: Clarendon Press, 1930); and *The Works of Sir John Suckling: The Poems*, ed. Thomas Clayton (Oxford: Clarendon Press, 1971). Poems will be cited in the text by line or stanza numbers, following the practice in these editions.

2. Arthur Marotti's *John Donne: Coterie Poet* (Madison: University of Wisconsin Press, 1986) and his ground-breaking article, "'Love Is Not Love': Elizabethan Sonnet Sequences and the Social Order," *ELH* 49 (1982): 396–428, have alerted us to the political dimensions of Renaissance love poetry. Marotti, relatively unconcerned with matters of gender, privileges politics and implies that love is merely a metaphor for political and socioeconomic ambition. On connections between love and politics, see also Louis Montrose, "'Shaping Fantasies': Figurations of Gender and Power in Elizabethan Culture," *Representations* 1 (1983): 61–94; and Lauro Martines, "The Politics of Love Poetry in Renaissance Italy," in *Historical Criticism in an Age of Deconstruction*, ed. Janet Smarr (Urbana: University of Illinois Press), forthcoming.

3. James Grantham Turner's *One Flesh: Paradisal Marriage and Sexual Relations in the Age of Milton* (Oxford: Clarendon Press, 1987) provides an illuminating discussion of attitudes toward sexuality and Edenic love in Milton and other seventeenth-century poets, though he does not include Behn. Kevin Sharpe, in *Criticism and Compliment: The Politics of Literature in the England of Charles I* (Cambridge: Cambridge University Press, 1987), 109–51, discusses the politics of love in Carew's poetry, rightly arguing that Carew's poetry of love is "a discourse through which he examined political relationships" (135), but Sharpe is indifferent to sexuality and matters of power inherent in sexual relations.

stand as having sexual, social, and political significance. Aphra Behn, however, presents a radically different, feminist libertinism that subverts both the sexual and political orders celebrated by these two Cavalier poets.

Carew's "A Rapture" offers Celia a vision of love in an Elysium where "All things are lawfull there, that may delight / Nature, or unrestrained Appetite" (111–12). This seems a place with no laws or prohibitions, no social institutions and conventions (like "honor," "marriage," or "chastity")—a place of Nature, as distinct from Society. But, in fact, the "natural" sexual relations between the male and female lovers in Elysium are carefully ordered: they represent an ideal that has implications for both private and public spheres.

The aggressive opening line of the poem—"I will enjoy thee now my *Celia,* come"—suggests pleasure, urgency, and the supposedly irresistible power of male desire. As in Donne's elegy "To his Mistris Going to Bed," which this poem echoes, male desire requires a small though not overwhelming amount of female resistance (something like Eve's "sweet reluctant amorous delay" that appeals so much to Adam in *Paradise Lost*) and is inextricably linked to power. The speaker wants to restore "free woman" (20) to her natural, original condition that was lost when "greedy men," with their invention of "Honour," sought to "enclose" her within the "private armes" of monogamous marriage (3, 19–20). The metaphor of woman as land which should be "common" property (19) suggests that relations between man and woman will be revised in ways that will reinforce, not erase, gender hierarchy.[4]

Once in Elysium, he "behold[s]" her "bared snow, and . . . unbraded gold" and her "virgin-treasure" (27–28, 32). Her "rich Mine" lies "ready still for mintage" (33–34). Carew stresses Celia's passivity, associating her with riches that the lover will possess. Despite the earlier rejection of private property, male sexual conquest turns out to be an individualistic, imperialistic, even capitalistic enterprise. In contrast to Donne's elegy "To his Mistris Going to Bed" where the mistress (as queen) has enfranchised her lover, giving him permission

4. John Donne, *The Elegies and the Songs and Sonnets,* ed. Helen Gardner (Oxford: Clarendon, 1965); John Milton, *Paradise Lost,* in *Complete Poems and Major Prose,* ed. Merritt Y. Hughes (New York: Odyssey Press, 1957), 4.311.

to explore her body, Carew's "enfanchiz'd hand" (29) seems empowered by itself or by the freedom of Elysium. Carew creates a fantasy of inexhaustible male potency and desire, fueled by the "delicious Paradise" of the woman's body:

> So will I rifle all the sweets, that dwell
> In my delicious Paradise, and swell
> My bagge with honey, drawne forth by the power
> Of fervent kisses, from each spicie flower.
>
> (59–62)

Carew invokes a long-standing tradition that identified woman with nature, and thus placed her "lower" than man and at his service. If Celia is paradisal nature, Carew's lover has dominion over it. Like Adam in the Garden of Eden, he rules in this kingdom. He is free to "rifle" (59), "seize" (63), "taste" (65), and "visit" (67) what turns out actually to *belong* to him.[5]

In Carew's libertinism, freedom clearly means something quite different for woman than for man. He tells Celia to "walke free" with neck "unyoak'd," un"fetter[ed]" by "Chastitie" (150–52). She can liberate herself by throwing off the authority of the "proud *Vsurper*" (150), Honor, and yielding to the rightful authority of man's desire. Far from achieving independence or equality, she must replace a "*Vsurper*" with a legitimate ruler. For woman as for subjects of a monarch, true freedom is in submission; for man, as for a king, it is possession.

Carew's sexual fantasy constructs a supposedly ideal order of harmony predicated on the enthusiastic submission of natural subjects to rulers. The fact that Carew repeatedly in his poems speaks of the poet-lover as monarch allows him to exploit powerful analogies between the sexual relations of lovers and the political relations of subject and monarch—both of which entail, for him, unequal yet comple-

---

5. See Aristotle, *De generatione animalium* [*Generation of Animals*], trans. A. L. Peck, Loeb Classical Library (Cambridge: Harvard University Press, 1953), for the association of the female with the earth (1.2.716a), and for the influential theory that in generation the male provides the "form" and "principle of movement" while the female provides "the body," the "material" (1.20.729a). Helkiah Crooke, *Microcosmographia: A Description of the Body of Man* (London, 1615), repeatedly cites Aristotle's description of the womb as "the fertile field of Nature" (200, 221, 270).

mentary distributions of power. The anthropologist Mary Douglas has shown how the human body functions as a "natural symbol" of society, a "model" symbolically expressing the values and orders of the social body.[6] I think a similar argument can be made for the symbolic function of what is thought to constitute the basic social unit, the relation between man and woman. The erotic fantasy of Carew's libertine "A Rapture" reaffirms both conservative, traditional notions of female obedience and male mastery and royalist, even absolutist notions of the relations of subject and prince. The female body becomes analogous to the body politic.

In Carew's poem and the political model inscribed in it, the issue of class is notable by its absence. There is, instead, a simple binary distinction between lover and mistress, between ruler and the body politic, which is defined in terms of its possession of riches that can be yielded, a definition that implicitly removes the lower social orders from consideration.

The political resonance of Carew's poem becomes clearer when we look at how relations between monarch and subjects were conceived in the earlier seventeenth century. James and Charles both spoke of themselves as fathers of their people. This conception of the relation between king and subjects as analogous to the relation between father and children found its fullest exposition in Sir Robert Filmer's *Patriarcha*.[7] According to Gordon Schochet, during the Stuart period the patriarchal family became a central, consciously recognized category in English political thought. Lawrence Stone suggests that the state deliberately encouraged patriarchy since "the subordination of the family to its head is analogous to, and also a direct contributory cause of, subordination of subjects to the sovereign." The notion of the king as father of his people is well recognized, but even more

6. See *Natural Symbols: Explorations in Cosmology* (London: Barrie and Jenkins, 1970), 12; and *Purity and Danger: An Analysis of Concepts of Pollution and Taboo* (New York: Frederick A. Praeger, 1966), 3–4, 114–28.

7. For examples of the "king as father" see James's *Trew Law of Free Monarchies,* in *The Political Works of James I,* ed. Charles Howard McIlwain (New York: Russell and Russell, 1965), 55; the Lord Keeper's speech for Charles at the summoning of Parliament April 13, 1640, in John Rushworth, *Historical Collections,* 8 vols. (London, 1721–1722), 3:1114; Charles I, *Eikon Basilike,* ed. Philip A. Knachel (Ithaca: Cornell University Press, 1966), 68; and Filmer's *Patriarcha,* in *Patriarcha and Other Political Works,* ed. Peter Laslett (Oxford: Basil Blackwell, 1949), the fullest articulation of this idea of kingship.

significant, for my purposes, was the analogy that compared the union between the monarch and his realm to marriage between husband and wife, an analogy which gendered the notion of obedience. James I, in his speech to his first English Parliament (March 19, 1603), put it boldly: "I am the Husband, and all the whole Isle is my lawfull Wife; I am the Head, and it is my Body."[8] The subjects are, in the double analogy, both effeminized and defined in terms of a body that is incapable of independent life or motion or reason, and that requires a head—all qualities that are assumed to apply to woman as well. For both James and Charles, the king is the owner of the realm (understood as both the land and the subjects), and has full rights to it.[9] Just as the head rules the body, and the husband the wife, so the king has authority over his subjects, whose duty is loyal obedience. The analogies serve to deprive subjects of power and rights as well as to "naturalize" the political order of divine right monarchy.

Charles was given to expressing his relationship with his subjects in amatory language. In his speeches to Parliament both in the 1620s and in the months following the opening of the Long Parliament on November 3, 1640, he spoke of the "Love and Affection of my English Subjects" and of Parliament. Such idealized descriptions of the relations of subject and monarch were clearly at odds with the actual opposition that had grown during the years of Charles's personal rule, when the king imposed various fines and taxes, such as ship money or "distraint of knighthood," in order to finance his projects. Charles's assumption of his right to his subjects' money was an extension of James I's sense of the people/realm as his property, possessing no rights of their own.[10]

8. Schochet, *Patriarchalism in Political Thought* (New York: Basic Books, 1975), 54–84; and Stone, *The Family, Sex and Marriage in England 1500–1800* (New York: Harper and Row, 1977), 152–54. The quotation is from Stone, 152. On the patriarchal idea of monarchy in this period, see also Michael Walzer, *The Revolution of the Saints: A Study in the Origins of Radical Politics* (1965; repr. New York: Atheneum, 1973), 183–98; and Laslett's Introduction to Filmer's *Patriarcha,* 11–33. James I, *Political Works,* 272.

9. See McIlwain's introduction to *Political Works,* xxxviii; and James I, *Trew Law,* 62–63.

10. Charles's speech is in Rushworth, *Historical Collections* 4:12; also in Charles I, *Reliquiae Sacrae Carolinae. Or, the Works of that Great Monarch and Glorious Martyr, King Charles the I* (Hague, 1650). Cf. the King's speech to Parliament, January 25, 1640/1 (Rushworth, 4:155). As the historian Esther Cope puts it, "Charles collected revenue,

For Charles, his subjects' "love and affection" could be shown only by submission and obedience understood in financial terms. This assumption characterizes his troubled dealings with Parliament in the late 1620s, his attempts throughout the 1630s to raise revenues by imposing "duties" by royal proclamation, and his parliamentary addresses 1640–1641. In the "Speech to both Houses at the passing of the Bill of Tonnage and Poundage, June 22.1641," for example, Charles interprets Parliament's action as "a testimony of [their] love" and "dutiful affections" and as an "occasion" for him to "shew that affection to my people, that I desire my people would shew to me." Charles's logic is: if you love me, you will give me your treasures which are really mine anyway; your *giving* these riches to me shows *your* love, and my *accepting* them is an expression of *my* love. Insisting that his only "designe" is "to win the affections of my People," Charles says he puts himself "wholly upon the love and affection of my people for my subsistence." This speech was written, of course, after Carew's poem, but it expresses an ideologically powerful conception of the relation between King and subjects maintained by Charles throughout his reign, despite its increasingly apparent fiction.[11]

The king's articulation of a mutual, inequitably reciprocal love between subjects and monarch is strikingly similar to the dynamics of love in Carew's poem, in which the male lover feeds off and is nourished and renewed by the mistress, who in turn becomes the happy recipient of his life-giving "soveraigne Balme" (77). In Carew the relation of the lovers is highly eroticized and thus differs from Charles's representation of his relation to his subjects; but Carew's eroticism is

but in doing so he lost affection." Communities, special groups, and individuals felt that their rights and property were being violated (see *Politics without Parliaments 1629–1640* [London: Allen and Unwin, 1987], 140). On Stuart absolutist ideology and the opposition to absolutism from those who stressed the subjects' liberties and property rights, see Johann P. Sommerville, *Politics and Ideology in England 1603–1640* (London: Longman, 1986).

11. See the Lord Keeper's speech for the king, February 5, 1625/6 (Rushworth, *Historical Collections* 1:202); and Charles's "Declaration to all his loving Subjects, of the Causes which moved him to dissolve the last Parliament [March 10, 1628/9]," in Rushworth, 1: appendix, 1–11. For his attempts to raise money during his personal rule, see Rushworth, 2:49–50, 70, 354. See also Sommerville's discussion of Charles's conflicts with Parliament over levying and collecting taxes (*Politics and Ideology,* 156–60). He also remarks that both Charles and James drew more money from extra-Parliamentary impositions than from Parliament (4, 151). The quotation from Charles's speech is from *Reliquiae Sacrae,* 12–13.

punctuated by words such as "soveraigne" that return us to the political world. I would suggest that the early Stuart convention of describing political relations in terms of affectionate love enables Carew's poem to envision an ideal political order as it constructs the supposedly ideal sexual relation between man and woman.[12]

The ease with which Charles, and James before him, used the language of love to express political and economic relations suggests the deep interconnection between domestic, amatory relations and public, political ones in the early seventeenth century. The king not only used amatory language in his political addresses, but, as Kevin Sharpe has observed, during the 1630s Charles "communicated his vision of the best government through his marriage [to Henrietta Maria] represented as a Platonic union of souls." Just as important as the Platonic assumptions, emphasized by Sharpe, that enabled the royal couple's chaste marriage to symbolize reason's control of the lower elements was the fact that the model of marriage gendered obedience as it sought to contain resistance. Carew paid tribute to Charles's vision in his masque *Coelum Britannicum* (1634), presenting the royal couple as an exemplary model of "conjugal affection" capable of reforming the world. Patriarchal marriage and divine right monarchy were mutually supportive, and the language of one could be invoked to support the other. And this should make us rethink how we read seventeenth-century love poetry.[13]

Carew's poem embodies both a prescription for female behavior and an idealized political order in which there is no threatening resistance or rebellion, no betrayal, in which the ruler is absolute in his pleasure and the "plyant" (118) subject (this mistress, the land, the people) willingly offers all her treasures in the confidence that she will be rewarded. "No rude sounds" or "observing spies" disturb the lovers'

12. Carew's eroticism contrasts with the fastidiousness of the king. As Charles's recent biographer notes, the king "was not a highly sexed man," and "the parsimony of Charles and Henrietta Maria's sexual habits was fairly well recognized at the time" (Charles Carlton, *Charles I, The Personal Monarch* [London: Routledge & Kegan Paul, 1983], 108, 131).

13. Sharpe, *Criticism and Compliment,* 143; see also 64, 68, and chap. 5, on "The Caroline Court Masque"). Carew, *Coelum Britannicum,* in *The Poems of Thomas Carew,* 160. Sharpe's emphasis on the importance of Platonism in Charles's ideal of marriage follows Steven Orgel and Roy Strong (*Inigo Jones: The Theatre of the Stuart Court,* 2 vols. [London: Sotheby Parke Bernet; Berkeley: University of California Press, 1973], 1: chap. 4).

"Halcion calmenesse" and "steadfast peace" (99, 101, 97–98). But the angry tone of the ending of "The Rapture" makes clear that the ideal, like Charles's descriptions of his subjects' "love and affection," is only a fantasy—at odds with the present state of things where false Honor (the "proud *Vsurper*" [150]) has perverted the proper order in both private and public spheres:

> When yet this false Impostor can dispence
> With humane Justice, and with sacred right,
> And maugre both their lawes command me fight
> With Rivals, or with emulous Loves, that dare
> Equall with thine, their Mistresse eyes, or haire:
> If thou complaine of wrong, and call my sword
> To carve out thy revenge, upon that word
> He bids me fight and kill, or else he brands
> With markes of infamie my coward hands,
> And yet religion bids from blood-shed flye,
> And damns me for that Act. Then tell me why
> This Goblin Honour which the world adores,
> Should make men Atheists, and not women Whores.
>
> (154–66)

The bitterness here and the reversion to the judgmental "Whores" explodes the fantasy of order that the poem has been celebrating, yet the exposure of hypocrisy and corruption in the present world makes that idealized order seem urgently necessary.[14]

Something of the anger that concludes Carew's poem surfaces at the end of Lovelace's "Love made in the first Age: To *Chloris*," probably written after 1649 but not published until after his death in *Lucasta. Posthume Poems* (1659). Charles was still in power when Carew was writing his libertine poem, but for Lovelace after the king's execution, it seemed impossible to hope for a restoration of order. Carew's Elysium, which was still potentially available to present day lovers ("come, / And flye with me to Loves Elizium"), has been replaced by a state of love that existed only in the very distant past, "In the Nativ-

14. Sharpe quite rightly sees in Carew's poetry advice to the court and king, not just flattery (*Criticism and Compliment,* 135), but I do not see the political criticism of "A Rapture" aimed in this direction.

ity of time" (st. 1). As the object of nostalgic longing, Lovelace's "golden Age" (st. 2) can only be recreated in the speaker's imagination.

In that first golden age, sex was direct, natural, immediately gratifying, free. A man could woo in "direct *Hebrew*" (st. 1) and have no fear of rejection since women were perfectly obedient and compliant: "cursed *No* stain'd no Maids Blisse, / And all discourse was summ'd in *Yes,* / And Nought forbad, but to forbid" (st. 2). Here was a state in which there was no resistance, no discord between the desiring male and the female object of desire, whose happiness consisted entirely in her willing submission:

> Love then unstinted, Love did sip,
> And Cherries pluck'd fresh from the Lip,
>   On Cheeks and Roses free he fed;
> Lasses like *Autumne* Plums did drop,
> And Lads, indifferently did crop
>   A Flower, and a Maiden-head.
>
> Then unconfined each did Tipple
> Wine from the Bunch, Milk from the Nipple,
>   Paps tractable as Udders were;
> Then equally the wholsome Jellies,
> Were squeez'd from Olive-Trees, and Bellies,
>   Nor Suits of Trespasse did they fear.
>   (sts. 3 and 4)

Lovelace's juxtaposition of flowers and maidenheads, cheeks and roses, "Olive-Trees" and women's "Bellies," erases differences between woman and nature while insisting on the disparity between woman and man. Part of nature's abundance, women existed simply to satisfy the appetites and desires of man. "Lasses . . . drop[ped]" like plums—conveniently ripe, with no volition of their own. As in Carew, the poem constructs a supposedly ideal sexual order in which the man is free and active, the woman passive and submissive; and this order of sexual relations enacts a socioeconomic political order in which subjects are fully cooperative, yielding their goods yet never depleted.

In Lovelace's version of the golden age, "free love" does not preclude marriage, which turns out to be the norm in his paradise:

> Their Troth seal'd with a Clasp and a Kisse,
> Lasted untill that extreem day,
> In which they smil'd their Souls away,
> And in each other breath'd new blisse.
>
> (st. 6)

Unions are permanent and lasting here. Lovelace emphasizes his lovers' constancy and loyalty, qualities that at first may seem surprising in a libertine poem, where one expects emphasis on sexual variety. But they are very appropriate once the representation of love is recognized as also being politically symbolic. The significance of loyalty would not have been lost on Lovelace's royalist readers.

This idealized picture of love, where each partner is forever faithful to the other, represents both a private and a public model of order. The reciprocal, yet essentially unequal relation between man and woman offers for Lovelace an image of permanence, innocence, and above all, perfect obedience. Woman's eager submission is rewarded by mutual constancy, loyalty, and security. This, Lovelace suggests, is the model of a happy marriage—and also of a social order composed of perfectly compliant, "tractable" (st. 4) subjects who are constant and faithful to a ruler who also does not break faith.

Lovelace was hardly alone in presenting the loyal, compliant wife as the example for political subjects. The figure appears in contemporary royalist tracts. Thomas Bayly's *The Royall Charter* (1649) argued that subjects, like wives, never have the right to rebel but must always remain faithful and obedient. In *Eikon Basilike,* published immediately after Charles I's execution, the king's wife, "eminent for love as a wife and loyalty as a subject," is held up as an example to his errant subjects (victims of an evil "seduction"), whose love he has lost. In both royalist texts, the loyal, constant wife provides the model for the behavior of subjects who are charged with having spurned the affection of a devoted husband, much as Celia at the end of Lovelace's poem is bitterly denounced for having rejected him.[15]

---

15. Thomas Bayly, *The Royall Charter* (London, 1649), 58–59: "King and Kingdome, are like man and wife, whose marriages are made in heaven" and allow of no divorce— even, Bayly says, if the king proves to be a bad and un-Christian husband. See *Eikon Basilike,* 31 and 169, on the wife as exemplar for the subjects, and 85, on the "seductions" of the people.

Lovelace's poem is, explicitly, about sex not politics, about how woman's false honor deprives her of pleasure. Chloris's refusal to accept him as a lover has ruined the "bliss" that she might have enjoyed. And yet it is crucial to see that the discussion of sex is also complexly political. The poem's narrative closely matches the trajectory of political events that Lovelace's poetry more largely records. Had woman (or subjects) not refused his (or the king's) affections, the lovers might have been able in some measure to recapture that original, harmonious happiness. But this happiness can now no longer be shared, socially or communally. Hence the poem's final turning from mutual love to onanism, the appropriate sexual practice for this fallen state. Chloris's punishment for resistance/disobedience will be to

> miserably crave
> The offer'd blisse you would not have;
>   Which evermore I must deny,
> Whilst ravish'd with these Noble Dreams,
> And crowned with mine own soft Beams,
>   Injoying of my self I lye.
>
> (st. 10)

In his masturbatory fantasy, the male speaker can reign supreme, dependent only upon himself and his own imagination ("Dreams") rather than on any untractable people that might resist his desires. From Lovelace's perspective, subjects need kings more than kings need subjects, just as women need men more than men need women.

The soft eroticism of Aphra Behn's poem "The Golden Age" contrasts sharply with Carew's and Lovelace's libertine fantasies of paradisal love.[16] The natural world is sexualized in ways that suggest a

---

16. I quote the text of the poem from *The Works of Aphra Behn,* ed. Montague Summers, 6 vols. (1915; repr. New York: Benjamin Blom, 1967), 6:138–44. Like others who have written on this poem, I treat it as reflecting Behn's own concerns. Frederick M. Link, *Aphra Behn* (New York: Twayne, 1968), discusses this poem under the category "original poems" (chap. 6) rather than under "translations." Angeline Goreau, *Reconstructing Aphra: A Social Biography of Aphra Behn* (New York: Dial Press, 1980), claims the poem gives "fullest articulation" to Behn's ideals (271–72). The convention of "paraphrase" allowed for considerable freedom and creative individuality, as Dryden remarked in his "Preface to the Translation of Ovid's Epistles [1680]," in *Essays of John Dryden,* ed. W. P. Ker, 2 vols. (New York: Russell and Russell, 1961), 1:237–43.

kind of peaceful, soft sensuality devoid of the inequalities and hierarchies engendered by disparities in power: the intertwined groves,
the proper setting for love, "Exchang'd their Sweets, and mix'd with
thousand Kisses"; the birds engage in "soft and tender Play" (st. 1–
2). In this "Blest Age" (st. 1), pleasure is associated with a natural
softness that is defined in striking contrast to the phallic hardness
Behn identifies with the corrupt, fallen world of civilization, culture,
and art. As part of their pleasure, the nymphs "Innocently play" with
snakes that cannot harm them: "No spightful Venom in the wantons
lay; / But to the touch were Soft, and to the sight were Gay" (st. 3).
This striking detail of the snakes may recall Euripides' *The Bacchae*
where the peaceful groups of women, sleeping in the grass "with
snakes that licked their faces," suddenly turn violent with the intrusion of man.[17] Like the snakes, the men in Behn's golden world are
soft, harmless, unthreatening: "every God his own soft power admir'd"
(st. 6). In this golden world, Behn humorously suggests, erect penises
were not necessary for female pleasure—apparently, they were not
even considered desirable by either sex. "Power" and "masculinity"
were entirely different from what we know in the modern world.
"Each Swain was Lord o'er his own will alone" (st. 4)—in the sense
both that he was not subservient to a superior and that he was not
lord over anyone else's, or any woman's, will.

In Aphra Behn's golden world there is no social or sexual hierarchy, no distinction between rulers and ruled, or between dominant
men and submissive women. The maids "yield" not to men but to
their own desires, and do so for *their* pleasure. This is a world of
reciprocity, a world of give and take where all is "lawful . . . that
Pleasure did invite" (st. 5)—where self-gratification seems indistinguishable from satisfying one's lover:

> The Nymphs were free, no nice, no coy disdain;
> Deny'd their Joyes, or gave the Lover pain;
> The yielding Maid but kind Resistance makes;
> Trembling and blushing are not marks of shame,

17. See Euripides, *The Bacchae*, in *The Trojan Women, Helen, The Bacchae*, trans.
Neil Curry (Cambridge: Cambridge University Press, 1981), 141–44. I am indebted to
Stella Revard for calling my attention to this passage, in which the Herdsman describes
the women he has seen to Pentheus.

> But the Effect of kindling Flame:
> Which from the sighing burning Swain she takes,
> While she with tears all soft, and down-cast-eyes,
> Permits the Charming Conqueror to win the prize.
>
> (st. 6)

The conventional description of the male lover as "Charming Conqueror" appears in a context that shows there actually is no conquest because there is no real resistance. Maid and Swain, both burning unabashedly with desire, are equal partners. In this golden world, there are no displays of male aggressive power either over women or over nature:

> The stubborn Plough had then,
> Made no rude Rapes upon the Virgin Earth;
> Who yielded of her own accord her plentious Birth,
>   Without the Aids of men;
>   As if within her Teeming Womb,
>   All Nature, and all Sexes lay,
>   Whence new Creations every day
> Into the happy World did come.
>
> (st. 3)

In this amusing description of the Virgin Earth's fertility, which looks a lot like parthenogenesis, the female contained within herself everything needed for generation. The "Aids of men"—both plow and penis—were no more necessary for reproduction than for pleasure. With this nice detail, which is a witty turn on Virgil's description of the world before Jove's time when the earth was not cultivated with the plow but freely produced her "fruits," Behn gives a sharp, feminist rebuttal to suggestions by Lovelace that men do not really need women.[18]

What is most important, though, is that Behn clearly shows the link between sexual practices and socioeconomic and political structures. For this nonaggressive, noncombative, soft and pleasurable

---

18. See *The Georgics of Virgil,* trans. C. Day Lewis (New York: Oxford University Press, 1947), 7: "No settlers brought the land under subjection" and "earth unprompted / Was free with all her fruits."

sexuality is part of a golden world where there was no cultivation of
the earth (seen as an aggressive enterprise of men), "no rough sound
of Wars Alarms," no "Ambition," no "Trade," no "Religion"—and no
monarchy. "Monarchs were uncreated then, / Those Arbitrary Rulers
over men" (st. 4–5). All these marks of civilization are interconnected,
for all involve an aggressively phallic, masculine thirst for power and
dominance:

> Right and Property were words since made,
>   When Power taught Mankind to invade:
> When Pride and Avarice became a Trade;
>   Carri'd on by discord, noise and wars,
>   For which they barter'd wounds and scarrs;
> And to Inhaunce the Merchandize, miscall'd it, Fame,
>   And Rapes, Invasions, Tyrannies,
>   Was gaining of a Glorious Name:
> Stiling their salvage slaughters, Victories.
>
> (st. 5)

Where Carew's and Lovelace's libertine sex enacts and supports a
monarchical structure based on a reciprocity defined in terms of dominance and yielding, possession and surrender, Behn's golden age calls
the whole structure into question and envisions an entirely different
order. Aphra Behn has been described as a strong supporter of monarchy and of the Stuarts, but I think the evidence of some of her
poems suggests otherwise. Her Edenic world where no invasive "Aids
of men" are necessary is also a world without monarchs. Far more
explicitly and directly than the Cavalier poets, she shows how private
sexuality is bound up with a whole range of practices in the public
sphere.[19]

19. Though Aphra Behn has usually been considered a staunch supporter of monarchy, Goreau well observes that Behn's "revolutionary attack on the concepts of social
hierarchy, property, and repressive social codes" in "The Golden Age" seems to contra-
dict her Tory allegiance fostered by the Popish Plot (*Reconstructing Aphra,* 272–73). But
Goreau concludes that this is yet another example of Aphra "at odds with herself" (273),
the recurring theme of her book. George Woodcock, *The Incomparable Aphra* (London:
T. V. Boardman & Co., 1948), sees the inconsistency in her "conservative" support of
the "reactionary Stuart kings" and her "revolutionary," "radical" ideas and attitudes as
reflecting "the confusion of social ideas in that age" (150–51).

After a long attack in stanzas 8 and 9 on "Honour," the embodiment of all the cultural pressures that prevent people from quenching their "amorous thirst" "At Loves Eternal Spring" (st. 8), Behn turns at the end to advise "*Sylvia,*" to whom we now discover the whole poem has been addressed:

> But *Sylvia* when your Beauties fade,
> When the fresh Roses on your Cheeks shall die,
>   Like Flowers that wither in the Shade,
> Eternally they will forgotten lye,
> And no kind Spring their sweetness will supply.
> When Snow shall on those lovely Tresses lye.
> And your fair Eyes no more shall give us pain,
>   But shoot their pointless Darts in vain.
> What will your duller honour signifie?
> Go boast it then! and see what numerous Store
> Of Lovers will your Ruin'd Shrine Adore.
>   Then let us, *Sylvia,* yet be wise,
>   And the Gay hasty minutes prize:
> The Sun and Spring receive but our short Light,
> Once sett, a sleep brings an Eternal Night.
>
> (st. 10)

Perhaps it seems odd that Behn would echo the carpe diem advice of Cavalier poetry, whose construction of sexuality and politics she has just been dismantling. But there is a new twist to the old line: the advice to seize the day, traditionally spoken by a male to a prospective female lover, is now spoken by one woman to another. The ending turns out to be subversive like the rest of the poem. Sylvia (and indeed, every woman) must reject the authority of "Honour" and seize the "hasty minutes" by openly "confess[ing]" and acting on her sexual desires. Only then will "the Golden age again, / Assume its Glorious Reign" (st. 10). Though the poem has shown how sexual relations have been culturally determined, how the corruption of male-female relations has been accompanied by other socioeconomic and politcal corruptions, Behn boldly concludes by asserting the efficacy of individual female agency to disrupt the established order. She thus both explodes cultural notions of female passivity and suggests that the only hope of change lies within the private sphere.

Several general conclusions emerge from reading these poems. Carew and Lovelace construct gender, sexuality, and desire in ways that reinforce female obedience and subservience, and that suggest how the submission of women in the private domain of love and the political obedience of subjects in the public sphere could be mutually reinforcing. The "discourse of desire" in this poetry is thus both sexual and political, in more than one sense. Behn makes the connection between sex and politics most explicit, exposing the interlocking paradigms of hierarchy and dominance that characterize erotic relations between men and women in her culture, on the one hand, and the political, social, and economic structures of society, on the other. In her libertine poem, which uses yet subverts conventions of Cavalier poetry, Behn seeks to dismantle the very structures of dominance and submission that Carew and Lovelace represented. But it is important to note that the poems of Carew and Lovelace themselves imply that the idea of female submission (and the correlative of political obedience) was hardly an uncontested "reality" in their society, since it is presented as an *absent* ideal, needing to be regained, perhaps something that never existed except in fantasy. Finally, these three golden age poems provide evidence that seventeenth-century writers actually recognized, as did Charles and James and even Elizabeth, a close relationship between sociopolitical structures and cultural conventions about sexual relations. In seventeenth-century England as in other cultures, sexual practices and codes for personal behavior existed in relation to the larger social order. Once we allow that these poets acknowledged and explored the interconnection between the sexual and political, we will better understand seventeenth-century love poetry.

Arlene Stiebel

Subversive Sexuality
Masking the Erotic in Poems
by Katherine Philips and Aphra Behn

Although in recent discourses of desire there has been polite acknowledgment of the importance of relationships among women,
much contemporary literary theory and criticism ignores the existence
of lesbians.[1] Critics tell us that there are women who were "autonomous," or unmarried; women who chose a "professional" or career
mode rather than a familial allegiance; women who, because they were
married, automatically qualify as heterosexual despite their primary
emotional and erotic bonds with other women; and some anomalous
women who had a hard time fitting in with societal expectations of
their time and so remained celibate. Only in a very few cases, and
usually famous ones, such as that of Gertrude Stein, is it openly stated
that literary women had sexual relations with other women and wrote
about them. Most literary critics, even some who themselves are lesbians, collude in the polite fiction of obscurity that clouds lesbian
literary lives. Bonnie Zimmerman confirms Marilyn Frye's analysis that
"we are considered to be both naturally and logically impossible."[2]

1. A version of some of the material in this essay appears in my article "Not Since Sappho: The Erotic in Poems of Katherine Philips and Aphra Behn," in *Homosexuality in
Renaissance and Enlightenment England: Literary Representations in Historical Context,*
ed. Claude J. Summers (New York: The Haworth Press/Harrington Park Press, 1992),
153–71, also published as a special issue of the *Journal of Homosexuality* 23 (1992).
2. Zimmerman, *The Safe Sea of Women: Lesbian Fiction 1969–1989* (Boston: Beacon
Press, 1990), 62.

The tradition of denial extends even to such distinguished works as Lillian Faderman's ground-breaking study and the most recent articles dealing with literature by lesbians. Through various critical representations, emotionally intense relationships between women are asserted to be nonsexual. Faderman insists not only that we do or can not know whether these women had "genital sex," but that even if they did, it is unimportant because historically there was no such thing as a "lesbian." Although it is now fashionable to exploit this notion of the social construction of sexual identity, such semantic hairsplitting seems to beg important questions of sexuality in literature.[3]

Adrienne Rich's theoretical observations in "Compulsory Heterosexuality and Lesbian Existence" lead to the position that choice for women was so restricted by patriarchal coercion that true sexual preference may often have been obscured or invisible, requiring conformity to a social norm in which even the acknowledgment of a sexual preference for a woman was a radical act.[4] Given these circumstances, the marriages of women known to have their primary emotional and sexual attachments to other women effectively provided them with the protection necessary to maintain respectability. Recognizing the historical circumstances of lesbian identity ought not to deprive it of sexuality.

Sandra M. Gilbert and Susan Gubar also relegate lesbians to the sexual sidelines. In their anthology of women's literature, they use every opportunity in footnotes, biographies, and glosses to explain away, where possible, evident same-sex choices in the lives and texts of lesbian authors. An example of how this bias works is evident in the way

3. Faderman, *Surpassing the Love of Men: Romantic Friendship and Love Between Women from the Renaissance to the Present* (New York: William Morrow, 1981). For some early examples of this critical approach, see Ellen Moers, *Literary Women* (New York: Doubleday, 1976); and Louise Bernikow, *Among Women* (New York: Harper and Row, 1980). For a contrary and unique appreciation of lesbian writers and themes, see Jane Rule, *Lesbian Images* (New York: Crossing Press, 1982). For an example of how this current theory relates to the English Renaissance, see Alan Bray, *Homosexuality in Renaissance England* (London: Gay Men's Press, 1982). For a more woman-centered treatment of some similar ideas, see Susan Cavin, *Lesbian Origins* (San Francisco: Ism Press, 1985). In their Introduction to *Hidden from History: Reclaiming the Gay and Lesbian Past* (New York: New American Library, 1989) the editors, Martin Bauml Duberman, Martha Vicinus, and George Chauncey, Jr., note that Faderman has been charged by other historians with denying the importance of sexual activity in lesbian women's lives (7).
4. In Rich, *Blood, Bread, and Poetry* (New York: Norton, 1986), 23–75.

they distort Katherine Philips's clearly erotic poems. In their analysis, the eroticism is diffused through disembodied generalization into a sterile intellectual bonding. Their approach robs Philips's work of its emotional intensity. Surprisingly, their refusal to acknowledge the erotic in Philips's poems comes more than fifty years after Philip Webster Souers's standard biography, which carefully and clearly presents the succession of women to whom Philips was attached.[5]

Harriette Andreadis, in an article in *Signs,* obscures the issue even further. She describes Philips's poetry as "desexualized—though passionate and eroticized." In Andreadis's argument, eroticism is not sexual, so she can claim for Philips a type of lesbianism that maintains the social respectability she sees as an important aspect of Philips's reputation and life. Andreadis rehearses in detail some recent arguments dealing with gay and lesbian sexuality to attempt a definition of what is "lesbian." According to her definition, Philips had "a lesbian experience," wrote "lesbian texts," but may not have "expressed her homoerotic feelings genitally." Andreadis's definition does not include women's experiences of physical desire as a component of lesbianism. By writing sensuality out of lesbian literature, Andreadis maintains the tradition of denial, which is perpetuated in Dorothy Mermin's more recent article. Refusing to acknowledge a lesbian sexuality, Mermin picks up Andreadis's assertion that Philips's poems "did not give rise to scandal" and were therefore "asexual, respectable." Mermin's characterization of "female homosexuality" as "unseemly" clearly indicates her approach to this literature.[6]

How can contemporary critics continue to overlook, if not deny outright, the lesbian content of poems so clearly erotically charged with the love of women for women? The fact is that they can if they

5. Gilbert and Gubar, eds., *The Norton Anthology of Literature by Women* (New York: Norton, 1985), 81; and Souers, *The Matchless Orinda* (Cambridge: Harvard University Press, 1931).

6. Andreadis, "The Sapphic-Platonics of Katherine Philips, 1632–1664," *Signs: Journal of Women in Culture and Society* 15, no. 1 (1989): 34–60 (quotations from 39, 59); Mermin, "Women Becoming Poets: Katherine Philips, Aphra Behn, Anne Finch," *ELH* 57 (1990): 335–56 (quotations from 343). Mermin also derogates Philips's poems for their lack of a particular kind of energy usually associated with heterosexual desire and not part of Philips's clearly lesbian tone: "Her celebrations of love usually lack, however, the dramatic tension between flesh and spirit that imparts nervous urgency to Donne's amatory verse" (343).

want to, for just as figurative language has the power to reveal more than it states, it can also conceal. When Muriel Rukeyser publicly wrote of her lesbianism, she noted in the content and title of her 1971 autobiographical poem "The Poem as Mask," a technique that lesbian writers have used for centuries to express their love for women:

> When I wrote of the women in their dances and wildness,
>   it was a mask,
> on their mountain, god-hunting, singing in orgy,
> it was a mask; when I wrote of the god,
> fragmented, exiled from himself, his life, the love
>   gone down with song,
> it was myself, split open, unable to speak, in exile
>   from myself.
>
>   (1–5)[7]

Stein encoded her work, Amy Lowell sometimes changed pronouns to disguise her speaker's sex, and Willa Cather changed her protagonists' gender. Katherine Philips and Aphra Behn also used masking techniques based in the literary conventions of their time, but although they used the same conventions as their male counterparts did, the effects of their verses were radically different.

Evident in the poems of Philips and Behn is the use of literary conventions we take almost for granted—the courtly love address to the beloved and her response, the idealized pattern of Platonic same-sex friendship, and the hermaphroditic perfection of the beloved who incorporates the best qualities of both sexes. The difference in the use of these conventions by the women poets lies in the significant fact that the voice of the lover is nowhere disguised nor intended to be understood as that of a male. Rather, Philips and Behn exploit the conventions to proclaim to all who would read their poems that the desire of a woman for a woman lover falls well within acceptable literary norms. The very transparency of their masking techniques is what makes them so fascinating.

Their contemporaries recognized the homosexual bias of the two

7. Quoted in Florence Howe & Ellen Bass, eds., *No More Masks: An Anthology of Poems by Women* (New York: Doubleday, 1973).

authors. Both women were praised by other, male, poets as "sap-phists," that is, women writers in the tradition of Sappho of Lesbos, whose verse fragments clearly celebrate the erotic attachments of women, lament their separation and loss, and generally become the first acknowledged model for female-identified love poems.

Katherine Philips (1632–1664) was known as "The Matchless Orinda" and "The English Sappho" of her day. Privately circulated in manuscript during her lifetime, her *Poems* were first published post-humously in 1664. That incomplete edition was superseded by the *Poems* in 1667, which became the basis for the subsequent edition of 1678. Of the collected poems, more than half deal with Orinda's love for other women. In addition to poems addressed to her beloved "Lu-casia" (Anne Owen), there are poems by Philips to "Rosania" (Mary Aubrey), who preceded Lucasia in her affections, and to "Pastora," whose relationship with "Phillis" is celebrated by Lucasia after her own female lover has gone. In addition to these poems using the names Philips bestowed on members of her "Society of Friendship," which was "limited . . . to persons of the same sex," Philips writes in her own historical voice openly to Anne Owen as well as "To the Lady E. Boyl" with declarations of love.[8]

Central to Philips's short life—she died of smallpox at thirty-one—was the romance with Anne Owen, and central to her poetry is the conventional representation of their involvement through the images of classical friendship and courtly love. "Orinda to Lucasia," in a tra-ditional pastoral mode, illustrates the importance of the presence of the female beloved. Lucasia is the sun who will restore the light and energy of day (life) to Orinda, who cries for her "friend" to appear as the birds, flowers, and brooks call for their own renewal at a delayed sunrise. The "sun" is "tardy," so that the "weary birds" must "court their glorious planet to appear." The "drooping flowers . . . languish down into their beds: / While brooks . . . Openly murmer and de-mand" that the sun come (8–12). But Lucasia means *more* to Orinda than the sun to the world, and if Lucasia delays too long, she will come in time not to save Orinda, but to see her die.

---

8. The texts of Philips's *Poems* in the 1664, 1667, and 1678 editions are identical. See also Philips's *Letters from Orinda* (London, 1705); Souers, *Matchless Orinda,* 41; and Philips, *Poems,* 1664, 149.

> Thou my Lucasia are far more to me,
> Than he to all the under-world can be;
> From thee I've heat and light,
> Thy absence makes my night.
>
> .   .   .   .
>
>   if too long I wait,
> Ev'n thou may'st come too late,
> And not restore my life, but close my eyes.
>
>   (13–16, 22–24)

Traditional lovesickness unto death from a cruel mistress becomes transformed here to an urgent request for the presence of the willing beloved who will grant life if she comes speedily, but will be her chief mourner should the speaker expire.

Conventional oxymoronic terminology permeates the verse—light versus dark, day versus night, presence and absence, life and death— while the elements of nature that reflect the lover's state of being are, in a reversal of the magnitude of traditional signification, portrayed microcosmically in relation to the macrocosm of Orinda's feelings. The true relationship between the lovers is clear, if we allow ourselves to read the text explicitly. But through the lens of customary literary metaphors, the relationship of the two women can be explained away as being only figuratively erotic—a clever reworking of the spiritualized romance tradition combined with idealized classical friendship to de-emphasize the sexual reality inherent in the concrete, physical terminology of the poem. That is, the familiar literary conventions of the poem may mask and diffuse its pervasive eroticism. But to recognize the use of conventions as an elaborate mask is to acknowledge the reality of sexual desire that the poem simultaneously reveals and cloaks.

The relationship between Lucasia and Orinda is further developed and clarified in "To My Excellent Lucasia, on Our Friendship," for which the traditional soul-body dichotomy is the metaphorical basis. In this poem, Orinda's soul is not only given life by Lucasia, but Lucasia's soul actually *becomes* the animating force of her lover's body:

>   the world believ'd
> There was a soul the motions kept;

> But they all were deceiv'd.
>
> . . . .
>
> never had Orinda found
> A soul till she found thine.
> (6–8, 11–12)

The lovers are united in one immortal soul, and their relationship grants to the speaker attributes similar to those of a "bridegroom" or "crown-conquerer." But here too, Philips presents the metaphor in hyperbole that extends the more orthodox presentation, "They have but pieces of the earth, / I've all the world in thee" (19–20). The echo of Donne's lines from "The Sun Rising," "She's all states, and all princes I / Nothing else is" (21–22), forces the reader to regard the lovers' relationship as one of traditional courtly desire transformed into the sacramental union with a soul mate through whose agency one participates in the heavenly. Further, their love also remains "innocent" because they are both women. Given their mutually female design, the speaker can "say without a crime, / I am not thine, but thee" (3–4) and encourage their "flames" to "light and shine" without "false fear," since they are "innocent as our design, / Immortal as our soul" (23–24).

The speaker is careful to invoke both spirituality and innocent design as justifications for such language of excess, even though convention would allow her the license to claim another's soul as her own because of their affection alone. But, as female lovers, they need more than a mere statement rejecting what Donne characterizes in "A Valediction: forbidding Mourning" as "Dull, sublunary lovers' love" (13), to make their union acceptable. So Orinda's argument is that she and Lucasia are "innocent."

We may read this assertion as a refutation of the guilt surrounding accusations of unnatural love between women, as an outspoken declaration that lesbianism is not to be maligned. But I read it another way, in the time-honored tradition of irony that finds answers to bigotry in terms of the ignorance of prejudice itself. Orinda can maintain that love between women is "innocent" because, as Queen Victoria much later asked, what could women do? In a phallocentric culture that defines sexual behavior according to penile instrumentality, sex exclusive of men is not merely unthinkable, it is impossible. Which of us is unfamiliar with the characterization of "sex" as "going all the way," and what woman has not at one time or another been reassured that if it did not go in "nothing happened"? In England, although male homosexuality was outlawed, women together could not commit a sexual crime. If the norm is androcentric, eroticism among women is illusionary, female "friendships" are merely spiritual bonds, and lesbians are nonexistent.

As long as the definition of the sex act is inextricably linked to male anatomy and behavior, the question of what can women do is moot. So in order to address the question of sexuality in these poems, we must reexamine what we mean by erotic attraction and sexual activity. If we confuse ejaculation with orgasm, and both of these with sexual satisfaction, and deny the realities of varied sexual responses that are not centered actually or metaphorically in male anatomy, the true nature of lesbian relationships will remain masked. And to the extent that the bias of heterosexual denial and ignorance maintains that intercourse is the sexual norm, then, by definition, activity from which a penis is absent provides women with a love that is "innocent."[9]

In "To My *Lucasia*, in defence of declared Friendship," Orinda openly argues, "O My Lucasia, let us speak our Love, / And think not that impertinent can be" (1–2). Unlike Donne's male speaker in "The Flea," who asserts that "use make you apt to kill me" (16), as women, Orinda and Lucasia "cannot spend our stock by use." Their "spotless passion never tires, / But does increase by repetition still" (27–28). So female "friends" may enact their sexuality on quite different terms than their male counterparts. Sometimes the terminology of Philips's poems, so frequently reminiscent of Donne's, presents a lesbian sexuality only slightly masked, as in her wholesale borrowing of what may be Donne's most celebrated metaphor, that of the "stiff twin compasses" (26) from "A Valediction: forbidding Mourning" in "Friendship in Embleme, or the Seal. To my dearest Lucasia":

9. Much has been written recently by women about female sexuality. See, for example, Shere Hite, *The Hite Report: A Nationwide Study of Female Sexuality* (New York: Macmillan, 1976); as well as two books by Joann Loulan, *Lesbian Sex* (San Francisco: Spinsters, Ink, 1984) and *Lesbian Passion* (San Francisco: Spinsters/Aunt Lute, 1987).

6.
The Compasses that stand above
Express this great immortal love;
For Friends, like them, can prove this true,
They are, and yet they are not, two.

7.
And in their posture is exprest
Friendship's exalted Interest:
Each follows where the other leans,
And what each does, this other means.

8.
And as when one foot does stand fast,
And t'other circles seeks to cast,
The steddy part does regulate
And make the wand'rer's motion straight.

(21–32)

Literary and cultural conventions of friendship here only partially mask the eroticism implicit in Donne's famous metaphor. The mask preserves Philips's respectability, while the sexual energy that infuses the women's friendship is highlighted by the use of the formerly heterosexual image.

As a representative of Sappho in the British Isles, Katherine Philips was praised for her poetic skills. Twenty years after her death and the first appearance of her poems in print, the Matchless Orinda was succeeded by the Incomparable Astrea, Aphra Behn (1640–1689), whose poetic reputation was enhanced by favorable comparisons with her well-known predecessor.[10] Behn was known primarily as a scandalous playwright, although she also wrote incidental poems and what is perhaps the first real novel in English, *Love Letters between A Nobleman and His Sister* (1682–1685), which set the generic model (epistolary) and topic (courtship) for future lengthy prose works.[11]

10. "*Greece* in *Sappho,* in *Orinda* knew/ Our Isle; though they were but low types to you." From "To the excellent Madam BEHN, on her Poems," J. Adams, in Aphra Behn, *Poems Upon Several Occasions: With A Voyage To The Island Of Love* (London, 1684).

11. Two recent biographies of Behn are Maureen Duffy's *The Passionate Shepherdess* (London: Cape, 1977); and Angeline Goreau's *Reconstructing Aphra: A Social Biography of Aphra Behn* (New York: Dial Press, 1980). Vita Sackville-West's brief life of Behn,

Behn was married and widowed early, and as a mature woman, her primary publicly acknowledged relationship was with a gay male, John Hoyle, himself the subject of much scandal. She celebrates gay male love between the allegorical Philander and Lycidas, as she describes her social circle in a poem called "Our Cabal." Her description of their "friendship" reflects the convention of androgyny, as it becomes the justification for "Tenderness . . . / Too Amorous for a Swain to a Swain" (187–88). Behn was herself apostrophized by her admirers for her androgyny, which was seen as the desirable reconciliation of an arguably masculine mind with her apparently feminine physique. The conventional reconciliation of sexual opposites was expressed in dedicatory poems to her collection *Poems upon Several Occasions: With A Voyage to the Island of Love.*[12] The hermaphroditic paradigm is the basis for so many of these verses that the conventional encomiastic mode itself becomes a masking device to acknowledge the sexuality of her poems. "Such work so gently wrought, so strongly fine, / Cannot be wrought by hands all Masculine," writes J. C., who, along with J. Adams, praises her for "A Female Sweetness and a Manly Grace." J. Cooper uses the conventional marriage of "*Venus* her sweetness and the force of *Mars* . . . Imbracing . . . in thy due temper'd Verse" to characterize what J. C. terms "the Beauties of both Sexes join'd . . . with a strange power to charm."

But the most complex presentation of the hermaphroditic ideal is Behn's own. "To the fair Clarinda, who made Love to me, imagin'd more than Woman" explicitly states in the title the true relationship between the two women, and the poem develops the concept of a love that is "Innocent" into a full exploration of the safety in loving an androgynous female.

> FAIR, lovely Maid, or if that Title be
> Too weak, too Feminine for Nobler thee,
> Permit a Name that more Approaches Truth:
> And let me call thee, Lovely Charming Youth.

The Incomparable Astrea (London: Russell & Russell, 1927), remains an interesting historical document. The standard edition of Behn's works is that edited by Montague Summers, *The Works of Aphra Behn,* 6 vols. (1915; repr. New York: Benjamin Blom, 1967).
    12. (London, 1684).

This last will justifie my soft complaint,
While that may serve to lessen my constraint;
And without Blushes I the Youth persue,
When so much beauteous Woman is in view.
Against thy Charms we struggle but in vain
With thy deluding Form thou giv'st us pain,
While the bright Nymph betrays us to the Swain.
In pity to our Sex sure thou wer't sent,
That we might Love, and yet be Innocent:
For no sure Crime with thee we can commit;
Or if we shou'd—thy Form excuses it.
For who, that gathers the fairest Flowers believes
A Snake lies hid beneath the Fragrant Leaves.
    Thou beauteous Wonder of a different kind,
Soft *Cloris* with the dear *Alexis* join'd;
When e'r the Manly part of thee, wou'd plead
Thou tempts us with the Image of the Maid,
While we the noblest Passions do extend
The love to *Hermes, Aphrodite* the friend.

If Clarinda's "weak" and "feminine" characteristics are insuffi-
ciently noble to evoke the superlatives of praise that are more appropriately addressed to a "Youth," then that very appellation lifts the
constraints on a woman-loving female in pursuit of her courtship.
The beloved's combination of masculine with female characteristics, the Maid and the Youth, the nymph and the swain, confers a sexual freedom on the lover, who can argue that friendship alone is addressed to the woman, while the erotic attraction is reserved for the
masculine component of her beloved androgyne. This makes their
love "innocent." Further, as we have seen, two women together can
commit no "Crime," but *if* they can, Behn argues with sophistical
Donnean wit, Clarinda's "Form excuses it." Katherine Philips relies
on her lover's "design" as the basis for the love that can be "innocent."
But Aphra Behn goes even further. Here Clarinda is not merely ob-
servably a female. As the Neoplatonic courtly beloved, her "Form"
partakes of the ideal forms of the universe, desire for which refines
the erotic to the highest plane of spiritual love, a morally acceptable transformation of mere physical attraction that might otherwise
offend.
    The serpent among the flowers imagery is a standard allusion to

the phallic, with Edenic associations of sin. But the "different kind" who is the beloved in this poem clearly mitigates against any aspects of sinfulness by allowing the speaker (in a multilayered and witty pun) to extend her love to Hermes, and her friendship to Aphrodite in a socially acceptable construction of their passionate attachment. Behn's argument here is reminiscent of Shakespeare's response to the "master mistress" of his "passion" in Sonnet 20, where the speaker distinguishes between the androgynous youth's physical attributes designed "for women's pleasure" and the kind of love that may be appropriately shared between men: "Mine be thy love, and thy love's use their treasure" (14). We can read Behn's poem as the speaker's justification of her own approach to a forbidden beloved. But Clarinda is no traditionally passive maiden fair. She is the one who, the title states, "made love" to the speaker, and, in the last quatrain, her "Manly part . . . wou'd plead" while her "Image of the Maid" tempts. Clarinda, therefore, may also be seen as the initiator of their sexual activity, with the speaker justifying her own response in reaction to the public sexual mores of her time. This reciprocal construction of the poem may suggest the mutuality of a lesbian relationship that rejects the domination and subordination patterns of traditional heterosexual roles.

Behn's verse entertainment, "Selinda and Cloris," portrays a reciprocal relationship between women as unparalleled. It includes both physical and intellectual attraction, friendship and sexuality. Cloris "will sing, in every Grove, / The Greatness of your Mind," to which Selinda responds "And I your Love" (74–76). They trade verses and sing together in a presentation of the traditional pastoral speaker as poet, lover, singer, and shepherd:

> And all the Day,
> With Pride and Joy,
> We'll let the Neighbr'ing Shepherds see,
> That none like us,
> Did e'er Express,
> The heights of Love and Amity.
>
> (77–82)

This celebration of the female lovers' mutual joy in a variant on the traditional masque of Hymen presents in song and dance a formal dramatic closure that emphasizes the eroticism of the women's relationship in a conventional representation that also may serve to disguise it.

Two other poems addressing women as lovers or potential lovers are also interesting. In each case, the combination of direct statement and literary convention highlights the erotic content of the verse. In "To My Lady Morland at Tunbridge," Behn employs the customary compliment to the beautiful woman, but expresses also a womanly concern for virginity. In a reversal of convention, the speaker's concern is for the chastity of the lover rather than that of the beloved, "A Virgin-Heart you merit, that ne'er found / It could receive, till from your Eyes, the *Wound*" (47–48). Behn was sufficiently interested in the unidentified woman whose eyes struck hers, or in the poem itself, to rewrite it as "To Mrs. Harsenet, on the Report of a Beauty, which she went to see at Church." Carola Harsnett Morland seems, in this case, to have been Behn's audience rather than the subject of the poem, and Behn writes to her openly of her physical attraction to another woman. In "Verses design'd by Mrs. A. Behn to be sent to a fair Lady, that desir'd she would absent herself to cure her Love. Left Unfinished," the audience is clearly the beloved, and the content of the poem as well as the title indicates that this love is unrequited, "The more I strugl'd to my Grief I found / My self in *Cupid's* Chains more surely bound" (18–19). Eros is clearly a factor in the lack of fulfillment this poem conveys.

The complexity of Behn's verse—its logical argument, pastoral and courtly conventions, biblical and classical allusions, and social comment—epitomizes the disguise that reveals meaning. Such eloquent masking allows the audience to go away satisfied that no breach of decorum has been made. It permits us to deny, dismiss, or marginalize that which we do not wish to acknowledge, and exempts the poet from social condemnation while bestowing critical acclaim for her ingenuity.[13] Just as in society the conventional polite fiction disguises true feeling, in literature conventional representations of friendship,

---

13. For a discussion of how Behn employs this technique to create a double perspective on rape and seduction in her most famous poem, "The Disappointment," see my essay, "Not Since Sappho."

courtly romance, and female androgyny may mask true meaning. In a male-dominated society, with a male-oriented literature, women authors who chose to write honestly about important issues in women's lives (and sexual issues may be at the core of these) needed to convey their experiences in ways that express meaning on more than one level simultaneously. By using conventions as maskings, invoking all the connotations of masquing as play, Katherine Philips and Aphra Behn present alternative views of sexuality that are still considered taboo. It is time for us as readers at least to acknowledge the lesbian content in these works. The real question is not how innocent were they, but how innocent are we?

Catherine Gimelli Martin

Demystifying Disguises
Adam, Eve, and the Subject of Desire

One of the chief innovations in Milton's conception of paradise is his frank acceptance of desire as an essential and inalienable attribute of the human condition. Free of "dishonest shame," Adam and Eve need neither the "mere shows of seeming pure" (4.313–16) nor any of the other "troublesome disguises which wee wear" (4.740).[1] Yet not merely the "Hypocrites austere" the poet condemns for "defaming as impure what God declares / Pure," but many modern readers also question the innocence of this portrayal of uninhibited "connubial Love" (4.743–46). What *seems* to be "free to all" (4.746–47)—desire— may not *be* free and, in fact, has been interpreted as something less than pure and more than patriarchal, as the mystified voice of patriarchy itself.[2]

In fact, though Adam demanded, and God seemed to grant, a consort fit "to participate / All rational delight" (8.390–91), our first view of the human pair suggests that they are unequal, "as thir sex not equal seem'd" (4.296). However, since this observation is conveyed not only through the potentially misleading verb of "seeming," but actually through the eyes of Satan himself, many of the poem's more

1. All quotations from *Paradise Lost* are taken from the Merritt Y. Hughes, ed., *John Milton, Complete Poems and Major Prose* (New York: Odyssey Press, 1957).
2. This view can be traced to Virginia Woolf's *A Room of One's Own*, which seems to have been a primary influence upon the version developed by Sandra M. Gilbert and Susan Gubar in *The Madwoman in the Attic: The Woman Writer and the Nineteenth-Century Imagination* (New Haven: Yale University Press, 1979), see esp. 187–247.

sympathetic readers have been inclined to reject these "appearances" as deceptive.[3] Yet unfortunately for this line of defense, all else that Satan observes about our "Grand Parents" turns out to be accurate not only from his own but from the narrator's point of view. If we are to dispute the inequality he attributes to Eve, then we must doubt both that she and Adam are "Lords of all," since they only *seem* so, and also suppose that Satan's gaze is no more correct in observing how they are *formed* than how they seem. Furthermore, although both male and female merely *seem* worthy of the image of their maker, it is their "seeming" to reflect this image that allows them to be "plac't" in "true filial freedom," while their purported inequality is reinforced by the description of Eve being "*form'd*" for "softness" and "sweet attractive grace," Adam "for contemplation . . . and valor." Finally, since Satan's observations prove especially reliable whenever his success is at stake, and since his observations here are not only useful to his plans but mixed with an unfeigned if ambivalent sense of admiration, it seems most plausible to assume that not merely his torment but his gaze is sharpened as he spies upon the pair, seeing

> Two of far nobler shape erect and tall,
> Godlike erect, with native Honor clad
> In naked Majesty seem'd Lords of all,
> And worthy seem'd, for in thir looks Divine
> The image of thir glorious Maker shone,
> Truth, Wisdom, Sanctitude severe and pure,
> Severe, but in true filial freedom plac't;
> Whence true autority in men; though both
> Not equal, as thir sex not equal seem'd;
> For contemplation hee and valor form'd,
> For softness shee and sweet attractive Grace,
> He for God only, shee for God in him.
> (4.288–99)

Whatever the conflicting connotations of the verbs in this passage, their ultimate effect is to confirm the ironically appropriate inconsis-

3. Prominent examples of this form of apologetic can be found in James Grantham Turner, *One Flesh: Paradisal Marriage and Sexual Relations in the Age of Milton* (Oxford: Clarendon Press, 1987), 266–67; and David Aers and Bob Hodge, "'Rational Burning': Milton on Sex and Marriage," *Literature, Language and Society in England, 1580–1680* (Dublin: Gill and McMillan, 1981), 143–46.

tency of Satan's gaze, a gaze not fundamentally different from our own. Sharing some of his dis-ease but also his awe, we are thus led into a paradisal paradox without any "seeming" resolution.

At the heart of this paradox lie the unresolved questions of whether Eve's weaker attributes can be reconciled with her full reflection of God's image, and whether her belatedness also implies a secondariness in dignity and power. The centrality of these issues is further stressed by the fact that the observation of her inherent "softness" is immediately followed and seemingly summarized by the most decisive statement of the difference between the two, their sequential and apparently subordinationist creation, "He for God only, Shee for God in Him." If this difference is taken literally, what, if anything, can remain of their "true filial freedom"; does it not thereby become an empty technicality, or even a covert form of domination that, as Christine Froula concludes, not only "transsexualizes" Eve's autonomous desire, but also serves as a means of "silencing and voiding . . . female creativity"?[4] However, like the defense of Edenic desire that would dismiss Satan's "seeming" point of view entirely, an unproblematic acceptance of this point of view—which requires dismissing Eve entirely—raises as many problems as it resolves. Like a large number of the solutions proposed both by Milton's detractors and his defenders, Froula's account omits many of the epic's actual ambiguities by drawing upon inherited assumptions about the "orthodoxly" Puritan, patriarchal poet and, consequently, about the uniform, didactic purpose supposedly informing what is actually an unconventional, evolutionary epic.[5] Yet just as surely as Milton's Eden contrasts with the

4. "When Eve Reads Milton: Undoing the Canonical Economy," *Critical Inquiry* 10 (1983): 338.

5. Criticism can be generally divided into three mutually opposing camps on this question: feminist scholars, Milton's "neo-Christian" apologists, and a third group, some members of which (like David Aers and Bob Hodge) have attached Empson's "neo-Christian" label to the latter but are not themselves as dismissive of Eve's authority as the former. See Aers and Hodge, "'Rational Burning.'" Stanley Fish's *Surprised by Sin: The Reader in Paradise Lost* (Berkeley: University of California Press, 1971) persuasively records without reducing the evolution of the poem's "constructive" tensions and paradoxes, although as William Kerrigan remarks, Fish has an unfortunate tendency to *re-allegorize* (and thus re-stabilize) the poem's dialectic. See *The Sacred Complex: The Psychogenesis of Paradise Lost* (Cambridge: Harvard University Press, 1983), 98–99. From a different perspective, Christopher Hill has forcefully refuted the myth of Milton as orthodox Puritan poet in *Milton and the English Revolution* (London: Faber and Faber, 1977).

conventionally static Paradise, his portrayal of the "yet sinless" Adam and Eve resists the conventional treatment by emphasizing the constant alteration, development, and reciprocity of capacities that belong at once to general human subjects and to specific male and female prototypes.[6]

Thus any atemporal reading of this "allegory of desire" tends to ignore how the poem exploits traditional, even courtly models of male and female subjectivity only to subvert them, just as it exploits Edenic gates and boundaries primarily to subordinate *them* to individual choice. As Adam's "sudden apprehension" reveals in the aftermath of Eve's "tainted" dream, even Satan's most forceful incursions into Eden can easily be undone by the willing subject: "Evil into the mind of God or Man / May come and go, so unapprov'd, and leave / No spot or blame behind" (5.117–19). Similarly, God's provisions for "advent'rous Eve" are not only ambiguous but also ultimately impermanent. Although she is initially depicted as the vine to Adam's elm, she later proves more of a quester, at least in the physical, heroic sense, than he is, while he takes on the guiding and corrective functions that Spenser would assign a feminine "conscience" or soul like Una's. In this way not only are both sexes "transsexualized," but the substitutions and transferences of this process are never stabilized into a new hierarchy. A dialectic of assertion and subversion is finally the *most* characteristic element of the landscape and life of this paradise; and in spite of the intimate connections between the former and the latter, no permanent alteration in matter or spirit ever occurs that is not subject to the reversal implicit in the free act of the desiring subject. Hence, lacking Eve's permission, Satan proves no Archimago; he can impose on her only the most transitory and ultimately unreal loss, a mere inquietude (5.10–11). Correspondingly, since all Edenic boundaries exist primarily to mark the threshold of choice, not of purity or contamination, its gender roles like its other "barriers" characteristically remain "virtue proof" *because*—not *in spite of*—the potentially "errant" suggestions that surround them.[7]

6. See Barbara Lewalski, "Innocence and Experience in Milton's Eden," in *New Essays on Paradise Lost,* ed. Thomas Kranidas (Berkeley: University of California Press, 1969), 86–117, esp. 94–101.

7. See Diane Kelsey McColley, *Milton's Eve* (Urbana: University of Illinois Press, 1983), esp. 110–86; McColley extols Eve for the seriousness of her vocation, sense of

For these as well as a number of related reasons, the paradisal paradox can only be untangled by emphasizing that although the epic portrayal of gender (as of all physical appearances) grants each a power and a dignity of their own, the poem's characteristic mode of emblematic outline and qualification, statement and revision, ultimately depicts Eve's subjection to Adam's authority as more apparent than real. "Impli'd" but not coerced, even the most fundamental precept of her submission—that it be "requir'd with gentle sway"—remains open to her own as well as to Adam's interpretation. In fact, the multiple meanings of "requir'd" underscore the ambiguity of Milton's interpretation of biblical headship (1 Cor. 11:3–10; Eph. 5:23) in ways that make the verbal qualifications surrounding this "sway" far more meaningful than those surrounding "seeming."[8] To *require* can mean either to request *or* to exact, but since the "yet sinless" Eve is not always "submiss," the former, not the latter sense predominates. Similarly, her emblematic role as Adam's vine fails to limit her to a largely passive or decorative function; while she may (and does) choose simply to complement his "masculine" sturdiness, she equally may and does choose to surpass and enthrall this "elm." Yet these like the poem's other vicissitudes are no more "tainted" than Eve's dream. While many critics have condemned this along with other aspects of her supposedly coy or flirtatious femininity, the variety of her moods, like the various walks and "seasons" of Eden, and like the "sweet reluctant amorous delay" with which she responds to Adam, supply an ambiguity necessary not only to the representation of her own freedom, but to that which she shares with all God's creation. The

responsibility, and commitment to liberty even in the context of the separation scene (154). For Eve's more explicitly "male" characteristics as well as her transcendence of them in becoming Christ-like, see Aers and Hodge, "'Rational Burning,'" 141. For a more detailed account of Eve's dream, see my essay on "Ithuriel's Spear: Purity, Danger and Allegory at the Gates of Eden," forthcoming in *SEL* (Winter 1993).

8. The fact that Milton cites Paul throughout the Edenic books of the poem should not mislead us (as it has misled many) into thinking that he adheres to the literal letter of the epistles any more than he adhered to the literal letter of the gospels in his divorce tracts. For instance G. K. Hunter, whose account of the poem's gender relations is in most respects a responsible one, feels that the relation between Adam and Eve can be simply described as the Pauline mystery of the union of man and wife as "the mind and the body, the head and the limbs." This ultimately affords a somewhat reductive (as well as narrowly traditional) formulation of the cluster of meanings that actually surround "Contemplation" and "Grace" (*Paradise Lost* [London: George Allen and Unwin, 1980], 194–95).

conditionality of her response and its complex potential for acceptance, withdrawal, or both, is the source and warrant of its independence as well as of its "attractive grace." Significantly, then, while
J. Hillis Miller objects to Eve's admixture of "coy submission" and
"modest pride" (4.305–10), qualities that for him suggest a "wantonness" too experienced for innocence, he cannot help noting that it
effectively places "her above Adam or outside his control and identifies her with Milton's independent power of poetry. Eve's curly tendrils imply independence as well as subjection."[9]

Yet if these observations cast considerable doubt upon Froula's charge
that "Eve is not a self, a subject at all; she is rather a substanceless
image, a mere 'shadow' without object until the voice unites her to
Adam," in some respects the human pair *does* appear to be separate
and not equal in a way that clearly implies Eve's inferiority.[10] Although both receive "true autority" in reflecting their maker's "Truth,
Wisdom, Sanctitude severe and pure," Adam seems the more exact
copy, as the contemplation of "His fair large Front and Eye" declare.
As noted above, Eve's gifts seem considerably less: softness, sweetness, attractiveness and Grace, even if the latter is taken to include
spiritual as well as physical gifts. If this in turn implies a relay system
of sexual authority and desire whereby Adam is made for God and
Eve for God-in-him, the "part-ness" of his partner can in fact be taken
as literally as Froula does. Must Eve interpret her creator only through
Adam, or even worship him only through him—a seemingly idolatrous possibility? Furthermore, if she independently understands the

9. "How Deconstruction Works: *Paradise Lost*, IV, 304–8," *New York Times Maga-
zine,* February 9, 1986: 25. Critics of this and related passages are, as I suggest, legion,
although William Empson somewhat characteristically regarded Milton's depiction of
Edenic sexuality "a splendid bit of nerve." A convenient overview of this and of other less
enthusiastic responses appears in Edward Le Comte, *Milton and Sex* (New York: Columbia University Press, 1978), esp. 92. However, it is important to observe that since these
views tend to center around Eve's aggressive role as active sexual partner and wedded
"temptress" (a variation of the "wedded virgin" paradox that appeals to the early Milton;
see "On the Morning of Christ's Nativity," 3), they actually supply evidence of the *anti*-
patriarchal bias of the poem. Of course, feminist critics are disturbed by these paradoxes
for different reasons, generally viewing Eve's behavior a dishonest manipulation of male
desire. A more positive (and I think accurate) appraisal of the same facts can be found in
William Kerrigan and Gordon Braden's view of Paradise as "depend[ing] upon a wise
management of temptation"; see "Milton's Coy Eve: *Paradise Lost* and Renaissance Love
Poetry," *ELH* 53, no. 1 (1986): 42.
10. "When Eve Reads Milton," 328.

will of the "presence Divine" directly, why does she so often need Adam's guidance, even in interpreting her own dream? In order accurately to define the nature of Eve's "subjection" to the God-in-him and the nature of a difference posed as a series of continuities-within-difference—as Eve's loose tendrils, for instance, at once repeat and modify the "manly clusters" of Adam's hair—we must then turn to the archetypal descriptions of awakening life to which Froula also turns: Eve's creation narrative in book 4, and Adam's parallel narrative in book 8. Only here and in what follows can we discover the cumulative effect of comparing Adam to Eve as contemplation to Grace, as clusters to tendrils, truth to quest, and finally, as vision to revision—comparisons that on at least three occasions relate them not only to each other, but to Raphael and finally to the whole heavenly order.

Although Eve relates the story of her awakening consciousness first, this fact need not, as several feminist critics remind us, grant it any kind of priority.[11] First and last, like "Great / Or Bright infers not Excellence" (8.90–91), as Raphael is at some pains to teach Adam. And while Adam finally understands what Eve earlier had "suddenly apprehended," that "to know / That which before us lies in daily life, / Is the prime Wisdom" (8.192–94), Raphael's implicit approval of her reliance on experience over abstraction, like his mild disapproval of Adam's more abstract "roving," fails wholly to elevate her form of apprehension over his.[12] As book 9 will make abundantly clear, not only do both modes have their dangers, but each is tied to clear-cut sexual differences that Raphael's ritual hailing of the pair reinforces. Playing upon his name, Raphael greets Adam as more than clay, as a creature fit to invite "Spirits of Heaven" (5.372–75). Eve is on the

11. Mary Nyquist is particularly clear on this point in "Gynesis, Genesis, Exegesis, and the Formation of Milton's Eve," in *Cannibals, Witches, and Divorce: Estranging the Renaissance,* ed. Marjorie Garber (Baltimore: Johns Hopkins University Press, 1987), 147–209.

12. Although it by no means *devalues* her experiential or even her explicitly domestic gifts, either. As William Shullenberger remarks, Raphael's admonition "directs Adam's attention to the existential fullness and immediacy which we have been led, by the eighth book of the poem, to associate with Eve. . . . Eve *is* Eden, and the poetry of pristine astonishment appropriate to that paradisal place is hers." A fuller discussion of this aspect of Eve is elaborated below; Shullenberger's comments appear in "Wrestling with the Angel: *Paradise Lost* and Feminist Criticism," *Milton Quarterly* 23, no. 3 (1986): 73–74.

other hand hailed as a type of Mary, "Mother of Mankind, whose fruitful Womb / Shall fill the World" (5.388–89). The implication here is that Adam is intrinsically closer to the Spirits of Heaven, and Eve to her nursery, for whose "tendance" she leaves the discourse on astronomy (8.45–47). Hence once again the apparent mutuality of gender roles appears to dissolve into what Froula terms the "ontological hierarchy" of *Paradise Lost*.[13]

However, this hierarchy is again modified or "corrected" by Raphael's narration of Satan's fall. The moral of this story is that "filial freedom" is opposed to the rigid "Orders and Degrees" that Satan upholds in the spurious name of "liberty" (5.792–93) and depends instead upon an acceptance of difference. Since Adam's role in regard to Eve is far less priestly or exalted than that which Satan envied in the Son, both humans uttering prayers "unanimous" (4.736), we must then question if their difference can also be a form of freedom, if not of equality as we have come to know it. This problem is magnified by the tremendous evolution in recent concepts of equality. As Joseph Wittreich points out in *Feminist Milton,* earlier female readers were likely to interpret gender differences as "evidence of distinction, not inequality"; early feminists, too, generally supported a concept of male and female mutuality in which "ideally their different qualities blend." For modern feminists after Freud, however, difference signifies domination. Thus for Froula, the whole point of the temporal priority of Eve's birth narration is to subsume it in Adam's; to inculcate the idea that "Eve can only 'read' the world in one way, by making herself the mirror of the patriarchal authority of Adam." The mothering waters of the lake to which Eve is intuitively drawn, like her own reflected image, are thus canceled by the "invisible voice" that leads her to Adam, the voice at once of God / Adam / Milton and Patriarchy.[14]

Yet as suggested above, this interpretation fails to account for the full scope of the mirroring process that connects Adam to Eve as vitally as Eve to her lake. In this process a recognition of difference *precedes* one of continuity, which in both narratives is represented as

---

13. "When Eve Reads Milton," 330.
14. Wittreich, *Feminist Milton* (Ithaca: Cornell University Press, 1987), 84; Froula, "When Eve Reads Milton," 329–30.

a gradual series of differentiations and corrections. The uniformity of this process is underscored by the fact that Eve's awakening response is *not* in fact to her own reflection, but like Adam's, to the questions surrounding her existence: "what I was, when thither brought, and how" (4.452). Her next response is to a "murmuring sound / Of waters" that brings her to "a liquid Plain . . . Pure as th' expanse of Heav'n" (4.453–56). Already aware of the existence of the Heavens, which symbolize the mental orientation of both human genders, her fascination with their replication both beneath and above her then causes her to seek an answering existence. While unlike Adam she finds this in the form of her own reflection, which Narcissus-like responds with "looks / Of sympathy and love" (4.464–65), Eve is an unfallen *anti*-Narcissus who, as she later acknowledges, is merely "unexperienc't" (4.457). Unlike the conceited creature who prefers self-absorption to another's love, but like the child of Lacan's mirror stage, initially incapable of separating self (the form recumbent on the green bank) from Other (reflection, watery womb, or Mother), and *like* Adam, she needs an external stimulus, God's voice, to help her make this distinction and hail her into the symbolic order. In this respect Eve provides an archetypal model of awakening consciousness fully as much as Adam does; her "hailing" into the symbolic order, like his, initiates her dis- and re-union with a creature like herself ("whose image thou art," 4.472), but *without* any confusion or shadow-barrier between them (4.470).[15]

Entering the landscape of names/language/difference, Eve thus gains a new title and position, "Mother of human Race" (4.475). This title, along with the acceptance and the renunciation it implies, exalts more than it limits her, since it allies her with the Son. Like him, she becomes an example of the interdependence of growth and sacrifice:

15. For a detailed description of the ways in which Milton reworks the Narcissus myth, see Kenneth J. Knoespel, "The Limits of Allegory: Textual Expansion of Narcissus in *Paradise Lost*," *Milton Studies* 22 (1986): 79–99. Both Kerrigan in *Sacred Complex* and Nyquist in "Gynesis, Genesis, Exegesis" find prototypes of Freudian psychology in *Paradise Lost;* the poem was, after all, on the list of Freud's ten favorite books (*Standard Edition*, trans. James Strachey, 11:245, quoted by Kerrigan, *Sacred Complex*, 286). Nyquist also argues (albeit in a less favorable sense than Kerrigan), that the epic makes possible the conditions of both Freudian and Lacanian psychoanalysis (201–2). Finally, Shullenberger ("Wrestling with the Angel," 81) fruitfully contrasts Eve's constructive use of the mirror stage with Satan's destructive "amnesia" about his own origins.

both are able to reflect the Father's creative design only by renounc-
ing self-love, yet both are appropriately rewarded by achieving the
potential to produce "Multitudes like thyself," not merely like the
Father or Adam. Hence, just as the Son's descent "to assume / Man's
Nature" neither lessens nor degrades his own (3.303–4) but grants
him even greater equality with God, "equally enjoying / God-like
fruition" (3.306–7), so Eve can enjoy "God-like fruition" only by quit-
ting her virgin, self-mirroring independence. In return she, too, gains
restoration and exaltation within an expanded mirroring process, the
potential for limitless reflexivity in the space of Edenic marriage, an
exchange of desire that is alone fecund.[16]

Hence the poet's striking revision, in fact reversal, of the Narcissus
myth also illuminates his use of pagan images to describe Eve in another controversial passage, when Adam on Eve

> Smil'd with superior Love, as *Jupiter*
> On *Juno* smiles, when he impregns the Clouds
> That shed *May* Flowers; and press'd her Matron lip
> With kisses pure . . .
>
> (4.499–502)

This, too, suggests that love, like life itself, can be created only by the
alternation of similarity with difference—as when God "conglob'd /
Like things to like, the rest to several place / Disparted" (7.239–41).
Extending the metaphor, Adam and Eve may be understood as a
primally innocent Jove and Juno "disparted" from all negative connotation, representatives of the masculine and feminine principles of
sunbeam and cloud, male seed and female mist mingling in a flower-
like, gentle form of "sway." The sun shines down on the cloud for
purposes of propagation inseparable from sexual delight, but inseparable also from the mysterious, asexual process of equality-within-
difference imaged by Father and Son. Yet here we must once again

16. Thus as Kerrigan remarks, "Femininity symbolizes the something 'more' in
Christ, the epistrophe of voluntary love that makes him exceed a mere echo of his creator.
For Christ, as for angels and men, femininity constitutes the sphere of freedom" (*Sacred
Complex*, 187–88). Kerrigan's insights into gender as well as into the monist continuum
of the poem are at times brilliant, but too often his work seems to suffer from the assumptions of a somewhat dated Freudian ego psychology; as I suggest, a Lacanian model
seems more immediately applicable to this dimension of the poem.

address our recurrent problem; if Eve is represented as Son/Juno/cloud, the necessary principle of reception and nurture, then perhaps, as Mary Nyquist proposes, her desire is after all secondary: her-story actually a his-story of learning the "value of submitting desire to the paternal law." Continuing to weigh these stories, then, as to whether they blend into a kind of ur-story, we must next turn to Adam's reminiscences to Raphael in book 8 to see what actual limitations are imposed on Eve's desires by their different births.[17]

Adam's first sensation, unlike Eve's, is tactile. While it is natural enough for him first to feel the sunlight on his skin, given that he awakes in sunlight, Eve in shade (4.450–51; 8.254–55), this difference again suggests that Adam is to Eve as strong "male" light of the Sun to shaded "female" light of the Moon. However, the passage primarily serves to emphasize that Adam's natural affiliation, like Eve's, is with the heavens; the sun causes him to look upward much as the reflection of the heavenly expanse led her to gaze downward. In both cases a sensation of touch or sound motivates their sight, and causes them to assume the "Godlike erect" inclination they share with the angels. This is the essence not of Adam's but of *their* kind, which "upright with Front Serene" displays a "Sanctity of Reason" (7.508–9) made "to correspond with Heav'n" (7.510–11). Like the Son worshiping equally "with heart and voice and eyes," the love they render the Father like that they give each other is the exclusive prerogative of neither. Yet as the contrast between their awakening in shade or sunlight and then gazing either upward or downward also suggests, the organs of "voice and eyes" are experienced differently by male and female. Eve is led upon her awakening from sounds to sights, and thence back again to the invisible voice. Adam, on the other hand, is led from tactile sensations to gaze at the "ample Sky," and finally to

17. C. S. Lewis, on the one hand, laments the openly erotic suggestions of the preceding lines, "half her swelling Breast / Naked met his under the flowing Gold / Of her loose tresses hid," while feminists, on the other, deplore Eve's "submissive Charms." Further objections have been raised by Aers and Hodge in "'Rational Burning,'" 149, some of which ("Did she 'press' back?") seem frivolous, although others clearly are not. However, an underlying problem in this line of argument is rarely addressed, which is that any doctrinairely egalitarian or "politically correct" form of Eros generally fails to maintain a genuinely erotic interest. Yet, as Kerrigan and Braden remark in "Milton's Coy Eve," Eve ironically *benefits* here from the libertine tradition, which affirms "the value of modesty and withholding" (41). Nyquist, "Gynesis, Genesis, Exegesis," 203.

see a "shape Divine" in his dream (8.295). So marked is his preference for the organ of sight that he even represents the "liquid Lapse of
murmuring Streams" as what he *saw* (8.261–63).[18]

Yet with an alternation characteristic of the poem, Adam's next
impulse reasserts his analogy to Eve. Seeking a creature with an answering face, he searches among all

> Creatures that liv'd, and mov'd, and walk'd, or flew,
> Birds on the branches warbling: all things smil'd,
> With fragrance and with joy my heart o'erflow'd.
> Myself I then perus'd, and Limb by Limb
> Survey'd . . . .
> But who I was, or where, or from what cause,
> Knew not;
>
> (8.264–68, 269–70)

First stopping to survey himself, Adam's attempt to find an answering
reflection of life does not then focus, as does Eve's, on his own image,
although his motive seems the same: to find a living being who will
return his gaze and fill his void. Moreover, his attempts like Eve's are
at once enabling and impairing; although he immediately perceives
his difference from the creatures who smile back at him, and thus
passes more spontaneously from the Imaginary to the Symbolic stage,
his difficulty in locating the Law's source—the Father himself—is actually greater than hers. Attempting to answer the questions that also
trouble Eve, "who I was, or where, or from what cause," he appeals
to the Sun and Earth: "ye that live and move, fair Creatures, tell / Tell,
if ye saw, how came I thus, how here?" (8.276–77). Eve's affinity both
with the sounds of creation and her own body is, taken as a whole,
inadequate; but Adam's sense of difference and alienation is, if anything, more so. The *natural* response of neither is sufficient to identify themselves *or* their creator; without direct revelation from God to
Eve through his voice, to Adam through his vision, both would become idolaters either of Mother Goddess or Father Sun.

Thus, these narratives show Adam and Eve erring in related but

---

18. Here Adam transfers what might have *begun* as a preeminently auditory experience, as stressed by the alliteration of "liquid Lapse" and its association with "murmuring," back into the visual field of *seeing* the lapsing current.

inverse directions. Adam attempts to "read" nature sheerly through tactile and visual stimuli and through analytic comparisons that allow him more rapidly to develop his symbolic consciousness. He questions his existence through rational contemplation, which allows him to conclude that his being is "Not of myself; by some great Maker then, / In Goodness and power preeminent" (8.278–79). Eve is also led to make comparisons but relies more on auditory sensations and on analogies rather than differences between inner and outer, higher and lower forms: her interest in the lake is prompted by the fact that it seems both a "liquid plain" (4.455) and "another Sky" (4.459). Yet if Adam is led by his sight, both physical and rational, into a more immediate entrance into the rational-symbolic order, Eve is equally adept in intuiting that her existence is alternately material and spiritual, just as the watery elements of earth and sky are alternately watery plain and fluid heavenly expanse. Neither Adam *nor* Eve is able to perceive the Deity unaided; God must intercept *both* Adam's confused search ("thus I call'd, and stray'd I knew not whither," 8.283) and Eve's pining with "vain desire." Adam is more dramatically depicted as seeking and conversing with his Maker, but only in a dream, and dream and voice are generally regarded as equivalent modes of prophetic knowledge. In any case, these modes reverse in books 9 and 10, where God speaks to Eve in a dream, to Adam through the prophetic voice of Michael.[19]

Since analogy as well as difference is stressed in these scenes, it is not surprising that the first decree of the "shape Divine" is strictly parallel, if gender specific. The Father names Eve "Mother of human Race" and Adam the "First Man, of Men innumerable ordain'd / First Father" (8.297–98). Following this, it is true, Adam is explicitly instructed in the uses and prohibitions of his garden, initiating a dialogue between Adam and his creator not later granted Eve. We must assume, however, that Adam instructs Eve in their joint authority over Eden, since Eve unequivocally considers the garden her responsibility, and since God declares both "authors to themselves in all" (3.122). Most significantly, neither Adam nor Eve knows God by

19. For an important commentary on the mythic significance of this reversal, see Northrop Frye, "The Revelation to Eve," in *"Paradise Lost": A Tercentenary Tribute,* ed. Balachandra Rajan (Toronto: University of Toronto Press, 1969).

any name more explicit than "Whom thou sought'st I am," an obvious variant of the Mosaic "I am that I am." Adam's question concerning intimate address, "O by what Name, . . . how may I / Adore thee" (8.357, 359–60), is never answered; Adam and Eve are to know the "author" through whom they become authors of mankind only through verbs of being and through spontaneous dialogue, listening, response, and vision. The Puritan poet carefully resists any suggestion of Adam's priestly functions in regard either to divine worship or to the prohibitions this authority could sanction. Nor is God's fatherly instruction of Eve actually less than of Adam, even if it occurs off-stage. As Adam describes his first sight of her to Raphael,

> On she came,
> Led by her Heav'nly Maker, though unseen,
> And guided by his voice, nor uninform'd
> Of nuptial Sanctity and marriage Rites:
> Grace was in her steps, Heav'n in her Eye,
> In every gesture dignity and love.
>
> (8.484–89)

With "Heav'n in her Eye" Adam must acknowledge Eve his sister as well as spouse, "one Flesh, one Heart, one Soul" (8.499). The name he gives her, "Woman," is not her name in the personal but only in the generic sense; Adam has wit enough to recognize his own species. Eve's name is no more "Woman" than Adam's is "Man"; titles are hardly names. It is only by a considerable distortion of the text, then, that Froula claims that God "soothes Adam's fears of female power . . . by bestowing upon Adam 'Dominion' over the fruits of this creation through authorizing him to name the animals *and* Eve." Far from subtracting from her female power, Eve's auditory response to the symbolic order forms a necessary complement to Adam's visual mode.[20]

Yet even if we can assert that Adam lacks the complete authority over Eve that Froula claims he has, and if, by now, it is clear that their difference is one of degree and not of kind, a final charge of the feminist critique of the hierarchy of Edenic desire remains to be ad-

---

20. "When Eve Reads Milton," 332.

dressed. Eve's more guided transition from the Imaginary to the Symbolic stage, her greater reliance on the intuitive, responsive ear as opposed to Adam's rational, active eye, appear in fact to suggest that Milton, like Freud, traces a "progress in spirituality" that places the female sex on a lower evolutionary rung. And this objection could in fact be supported, had not the Christian poet set a much higher value than Freud upon the primacy of the Imaginary, which for him performs an intuitive, wholistic communion with the body of a universe he insists is divine, and had not Eve's greater access to this communion actually granted her a source of authority fully equivalent—and hence potentially even superior—to Adam's. In this respect Froula, too, must accord Eve abilities that are more than merely complementary; she remarks that while "Adam's need to possess Eve is usually understood as complemented by her need for his guidance, [yet] . . . Milton's text suggests a more subtle and more compelling source for this need: Adam's sense of inadequacy in face of what he sees as Eve's perfection."[21]

However, Froula sees Adam's "alienation from his body" and even from God not as parallel to the sense of inadequacy Eve also feels, but as the direct cause of his subjugation of her. This view is challenged by the fact that Eve's ability to arrange thoughts and words, not merely domestic delights, clearly surpasses Adam's in a way that he finds both sustaining and inspiring. In highly cadenced and evocative blank verse, she turns her love for him into what James Turner calls an "aria," eighteen lines that have "the grace and recapitulative pattern of an Elizabethan sonnet." The author and not merely the singer of the piece, her voice is as authentic as her verse original; she creates a form that claims Adam as the demystified object of her own desire. Not Adam's "coy mistress" forever eluding him on the banks of an Edenic Umber, *she* is the sonneteer praising him because "With thee conversing I forget all time." Inverting Marvell's clever carpe diem to his lady,

21. See, "When Eve Reads Milton," 338, where Froula observes that Milton's "silencing and voiding of female creativity" recalls "all the elements of Freud's 'progress in spirituality.'" For a related argument, see Nyquist, "Gynesis, Genesis, Exegesis." As Paul Stevens points out, for Milton the "imagination at its highest potential is not simply a necessary evil. . . . It is a God-given faculty which has a specific purpose in assisting man toward knowledge of his Maker . . . the *educated* imagination is the peculiar instrument of grace" ("Milton and the Icastic Imagination," *Milton Studies* 20 [1984]: 44). "When Eve Reads Milton," 331.

this lady seizes the day and the object of a desire to which she is also subject. Hierarchy is undermined by role reversal, which, as Turner notes, blurs "the usual division of faculties into 'male' and 'female'; . . . [Milton's] Eve is more logocentric and intelligent than the conventional treatment, and his Adam, even in his prime, more emotionally susceptible."[22]

Yet the implications of Eve's invention are broader still. She concludes her aria with a question suggested by the theme of her composition; tracing the course of an Edenic day, its "seasons and thir change" (4.640), she wonders what the purpose of the most mysterious of these changes, the procession of "glittering Star-light," might mean: "But wherefore all night long shine these, for whom / This glorious sight, when sleep hath shut all eyes?" (4.657–58). Adam is immediately aware both of the skill of her song and the importance of this question; addressing her as "Daughter of God and Man, accomplisht *Eve*" (4.661), his reply supplies "manly" balance to her poetic skill as he offers a "hymn" to God's providence. Yet neither here nor elsewhere does his authority silence Eve; it only complements hers. Further, his conjecture that the stars "shine not in vain" (4.674) is in turn supplanted by a higher authority, and what this authority reveals combines as it elevates the male and female responses to creation. Before informing them of the several possible arrangements of the universe and even hinting at the possibility of life on other planets (8.172–76), Raphael cautions that although experiential knowledge may at times exceed abstract, all forms of knowledge, in fact all life, are ultimately relative. Each should "Solicit not thy thoughts with matters hid" (8.167), but instead invest their energies in affairs closer to hand—not because of any divine prohibition or even because of the threat now posed by Satan, but because human understanding like the human body itself will be refined by obedience, so that in "tract of time" the human couple may become "Ethereal, as wee" (5.498–99). At this point they would enjoy not only the intuitive understanding of the angels, but also their fully unencumbered sexual freedom, which can "either Sex assume, or both" (1.424). Yet

22. *One Flesh,* 245 and 237, where Turner contrasts her aria with a fallen form of verse where love becomes "a specialized area or subcategory of experience, as it is in 'Court Amours.'"

Raphael also acknowledges that their present state is not lacking sufficient perfection that they might then actually prefer to continue their earthly existence (5.499–506); no simple value can be attached to the process of "rising" in and for itself.[23]

However, Raphael's final, private discourse with Adam also offers the most problematic representation of the poem's hierarchy of desire. Although seeming to agree with Adam in his opinion of Eve as "resembling less / His Image who made both, and less expressing / The character of that Dominion giv'n / Oe'r other Creatures" (8.543–46), he adds that Adam's ambivalence as to whether Eve corresponds to this, or to his other view of her "As one intended first, not after made / Occasionally" (8.555–56), lies in his own perceptions, not in Nature. Yet Raphael never precisely reveals what "Nature" dictates concerning Eve's role; he simply warns against "attributing overmuch to *things* less excellent" (8.565–66; emphasis supplied). Since these "things" refer neither to Eve nor to her accomplishments per se but only to her "fair outside" (7.569), Raphael suggests that Adam can best appreciate and guide her by weighing her merits against his. Even this vaguely patriarchal advice must, however, in turn be weighed against its broader context, one in which the entire discussion between Adam and Raphael mirrors those previously initiated between Adam and Eve. As the prelude to Eve's sonnet included a didactic statement of obedience, a summation of the Pauline doctrine of headship— "what thou bidd'st / Unargu'd I obey; so God ordains, / God is thy law, thou mine" (4.635–37)—so Adam now mimics Eve's procedure in conversing with Raphael. A statement of submission is followed by a tribute to Raphael's sensory powers—a tribute that similarly bestows the powers of the subject on their object. Just as Eve had deferred to

---

23. In "'Rational Burning,'" Aers and Hodge find true equality of desire only in the angelic state; yet if angels are Milton's "chief means of conceiving satisfactory sexual relations," they hardly seem to be his *only* means, as they assert (142–43). Sandra Gilbert even more radically misinterprets the nature of angelic bisexuality in claiming that the female gender is excluded from heaven; yet as Joan M. Webber has shown, evidence for this view is equally shaky. See "The Politics of Poetry: Feminism and *Paradise Lost*," *Milton Studies* 14 (1980): 3–24; Webber is responding to Sandra Gilbert's article, "Patriarchal Poetry and Women Readers: Reflections on Milton's Bogey," *PMLA* 93 (1978): 368–82. An even more trenchant critique of Gilbert's preference for a narcissistic Satan-hero who *exalts* rising at the expense of others (and a modification of Webber's view of Milton's God, 73) is offered by Shullenberger, "Wrestling with the Angel," 79.

254 Catherine Gimelli Martin

Adam by attributing her rich sensory experience of Eden, her "nursery," to his presence, by her example Adam now demonstrates his humility (which is also his authority) by granting Eve his first-born prerogatives of Wisdom, Authority, and Reason. The result of this exchange is simultaneously to exalt masculine and feminine dignity; Eve is its synthesis for him as he had been it for her. She now becomes a vision of masculine virtue in feminine form: "Greatness of mind and nobleness thir seat / Build in her loveliest" (8.557–58).

Still, like Raphael, the reader cannot immediately evaluate the full meaning of this transference, let alone how patriarchal, antipatriarchal, or even uxorious its assumptions may be, until it is tested against the background of Edenic gender relations as a whole. Here for the third time we have observed Adam and Eve performing a similar interchange, Eve responding, Adam recapitulating and interpreting her more spontaneous activity.[24] She first questioned the purposes and motions of the stars, a query that Adam elaborates and poses to Raphael (8.25–28), while a little earlier she had narrated her experience of creation to Adam, a story that so delights him that he then adopts it as a means of entertaining the angel. On the third occasion Eve set another pattern by first acknowledging the principle of marital headship, then giving Adam a verse account of the experiential value, greater than all of Eden, she found in his company; she made her gifts, her perceptual and poetic skill, a supreme tribute to him. Later Adam gives Raphael a similar acknowledgment of his "official" superiority, then adds an experiential account of the supreme value of his conversation, a "process of speech" that figuratively synthesizes

24. Thus as Barbara Lewalski observes, "Adam raises to higher perfection the several literary forms Eve invents. . . . In Milton's universe each individual is stimulated to intellectual and literary expression in relationship to and in conference with a superior. Eve is stimulated in this way by Adam, and Adam by Raphael" (*Paradise Lost and the Rhetoric of Literary Forms* [Princeton: Princeton University Press, 1985], 218–19). However, if accurate in outline, this reading unfortunately incorporates several erroneous assumptions: (1) that the relationship between Adam and Eve is an essentially one-way process, and thus (2) that instead of exchanging the role of "stimulating superior" (as Adam and Raphael do when the first man corrects the angel's narrowly Neoplatonic view of human sexuality), Adam provides the superior human role model in all things. As a result, she places Adam's conventional *aubade* above what she nevertheless describes as "Eve's exquisite, rhetorically complex love sonnet in Book Four" (200–201). This restrictive view of male and female gifts should be weighed against Earl Miner's less biased opinion of Eve's sonnet as the "highest moment of human lyricism in the entire poem." See "The Reign of Narrative in *Paradise Lost,*" *Milton Studies* 17 (1983): 16.

and transcends "masculine" and "feminine" gender traits. His compliment in fact paraphrases the very words that Eve had used to express her love for him. He tells Raphael,

> For while I sit with thee, I seem in Heav'n
> And sweeter thy discourse is to my ear
> Than Fruits of Palm-tree pleasantest to thirst
> And hunger both.
>
> (8.210–13)

While Adam recognizes Raphael's differing "Grace Divine" as superior just as clearly as he sees that Eve's difference from himself can imply some relative superiority or inferiority between them, at the same time he can do no better than follow her example. While for Eve "Nor grateful Ev'ning mild, nor silent Night / With this her solemn Bird, nor walk by Moon, / Or glittering Star-light mild, without thee is sweet" (4.654–56), now for Adam no fruits of Eden can supply the sweetness of Raphael's words. Significantly, their theoretical affinities here reverse, since Adam is more domestic and Eve more astronomical in her metaphors.

Whatever this reversal may mean in the abstract, the concrete result is the same. As in the Father's relation to the Son, submission merits exaltation and, more importantly, reciprocity. Orders exist to be broken and transformed: as in the "one first matter" Raphael describes, energy and light flow both upward and downward. Anything more rigid or circumscribed would disturb the harmonious intercourse of the universe, as Raphael in response acknowledges:

> Nor are thy lips ungraceful, Sire of men,
> Nor tongue ineloquent; for God on thee
> Abundantly his gifts hath also pour'd
> Inward and outward both, his image fair:
> . . . .
>   Nor less think wee in Heav'n of thee on Earth
> Than of our fellow servant, and inquire
> Gladly into the ways of God with Man:
> For God we see hath honor'd thee, and set
> On Man his Equal Love.
>
> (8.218–21, 224–28)

In this exchange, the discourse of "rational delight" is made the simultaneous prop and leveler of hierarchies; Adam can scarcely be as
superior to Eve as Raphael is to himself, and yet his graceful deference
merits acknowledgment of angel and man as "fellow servants" enjoying God's "Equal Love." In contrast, duplicitous self-promotion leads
Satan, like Adam and Eve after their fall, to bestiality. Nor is their
postlapsarian descent depicted as the effect of a divine curse upon
those who exceed hierarchical boundaries, but merely as the natural
and immediate outcome of Adam's failure correctly to apply Raphael's
advice. Instead of skillfully weighing Eve's gifts with his, which would
include balancing her more accurate interpretation of Raphael's instruction against his equally accurate intuition about Satan's most
likely strategy, Adam is distracted by a temporary loss of face that he
fails to see has little or nothing to do either with his true authority or
with Eve's true love for him.[25] Atypically yet fatally, his regard for her
sense of responsibility toward her garden, her determination, and her
well-reasoned (if over-confident) acceptance of trial as a concomitant
of Edenic life makes him lose his ability to direct and guide the admi-
rable qualities that, unmodified, like both their garden and his own
desire, "tend to wild." Yet if his error perhaps increases Eve's all-too-
human liability to err, it cannot be said to produce her fall unless all
we have seen of her, including God's pronouncement that *both* were
created "sufficient to have stood," is rendered meaningless. Rather,
Adam's failed conversation with Eve, his temporary but not-yet-tragic
loss of appreciation for their radical relativity, becomes truly tragic
only when Eve, like Adam overvaluing her momentary victory, chooses
to forsake successful conversation not merely with Adam but with
herself and her God. Indulging in a "process of speech" that is actually a process of rationalization, she begins to dream of synthesizing
and supplanting Adam's gift for abstract understanding with her own
for intuitive thinking and experimentation. Inevitably, this self-cen-
tered desire for rising leads her to overvalue the fallacious "evidence"
of the wily serpent/Satan. Then and only then does she develop a
sinful appetite for what is neither properly hers nor Adam's, the seem-

---

25. See Diana Benet's exemplary treatment of Adam's failure in "Abdiel and the Son
in the Separation Scene," *Milton Studies* 18 (1983): 129–43, esp. 138–39.

ingly effortless but ultimately illusory ascent that throughout the poem is shown to be the essence of all descent.[26]

Yet finally, the eternally authentic and not exclusively Edenic power of innocent desire is confirmed both because and in spite of loss of Eden. Self-knowledge and recognition of difference, the basis of both growth and exchange, are reestablished as the proper and in fact only channels of true union and communion between spiritual beings. And while both before and after the Fall this union is only temporary, this is because it must first be temporal, the result of free and rational choice in time, the mark of "Grace Divine." It is not God alone who raises his creatures "deifi'd" by his communion to "what highth thou wilt" (8.430–31), but Adam can merit and Raphael bestow this same equality. By precisely the same means, the human genders may alternately exalt one another, so that ideally each is fit both to initiate and "to participate / all rational delight" (8.390–91). Further, their capacity to do so directly follows from the fact that Eve is *not* the body to Adam's head nor the senses to his intelligence; as experience, beauty, hearing, Eve is analogous not merely to Christ, but to the poet himself. Milton can conceive her function in this way because he conceives poetry, like reason, as the necessary but not sufficient condition of Grace. Its sufficient condition depends neither exclusively upon Adam's more visual and analytic understanding nor upon Eve's auditory and intuitive imagination, but upon a process of "weighing" and blending both. This process of harmonizing her gifts with his is what Raphael recommends to Adam after showing him how dialectically to sift through his motives, and what allows Eve to initiate their recuperation after the Fall. Then, significantly, Eve again spontaneously intuits the necessity of weighing and accepting responsibility, while Adam's self-righteous sense of the betrayal of his "higher" functions

26. In this sense Eve rejects not merely true obedience but true love. In "Milton's Coy Eve," Kerrigan and Braden point out that "Love is a fragile knot woven of narcissism— the consummate pleasure of paradise, but equally the precondition of paradise lost" (47). However, one might add that the "fragile knot" contains both positive and negative narcissism, the latter a reductive form of the more inclusive or healthy version. Hence Eve is here not merely choosing her own image, which Kerrigan and Braden claim "was never abandoned," but actually a narrower and more intense—and not, as Eve thinks, thereby more exalted—reflection of it.

(as well as his emotional confusion) leads him into a momentary loss of all hope and even all remembrance of Raphael's subtle lessons.[27]

Thus the question of "whence true autority in men," in Milton's universe one among many variants of the question of "whence true autonomy," can be accurately resolved only by at once refining and broadening our understanding of the universal basis of "Union or Communion" (7.431), that semimysterious conversation in which difference, including the ultimate difference between God and his creation, is resolved in an act of complementarity inseparable from simultaneous Other and self-reflection. Autonomy hence becomes a metonymy of male and female gifts and desires that, in perfect balance, generates the synecdoche of divine intercourse and human marriage alike. Raphael counsels Adam (and his heirs) not to upset the balance of this exchange, which by resting upon an unstable and thus freely adaptable form of reflexivity, can achieve a liberating potential that is neither moderate nor conservative but extreme. Because in this system hierarchy is dependent upon temporal interpretation and initiative, not upon innate "natural dispositions," the inner harmony of its balance is at once subject to radical alternation and role reversal and to radical joy, the true analog of the heavenly union revealed/ concealed behind Raphael's rosy blush, "Love's proper hue" (8.619). Yet behind even this disguise are demystified glimpses—of an original sexual union precedent to original sin, of the unencumbered embraces of the angels, "Union of Pure with Pure/Desiring" (8.627–28), and of the mutual glorification of the Father and Son, whose balanced energies produce the spontaneous desire to exalt and multiply the Other, the *universal* desire that "to fulfill is all . . . Bliss" (6.729).

27. See Joseph Summers's influential account of the analogy between Eve and Christ in *The Muse's Method* (Cambridge: Harvard University Press, 1962), 175–85. In "The Revelation to Eve," Frye argues that in the later course of the epic a mother-dominated mythology of salvation comes to replace a father-dominated one, a view at least partially supported by Earl Miner's assessment that "Books IX and X constitute an Eviad" ("The Reign of Narrative in *Paradise Lost*," 20).

Paul G. Stanwood, Diana Treviño Benet, Judith Scherer Herz, and Debora Shuger

Excerpts from a Panel Discussion

Paul G. Stanwood

The lively and varied academic responses to the general theme of "Discourses of Desire" prove yet once more that everyone has something to say about sexuality. In the seventeenth century, Robert Burton addressed the subject of "love-melancholy" in his discourse about desire, remarking in *The Anatomy of Melancholy* of "what fires, torments, cares, jealousies, suspicions, fears, griefs, anxieties, accompany such as are in love" (3.4.2). The concern for and the treatment of these melancholic miseries afflict most persons and have both a universal and particular significance that could make Burton's great work the subject worthy of a universal synod.

When offered so broad a topic, however, most people naturally wish to focus narrowly on some special issue related to Renaissance England, probably an unfortunate and fortuitous limitation along linguistic lines. With an easy leap, therefore, sexuality may be variously defined; the term can describe almost any sort of human relationship, usually with some erotic dimension, for the language of love prefers neither nations nor special parties. Thus, Aretino is well known as one who describes certain sexual practices; and if he sets us in the appropriate mood, we may find that familiar locations, such as Donne's Twickenham garden, possess envious spiders that sting in erogenous places. To be sure, we should know already that Donne's customary spectator, as in "The Sun Rising," may remind us of our own voy-euristic pleasure.

Yet Petrarch and his situation in literary history and convention is largely absent from contemporary deliberations, the concern now, in fact, perhaps pointing to specific ways in which poets tried to avoid his influence. If Carew's relationship to the court of Henrietta Maria demanded that he establish his own personal identity, for example, with amatory circumstances calling for a practical cynicism and scorn for authority, then he would have wished deliberately to avoid "Petrar-chanism." But was not Carew also affected by the *précieux* and liber-tine poets? Should we not study Malherbe or Théophile de Viau to learn more about Carew? Is there not still currency in the old judgment?

> Un libertin est un homme aimant le plaisir, tous les plaisirs, sacrifiant à la bonne chère, le plus souvent de mauvaises moeurs, raillant la religion, n'ayant autre Dieu que la Nature, niant l'immortalité de l'âme et dégagé de erreurs populaires. En un mot c'est un esprit fort doublé d'un débauché.[1]

> A libertine is a man who loves pleasure, all the pleasures, sacrificing to good living, more often than not of bad morals, deriding religion, having no other god than nature, denying the immortality of the soul, and free from popular errors. In a word, he combines a strong spirit with the character of a debauched one.

But modern ideas move easily into the *régime nouveau* of the so-called "New Historicism," perhaps well manifested in readings that urge us to recognize "the eroticization of power" and meanwhile to scorn the familiar categories of literary history.

The political order (*any* political order) and its supposed impinge-ment on sexual relationships may be a fresh way of seeing stuffy rooms and old furniture. Let us suppose that Carew's "Rapture" con-structs a happy sexual relationship by recalling an absurdly delicious Edenic world chiefly for the sake of contrast with the strains of ordi-nary court life. We are nowadays beset by such ideological intuitions, while the best kind of criticism yet remains the sort that illuminates a

---

1. F. O. Henderson, "Traditions of *Précieux* and *Libertin* in Suckling's Poetry," *ELH* 4 (1937): 278–79, quoting Frédéric Lachèvre in *Le Procès du Poète Théophile de Viau* (1909).

text, the kind of study that locates, for example, Donne's "Sapho to Philaenis" within his usual range of subjects, not necessarily in any court or patriarchal power struggle, nor in any special fascination with "Sapphic love" or experience. We must try, above all, I think, to uncover the obvious literary associations and traditions of a text; this activity surely precedes further explorations, especially those conducted through theories of sex, or power, or dominance. The idea that we know more than our predecessors, or that they might have acted differently with the advantage of our knowledge, is a notion that responsible historians gave up years ago, and against which Herbert Butterfield dealt most fiercely in his *Whig Interpretation of History* (1931). Historical "process" is a fantasy, urging its followers into discourse for the sake of a "disconsolate chimera."

Before we can begin to form ideologies around Renaissance devices and desires, we need to assess the extraordinary range and abundance of this literature, and then we may ask questions about its supporting culture. Some concern must be given to the old chivalric ideas and their direction or dispersal in the sixteenth century. How may we best understand Ariosto, or Sidney, or Spenser? Is *The Faerie Queene* really "the most extended and extensive meditation on sex in the history of European poetry"? If so, and there are compelling reasons for agreeing with Camille A. Paglia, then how does Spenser define fertility, nature, aberration, chastity, erotic joy—to mention only a few issues in which sexuality is obviously preeminent?[2]

In thinking of Spenser and the romance tradition, one inevitably draws near to the link between religious faith and profane desire. While generally exalting the spiritual and physical communion of chaste love in marriage, Spenser reveals the different qualities of excitement aroused by the Bower of Bliss (2.7) as well as by the gardens of Adonis (2.10.70-73; 3.6). Gardens are usually enticing, but few of them remain comfortable and most suffer from the wounds of such fond lovers as Marvell imagines, who cut their names into the very trees. Paradise, that "happy rural seat of various view," too soon becomes a scene of sorrow and dismay.

Now the lost fragrance of the Hesperides and the beckoning images

---

2. "Sex," *The Spenser Encyclopedia*, gen. ed. A. C. Hamilton (Toronto: University of Toronto Press, 1990), 638.

of the Golden Age invite us to enter the passages that lead us to think about the erotic imagery that shapes so much religious poetry and prose. Should we not think yet more eagerly of the Canticles? In their extraordinary mixture of hot and chaste desire, we read of the consummation of secular life that seems to demand the touch of divine love, a theme that persists across the ages, finding renewed emphasis in the literature of the Renaissance, including not only Spenser, but notably also Marino, Richard Crashaw, and of course (and above all) Milton. To reflect on the theme of sexuality in Renaissance nondramatic literature is to remember that much of it returns us to the warmth of holy and flaming hearts, which weep and die and long for snowy doves and "a Bosom big with Loves." Burton was right to treat religious melancholy as complementing love melancholy—both of them being common species of the universal dotage that governs us all.

The study of discourses of desire inevitably leads in many directions, yet inexorably "Towards the door we never opened"; for all discrete places unlock some part of a greater design. We need to be wary of assigning too much value to one or another discourse lest we lose this pattern and miss the meaning. But to enter into any of these discourses is to grasp at least some fragment of the general conversation.

Diana Treviño Benet

Exploring "Discourses of Desire" in the light of feminism and the "New Historicism," we have some suspicions confirmed as scholarship catches up with experience—experience of the kind that sufficed the Wife of Bath. We are enlightened but not surprised to learn, for instance, that male poets favored intimate relationships reflecting male-centered political models. Similarly, we appreciate the concrete proof but are not startled to hear that male poets elaborated and glorified myths centered on male satisfaction and dominance. Given the usual poetic suspects and their usual crimes, the introduction of relatively "new" authorial voices is a welcome development, one that can only enliven our professional conversation by leading us to examine, modify, or perhaps even discard some ideas. More immediately, however, these unfamiliar voices made at least one participant at this conference feel that we had discovered or rediscovered some new figures in the landscape. We have acknowledged the importance of what has been occluded or marginalized (for various reasons) until fairly recently: the author, women writers, and gay male and lesbian lovers have made their appearances.

The author has emerged from the closet in which he had been locked by New Criticism. Freed from the strictures that insisted poems were isolated artifacts, we have become newly appreciative of the utility of the psychological perspective and of biographical materials. Whether scholars take an overview of poets negotiating the conflict between their personal perspectives and their society's values, or whether they focus on the inner life and unique experience of the author to show how it shapes his work, they have reclaimed an invaluable tool with which to explore matters of artistic substance.

The emergence of women writers marks another rich area for scholarly work and indicates new questions for investigation; for example: when women are the speakers of love poems, do they, in fact, construct entirely new stances vis-à-vis their lovers? If they appropriate postures already made familiar by men, what becomes of our critical assumptions about the political and patriarchal import of male inscriptions of desire? The current emphasis on the cultural implications of masculine views of amorous relations suggests that a parallel line of study might be fruitful: what can the stances and conventions adopted by women writers reveal to us?

The reaction prompted by the new prominence of gay and lesbian topics in Renaissance literature may be seen as a paradigm of the challenge confronting us in our approaches to plural *discourses* of desire. As our awareness and acceptance of different sexual orientations have increased, and as we have seen the lines drawn in the politico-erotic battles of our own day, the difficulties we face as scholars become more apparent: the challenge is to navigate between the Scylla and Charybdis of zeal and denial. I will explain by referring to matters that some of the papers raised but did not specifically address: the issue of the private versus the public and, related to that, of implicit versus explicit forms of expression. Analyzing and writing about literary sex and love, it is imperative to remember the distinction between the private and the public domains: surely, we need to take into account the difference between works circulated among friends and work published to the world at large. What authors permit themselves or feel they can permit themselves in public and what they choose, or are compelled, to keep private are matters that should figure clearly and sensibly in the critical equation.

Our public language about sexuality grows ever more explicit, as do the publicly acceptable expressions of sexuality. Given such a climate, we may be inclined to slight or even to ignore the different attitudes of another age. There can be no doubt that we gain something essential to our understanding of Renaissance poetry when we learn, for instance, that sexual preferences and practices in the Renaissance were not substantially different from those of today; but we may misrepresent that poetry if we forget that, in general, the age favored subtle over explicit expression of sexual matters. Poetry that aspires to appeal to the mainstream or to one's peers or patrons (as well as to one's lover) must maintain a certain decorum. Poetry with agendas other than humor, shock, or titillation cannot easily accommodate too much physical detail.

Moreover, subtlety is a corollary of desire, which is the keen experience of lack or absence. Being an actual or pretended substitute for physical satisfaction, the discourse of desire gives substance to absence through language. The forms meant to express the felt condition of lacking or unfulfillment must convey a certain sense of immateriality. As Kenneth D. Weisinger remarks, "A thousand words can be stilled by one sexual act, . . . for [poet-lovers] language simply marks the contours of an absence of sexual gratification and can be quieted only when that absence is filled. . . . [A poet is] everywhere converting his sexual desire into the complexities of language."[3] With a few notable exceptions, Renaissance authors do not seem as interested in representations of the sexual act itself as they are, say, in the solitary inscriptions of longing, or in the arguments meant to change frustration into fruition. We misrepresent the literature if we ignore the difference between explicit statement and implicit suggestion. These works are not, as some scholars feel compelled to remind us, sociological texts to be mined for facts or figures.

If we are bound, in our zeal, not to ignore the Renaissance preference for subtlety, or the fact that metaphors are sometimes only *figuratively* erotic—equally, on the other side, we are obliged not to ignore

3. *The Classical Facade* (University Park: Penn State University Press), 144.

the existence of conditions and pressures that necessitated the privatization or the encoding of texts. Dealing with a culture that preferred, for the most part, subtlety and indirection even in the service of the dominant sexual orientation, we must not underrate the genuine constraints on the open expression of same-sex love. Finally, we are obliged not to deny that erotic language *is* erotic, though it may be encoded or metaphorical and sanctioned by literary tradition.

The public versus the private domains, the essential difference between subtle and explicit forms of expression: these are simple issues, indeed. But inasmuch as they bear directly on the tone, emphasis, and purposes we attribute to the texts that embody the discourses of desire, they are fundamental.

Judith Scherer Herz

What is the relationship between the writer as desiring subject and as writing subject? What indeed constitutes subjectivity at the turn of the seventeenth century? How do we gain access to the network of allusions, assumptions, commonplaces, and associations that would have been recognizable and normative in the seventeenth century in order to articulate this subjectivity? These seem to me to be a set of interrelated questions that the conference, taken as a whole, asks that we address. There are certainly other issues. I shall, however, confine my remarks to these.

If we attempt to answer the first question in terms that are relatively independent of the linguistic practices and cultural assumptions of a specific period, we might arrive at something like Barthes's description of the desiring subject as one "speaking within himself, amorously, confronting the other (the loved object) who does not speak." Such a desiring/writing subject operates under the "illusion of expressivity: as a writer, or assuming myself to be one, I continue to fool myself as to the effects of language: I do not know that the word 'suffering' expresses no suffering and that, consequently, to use it is not only to communicate nothing but even, and immediately, to annoy, to irritate."[4]

This model of textual solipsism is compatible with readings of

4. *A Lover's Discourse,* trans. R. Howard (New York: Hill and Wang, 1978), 3, 98.

Donne, for example, that argue that textuality is both source and end of its quest for pleasure, that desire finds fulfillment in the play of language. Although lyric language may be primarily affective, in a Donne text it projects a performative or dramatic illusion. It is as if, to turn Barthes's statement around, the Donnean subject believed that his words not only pointed to his desires but constituted them as well, as if "suffering" carried suffering and "I love," love. But when such a position was invoked at the conference, it was at the same time historicized in arguments that explored the public dimensions of this private language. We heard this, for example, in discussions of the simultaneous construction of the idea of privacy and the houses that allowed for it, or in the examination of the relationship between Elizabeth's body natural and body politic, or in discussions of the cavalier poet's textual enactment of the politics of patronage and of the nascent imperial politics of exploitation and domination in a rhetoric of courtship and seduction.

However, to historicize may, oddly enough, be to allegorize. For the self that is now located in a network of objective relations is also made to mean something other than the self (the politics of the court, the economics of colonization). It is an interesting and productive approach particularly when one's focus is on the text as an index of and participant in a process of social exchanges. But the very act of identifying these relations either in the form of event or of ideology (in the sense of a shared social-cultural consciousness that allows one to make sense of an event) may require a conception of the self that will turn out to be as socially constructed and historically determined as the events and relationships it is troping. Yet that self is too often unquestioned, subjectivity functioning as an atemporal given, especially in discussions that turn on gender, on ideas of difference.

Establishing the boundaries of the self and establishing the boundaries of the text are indeed closely related undertakings. But the relationship is problematic and nowhere more so than when we use literary language as a key to actual social relations and then use these hypostatized relationships to decode the literary language. We speak of language as disguise or mask. The lesbian poet, it is often argued, seems to borrow a conventional language in order to make it mean something particular to her. Since institutional critical practice too often occludes such a subject position, this is a point that needs reiteration. But how does one develop a decorum of reading to hear the distinction between the convention as commonplace and as subversion? What is the relationship between this activity, essentially rhetorical, and the necessary process of historical recovery, the unevasive, uneuphemistic identifying of a writer's real life and loves? What indeed does it mean to identify Katherine Philips or Aphra Behn as lesbian poets? Does it mean something different in the 1990s than it would have in the 1650s?

To answer such questions, one needs to address the idea of the constructed self as it has been elaborated by historians of homosexuality such as Alan Bray or David Greenberg. To what degree is the self identifiable as an essence? To what degree is it culturally determined and made? Such a profoundly contested subject cannot be resolved here. But it is necessary, I think, to extend the argument offered by the constructivist historians of homosexuality to heterosexuality as well, sexuality in either case understood as a concept of the self and not as a designator of a type of sexual activity. Situating this discussion at the transition point that Raymond Williams identifies between individual in its meaning of undivided from the community and in its meaning of the (currently besieged) autonomous self, we need to understand what constituted the boundaries of the self and in what terms those limits were conceived. How primary is the idea of a gendered self to a conception of the self? How do we distinguish between experiencing the self and conceptualizing it? Am I what I do? There were obviously lesbian and homosexual acts in the seventeenth, sixteenth, and minus "nth" centuries. There were as obviously sexual preferences. When, however, did a lesbian or homosexual consciousness of difference emerge? What is the relationship between this form of identity and gender identity? What is the relationship between gender and sex?[5]

Recent work by Thomas Laqueur and Judith Butler provides useful ways of talking about these questions. Laqueur argues, for example, that "to be a man or a woman was to hold a social rank, a place in society, to assume a cultural role, not to *be* organically one or the

5. Bray, *Homosexuality in Renaissance England* (London: Gay Men's Press, 1982; Greenberg, *The Construction of Homosexuality* (Chicago: University of Chicago Press, 1988).

other of two incommensurable sexes. Sex in the seventeenth century
. . . was still a sociological and not an ontological category." His
work with medical and anatomical history as well as with records of
judicial proceedings leads him to conclude that "so-called biological
sex does not provide a solid grounding for the cultural category of
gender." Butler's critique of what she calls "the heterosexual matrix
. . . the grid of cultural intelligibility through which bodies, genders
and desires are naturalized" problematizes heterosexuality in precisely the way called for at the conference. The essential question of
her study is: "How is desire established as a heterosexual prerogative?"
For Butler, "anatomical sex, gender identity and gender performance
[are] contingent dimensions" (Laqueur's reading of medical history
provides powerful evidence for this claim). Her performative theory
of gender denies "the very notion of an essential sex and a true or
abiding masculinity or femininity."[6]

Within such a conceptual framework, one might reexamine the
nature of lyric subjectivity in a wide range of texts. It could help
explain Donne's sense of empowerment by Sappho both as poet and
as desiring subject in "Sapho to Philaenis" and help identify the gender fluidity in poems like "Aire and Angels." It could also provide an
explanatory model for identifying the self-fashioning of the Katherine Philips or Aphra Behn speaker by providing a way to distinguish between the normative and the transgressive.

Finally, I think one might ask how one could use such a framework
to discriminate between historical and textual reality. That is, how
does one distinguish between the writer and her desire (both the
biographical facts and the language in which they are inscribed) and
the writer and her sense of herself as both a desiring subject and, what
is not necessarily the same thing, a writing subject who need not be
writing *her* desire, who, in being written by her language, must inscribe another's (Philips's Donnean mode, Behn's cavalier idiom)
even as she strives to make it her own? Furthermore, as readers we
also have to clarify our own subject positions. We may learn how
nontransparent are our assumptions about sex and gender, especially
those concerning the naturalness of these categories, but equipped

6. Laqueur, *Making Sex* (Cambridge: Harvard University Press, 1990), 9 and 122;
Butler, *Gender Trouble* (London: Routledge, 1990), 151, 42, 17, and 141.

with our own biographies and beliefs, how do we negotiate texts where our own desires and assumptions about desire are enacted? Do we not necessarily, albeit often anachronistically, read our own texts? Is there any other kind of reading this side of philology?

Language is no doubt as recalcitrant as desire, and as difficult to reconcile with its object. For Barthes the discourse of desire is the speech of those enclosed in their own solitude: "To know that one does not write for the other, to know that these things I am going to write will never cause me to be loved by the one I love (the other), to know that writing compensates for nothing, sublimates nothing, that it is precisely *there where you are not*—this is the beginning of writing" (100). And the end of these remarks, but with the cautionary post scriptum, "As Bunuel's l'homme moyen was to discover / The one one loves is pretty sure some other."

Debora Shuger

In a recent article Valerie Traub comments, "In the Renaissance the fear of being turned back into women was constitutive of masculine subjectivity." Unfortunately, Thomas Laqueur, whom Traub cites to support her intriguing generalization, makes exactly the opposite point: on the single-sex model, women could turn into men (the womb could "get out" and become a penis); the reverse was not considered possible. Presumably, Traub has accidentally reversed her evidence under the influence of post-Freudian expectations about little boys and castration complexes.[7] Another castration story, this time belonging to the sixth rather than the sixteenth century, may further illustrate the problem inherent in theorizing the sexualized body of

7. Traub, "Prince Hal's Falstaff: Positioning Psychoanalysis and the Female Reproductive Body," *Shakespeare Quarterly* 40 (1989): 457; Laqueur, "Orgasm, Generation, and the Politics of Reproductive Biology," *Representations* 14 (1986): 1–41; Stephen Orgel, whom Traub also cites, is partly responsible for the confusion, since his "Nobody's Perfect: Or Why Did the English Stage Take Boys for Women?" *South Atlantic Quarterly* 88 (1989): 7–29, tends to elide the distinction between the modern meaning of "effeminate" (a male who exhibits the characteristics of a woman) and its Renaissance sense (a male given to the love of women at the expense of more martial pursuits). Orgel, however, correctly interprets Laqueur as saying that, according to Renaissance biology, gender transformations "work in only one direction, from female to male" (13).

the pre-modern period. This has to do with angels, particularly early Christian angels—the beautiful beardless adolescents of the Ravenna mosaics, who wear the robes of Imperial eunuchs. Eunuchs, it would seem, remind Byzantine Christians of angels, probably because they attend on the persons of the Emperor and Empress just as angels wait upon the throne of God.[8]

Modern theories of sexuality have very little to say about female fears of sprouting penises or castrated angels. In fact, the contradiction between the dual contemporary imperatives to historicize and to theorize (that is, use late nineteenth- and early twentieth-century paradigms) emerges with particular urgency in dealing with pre-modern discourses of desire. It does not follow, however, that historicism requires theoretical naivete. The major contribution of theory to cultural and literary studies—the disciplines primarily engaged in tracing the discourses of desire—has been its denaturalization and problematization of such central concepts as power, gender, subjectivity, and the body. To problematize something is to make it interesting, to make it a subject of inquiry, and this is not equivalent to the rather questionable practice of retrojecting modern theories onto Renaissance texts and practices. Rather, it is precisely the intractability of Renaissance texts to theory that is significant—because this intractability discloses the historical specificity of the Renaissance. Theory is thus invaluable for Renaissance scholars because it is usually wrong. Renaissance discourses of desire become visible as *that which has been substituted* for the absent objects of our (theoretically informed) investigations; theory, that is, proffers metonymic access to history. Stephen Greenblatt's "Psychoanalysis and Renaissance Culture" nicely exemplifies the conceptual benefit of this sort of metonymic (as opposed to metaphoric) substitution, since his point is that Freudian theory is *not* applicable to Renaissance conceptions of selfhood, although the latter only come into focus in the process of being distinguished from modern theoretical presuppositions. Such a flexible use of theory may even clarify the cultural semiotics of castration; thus, in his study of George Herbert, Michael Schoenfeldt traces the complex links between Herbert's anxiety about the phallic aggres-

8. I owe this bit of iconography to a comment made by Peter Brown in his 1989–1990 UCLA seminar.

siveness concealed in the aristocratic practices of courtesy and his repeated longings for castration, for escape to a childlike "softness," for release from the linked tumescences of body and spirit. Here again, although theory, whether Freudian or feminist, does not directly address the problematics of desire for Christian men in the Renaissance, it makes their recognition possible, if only by raising the questions of sexuality and repression in the first place.[9]

The need to "respect [the] irreducible particularity" of earlier cultures impinges with a special acuteness on the study of sexuality and desire, perhaps because—unlike the cult of the saints or court ceremony—these experiences can be misleadingly familiar.[10] To take one example, most recent work on the body tends to presuppose that erotic desire (the longing for union with the beloved) *is* sexual desire (genital arousal). Whether true or false, this presupposition is not characteristic of the Renaissance and can only impede efforts to grasp its discourses of desire. For instance, in Juan Luis Vives's chapter on love in *De anima,* he consistently uses the terms *amans* and *amatus* (both with masculine pronouns) for the lover and beloved, and yet clearly Vives is not discussing homosexual love. The gender here is generic; as Vives's examples make clear, the *amans* and *amator* can be parent and child, husband and wife, two friends, God and man, teacher and student.[11] The *amans* and *amatus* constitute an erotic relationship not necessarily sexual at all. Heterosexuality and homosexuality are both misleading terms, not because Renaissance persons were bisexual, but because desire was not identified with sexuality before the late seventeenth century; as Ioan Culiano observes, in pre-modern culture "physical desire, aroused by the irrational soul and appeased by means of the body, only represents, in the phenome-

9. Greenblatt, *Literary Theory/Renaissance Texts,* ed. Patricia Parker and David Quint (Baltimore: Johns Hopkins University Press, 1986), 210–24; Schoenfeldt, *Prayer and Power: George Herbert and Renaissance Courtship* (Chicago: University of Chicago Press, 1991).

10. Peter Brown, *The Body and Society: Men, Women, and Sexual Renunciation in Early Christianity* (New York: Columbia University Press, 1988).

11. *De anima et vita* (Basel, 1538; repr. Turin: Bottega d'Erasmo, 1959). For example, "Quum ergo amatus in amantis sese animo intuetur, & recognoscit, amare illum compellitur, in quo quasi se habitare intelligit. . . . Ad haec amans semetipsum sibi aufert, & dedit ac mancipat amato. hunc ergo iam amatus, ut rem suam, charam habet, curatque . . . et quemadmodum amatur beneficus, ita & benefaciens amat eum, cui profuit, non secus quam opus suum: ut filium pater, & magister discipulum" (159–60).

nology of love, an obscure and secondary aspect."[12] In any culture where erotic longing provides the central metaphor for spirituality, desire cannot be equivalent to sexuality. Even when writing about romantic love (which, of course, does have a sexual component), Renaissance authors tend to assume a distinction between erotic and sexual response—which is not the same as a distinction between spiritual and physical love. Erotic desire is physical, but it primarily affects the upper body; it is engendered in the eyes and dwells in the heart. Even where a character is clearly suffering from sexual frustration—for example, the Jailer's Daughter in *Two Noble Kinsmen*—the diagnosis does not map her sufferings on the body's sexual organs; instead, as the Doctor observes, "that intemp'rate surfeit of her eye hath distemper'd the other senses" (4.3.70–71). In Renaissance texts the movement of eros is inward and down, so that sexuality becomes an inflection of erotic longing, not its origin or essence, whereas in modern thought, which privileges genital sexuality, movement takes place outward and up via cathexis and sublimation. The whole "point" of a poem like Donne's "The Extasie"—that true love can also be sexual—would be incoherent were there not a prior distinction between them. The same is true of Sidney's *Astrophil and Stella,* where Astrophil's horrified surprise that his "pure love" has a strong phallic component again presupposes the same at least conceptual differentiation.[13] This distinction is likewise crucial for Shakespeare's *Sonnets,* which are explicitly homoerotic but not therefore homosexual, or, at least, were not initially perceived as homosexual (and consequently unprintable)—again, what is at stake is not Shakespeare's sexuality but the cultural semiotics of desire. But if the erotic was not seen as *essentially* sexual, then efforts to construe the discourses of desire in the Renaissance in terms of gay, straight, anal, and oral seem unhistorically restrictive.

For if we allow this distinction between eros and sexuality, then the discourses of desire in the Renaissance, it seems to me, need to be understood not in terms of specific sexual practices but of cultural

12. *Eros and Magic in the Renaissance,* trans. Margaret Cook (Chicago: University of Chicago Press, 1987), 4.
13. Debora Shuger, "Saints and Lovers: Mary Magdalene and the Ovidian Evangel," *Reconfiguring the Renaissance: Essays in Critical Materialism,* ed. Jonathan Crewe, special issue of *Bucknell Review* 35, no. 2 (1991): 80–91.

forms. Just as the discourse of "food" in the Renaissance is not primarily a matter of cookbooks but rather penetrates the language of hospitality, power, patronage, eucharistic theology, aesthetics, and so forth—which is why it is interesting—so too the discourses of desire (including but not confined to sexual desire) suffuse and are suffused by religion, philosophy, medicine, the family, rhetoric, and politics. It is Luther who remarked that kings and princes "compose and sing amatory ballads which the crowd takes to be songs about a bride or a sweetheart, when in fact they portray the condition of their state and people with their songs."[14] The history of eros (as opposed to a history of sex) concerns the changing functions of the discourses of desire with respect to the totality of available discourses, that is, with respect to a specific culture.

Viewed this way, investigation into the discourses of desire in the Renaissance opens on to several intriguing problems. For example, when and why does epistemology cease to be structured erotically—in terms, that is, of desire climaxing in union?[15] Or what is to be made of the fact that, beginning in the Roman rhetorics of the first century A.D., the body of the catamite—the soft, delicate, languid body of the (castrated?) boy—becomes the dominant metaphor for both civilizational and stylistic decline?[16] What is the significance of

14. *Lectures on the Song of Solomon,* trans. Ian Siggins, *Luther's Works,* ed. Jaroslav Pelikan (St. Louis: Concordia Publishing House, 1972), 193. And, indeed, the reverse (theme little heard among New Historicists) may also be true; see W. H. Auden's "The Truest Poetry is the most Feigning," in which the language of politics allegorizes erotic desire.

15. See, for example, Vives: "Cognoscitur autem res primum, ut ametur: sed cognitionem esse oportet tantam, ut quae ad eliciendum amorem sufficiat . . . quocirca amoris fructus fruitio est, qui est delectationis actus, non solum voluntatis, sed etiam intelligentiae, ut in Deo. Itaque amor medius est inter cognitionem inchoatam, & plenam, quae est in unione: in qua desiderium semper aboletur, non semper amor. imo inflammatur acrius" (178).

16. The Loeb Classical Library translations almost invariably mistranslate as "effeminate" terms like *mollis, delicatus, impotens, elumbum.* Although these texts do at times describe the catamite's body as being like a woman's, the central opposition is not between male and female but between "hard" and "soft" males—the adjectives not referring primarily to the phallus but to the texture of the flesh (see the Loeb editions of Seneca, *Epistulae morales,* 104:3–4, 8, 20, 24; Tacitus, *Dialogus,* 18; the Elder Seneca, *Controversiae,* 1 pref. 8:10; 2 pref. 1; 9 pref. 4–5; 10.4.17–18). In the rhetorical tradition, the female body is generally represented in terms of clothing and make-up (*ornata, fuscata*) and is not contrasted to the male, but to a more natural and casual mode of woman's dress (cf. Jonson's "Still to be Neat" and Herrick's "Delight in Disorder").

the eroticization of spirituality that floods religious discourse from antiquity to the late seventeenth century—particularly its construction of a feminized, erotic religious subjectivity. So Donne speaks of how Christ's body "covers me by touching me . . . by comming to me, by spreading himself upon me . . . Mouth to mouth, Hand to hand."[17] The Jesuit martyr Robert Southwell dwells lovingly on Mary Magdalene's longing "to touch [Jesus], yea to embrace and carry him naked in thy armes" and imagines her joy "if lying in thy lap, thou mightest have seene him revived, and his disfigured and dead body beautified in thy armes with a divine majesty." And this is a work that ends, "O christian soule take Mary for thy mirrour. . . . Learne O sinfull man of this once a sinfull woman."[18] Especially in Donne, this erotic spirituality is further suffused by desire for subjugation and therefore implicated in the political discourses of power and submission. What are we to make of Donne's depiction of God as an aristocratic rapist, who "loves us, but with a Powerfull, a Majesticall, an Imperiall, a Commanding love: He offers those, whom he makes his, his grace; but so, as he sometimes will not be denyed"? This sort of subjectivity presents problems for modern scholarship, which has difficulty grasping the desire to submit—although Camille Paglia's work on the pervasive sadomasochism of Western erotics is often profoundly smart on this.[19]

I am not suggesting that we should reobscure the sexual body and become a sort of cultural platonists, although it would also be well to keep in mind recent work by medievalists like Peter Brown and Caroline Bynum, which throws serious doubt on the modern assumption that sexuality is at the center of what it means to be human.[20] Augustine's image of the phallic fall, where the involuntary erection signifies man's loss of psychic freedom and integrity, encapsulates a remarkably popular tradition in which sexual abstinence figures the

17. *The Sermons of John Donne,* ed. Evelyn Simpson and George Potter, 10 vols. (Berkeley: University of California Press, 1953–1962), 9:261. The subsequent quotation is from 9:103–4.
18. *Marie Magdalens Funeral Teares (1551),* Scholar's Facsimiles (Delmar, N.Y.: Scholars' Facsimiles & Reprints, 1975), 54 and 67.
19. *Sexual Personae: Art and Decadence from Nefertiti to Emily Dickinson* (New Haven: Yale University Press, 1990).
20. Brown, *Body and Society;* Bynum, "The Body of Christ in the Later Middle Ages: A Reply to Leo Steinberg," *Renaissance Quarterly* 39 (1986): 399–439.

possibility of liberation from all the painful and frustrating violence of appetite. We must nevertheless be wary of falling into the hyper-historicist error of a recent undergraduate who observed: "In the Sixteenth Century orgasm was associated with death because of sperm lost. Certainly sex is not connected with pleasure as it is in the Twentieth Century."

The erotic, furthermore, cannot be studied apart from gender. This is something no modern scholar seems likely to deny, but despite the attention this subject has received in the past decade a good deal of fertile terrain remains either uncultivated or unweeded. I would like to end, therefore, with a couple of brief comments on what seem to me problems or omissions in recent scholarship on gender and sexuality. First, I think we need to reexamine the claim that the Renaissance demonized female sexuality. On the one hand, many Renaissance texts follow Augustine in using male sexuality as a privileged symbol of evil (for example, Shakespeare's Sonnet 129 and *Comus*). Fulke Greville's little-known *Letter to an Honorable Lady,* written to an aristocratic woman suffering from an abusive husband, seems of particular interest here, since it posits male sexual desire as the cause of the Fall and subsequently all forms of oppressive hierarchy in a rather startling argument that begins by counseling patience and obedience and ends recommending subversion, republicanism, and playing Brutus to one's domestic (or political) Caesar. In addition, other Renaissance texts seem at least sympathetic toward explicitly female sexuality: the moving portrait of Jane Shore in Thomas More's *Richard III* and of the Jailer's Daughter in *Two Noble Kinsmen,* Kenelm Digby's defense of his wife in his *Private Memoirs,* Ariosto's *Orlando Furioso,* and Guarini's *Il Pastor Fido.* Moreover, the assumption that Renaissance men *simply* feared and mistrusted female sexual desire has obscured the extent to which such desire functions as a dominant metaphor for religious inwardness and has therefore also concealed the connection between female sexuality and the construction of subjectivity.[21] Judith Gardiner's claim that "patriarchal cultures, cultures like ours . . . define 'mind' as male and immaterial and mother as mindless mat(t)er" is not without historical basis, but neither is it an acceptable generalization about Renaissance culture, since the Re-

---

21. See Shuger, "Saints and Lovers."

naissance *also* represents selfhood or the soul as female—a paradigm in part derived from the grammatical gender of *anima,* in part from traditional allegorizations of Canticles, where the bride becomes a figure of the self.[22] In this paradigm, the *radix* and voice of the soul is always immaterially female.

Second, I am curious about the fact that so many Renaissance narratives—especially Petrarchan ones and versions of the Troilus story—treat male abandonment, whereas post-Restoration narratives seem generally about female abandonment. Astrophil never gets his Stella, and the speaker of Lovelace's "Love Made in the First Age" ends up masturbating in solitude. Even the one extant piece of English sixteenth-century pornography, Nashe's *Choice of Valentines,* describes a sexual encounter where first the narrator cannot perform and then is unable to contain himself long enough to satisfy his partner, who finishes up with an artificial surrogate. What are we to make of the pornography of male impotence and premature ejaculation? Why do Renaissance men write not about their power but their vulnerability and failure?

Finally, I am generally suspicious of the argument that male narratives are about domination, female about mutuality and equality. At least since Foxe, politically correct histories have told the story of how They want to dominate while We only want to share. This is, to coin a phrase, ideological mystification, and persons angry at the injustices authorized by politically motivated myths ought to mistrust all binary and hierarchical totalizations.

---

22. "Mind Mother: Feminism and Psychoanalysis," *Making a Difference: Feminist Literary Criticism,* ed. Gayle Greene and Copelia Kahn (London: Methuen, 1985), 114.

Notes on the Contributors

DIANA TREVIÑO BENET teaches at New York University. She is the author of *Secretary of Praise: The Poetic Vocation of George Herbert* and *Something to Love: The Novels of Barbara Pym,* as well as numerous essays on seventeenth-century literature.

JOSEPH CADY teaches literature and medicine in the Division of Medical Humanities at the University of Rochester Medical School and gay and lesbian literature at the New School for Social Research.

EUGENE R. CUNNAR has published articles on Donne, Herbert, Milton, Crashaw, Vermeer, and Zurbaran, as well as on other seventeenth-century literary and artistic figures. He has completed a book on Crashaw and baroque art.

THERESA M. DIPASQUALE is Assistant Professor of English at Florida International University. A specialist in seventeenth-century poetry, she is particularly interested in the connections between theological controversy and secular lyric.

M. L. DONNELLY is Associate Professor of English and Assistant Dean for Honors at Kansas State University. He has contributed to *The Milton Encyclopedia* and *The Spenser Encyclopedia* and has published articles on Bacon, Donne, Marvell, Milton, and Caroline panegyric. He is currently working on problems of self-representation and political psychology under the patronage system in the seventeenth century.

ACHSAH GUIBBORY, Professor of English at the University of Illinois, is author of *The Map of Time: Seventeenth-Century English Literature and Ideas of Pattern in History* and of numerous articles on Donne, Jonson, Herrick, Bacon, Browne, Cowley, and Dryden. In addition to exploring the representation of women and sexual love in seventeenth-century poetry, she is currently writing a book on the relationship between literature and religious conflict during the period of the English civil war.

JUDITH SCHERER HERZ is Professor of English at Concordia University, Montreal. She has written articles on medieval and Renaissance poetry (Chaucer, Shakespeare, Donne, Milton, Jonson, and Marvell), on E. M. Forster, and on literary biography. She is co-editor of *E. M. Forster: Centenary Revaluations* and author of *The Short Narratives of E. M. Forster* and *A Passage to India: Nation and Narration.*

ANTHONY LOW is Professor of English at New York University and Chair of the department. His books include *Augustine Baker, The Blaze of Noon, Love's Architecture,* and *The Georgic Revolution.* His essay on Carew in this volume is part of a book in progress with the working title "The Reinvention of Love: Cultural Change and Seventeenth-Century English Poetry."

CATHERINE GIMELLI MARTIN is Assistant Professor of English at Memphis State University, where she is completing a book-length study of the uses of allegory in *Paradise Lost.* She has published several essays on literary theory; other recent work includes a forthcoming article on the subject of ideology in Althusserian theory, and another on the subject-position of Eve in Milton's epic.

TED-LARRY PEBWORTH is William E. Stirton Professor in the Humanities and Professor of English at the University of Michigan–Dearborn. He is author of *Owen Felltham;* coauthor of *Ben Jonson;* and coeditor of *The Poems of Owen Felltham* and of collections of essays on Herbert, on Jonson and the Sons of Ben, on Donne, on the seventeenth-century religious lyric, on poetry and politics in the seventeenth century, and on Marvell. A textual editor and member of the Advisory Board of *The Variorum Edition of the Poetry of John Donne,* he has served as president of the John Donne Society of America.

STELLA P. REVARD is Professor of English at Southern Illinois University, Edwardsville, where she teaches courses in both English literature and Greek. Her book *The War in Heaven: "Paradise Lost" and the Tradition of Satan's Rebellion* received the James Holly Hanford Award of the Milton Society of America. She is currently completing a book on the influence of Pindar on sixteenth- and seventeenth-century English poetry.

ROGER B. ROLLIN is William James Lemon Professor of Literature at Clemson University. His revision of his 1966 critical study, *Robert Herrick,* has recently been published by Twayne. He is coeditor (with J. Max Patrick) of *"Trust to Good Verses": Herrick Tercentenary Essays.* He has also published essays on Donne, Jonson, Herbert, Marvell, and Milton. His other academic interest is popular culture, in which he has published articles on movies, television, and popular culture theory. A past president of the Popular Culture Association in the South, he is currently President of the American Popular Culture Association.

WINFRIED SCHLEINER, Professor of English at the University of California, Davis, is the author of *The Imagery of John Donne's Sermons* and of *Melancholy, Genius, and Utopia in the Renaissance.*

DEBORA SHUGER is Associate Professor of English at the University of California, Los Angeles. She is author of *Habits of Thought in the English Renaissance.*

WILLIAM SHULLENBERGER is Professor of Literature at Sarah Lawrence College. He has published essays on Milton, Herbert, and Beaumont and Fletcher, as well as on Wordsworth, Keats, and Dickinson. His ongoing interest in the relation of theology and poetics has led most recently to an article on Luther and Zwingli.

P. G. STANWOOD is Professor of English and Director of Graduate Studies in English at the University of British Columbia, and author of many essays and reviews on Renaissance poetry and prose. He has edited a number of texts, including John Cosin's *A Collection of Pri-*

vate Devotions, Richard Hooker's *Lawes, Books VI-VIII,* and, in two volumes, Jeremy Taylor's *Holy Living and Holy Dying.*

ARLENE STIEBEL is Professor of English at California State University, Northridge, and has published on both seventeenth-century literature and women's studies.

CLAUDE J. SUMMERS, William E. Stirton Professor in the Humanities and Professor of English at the University of Michigan–Dearborn, has published widely on both seventeenth- and twentieth-century literature. Coeditor of collections of essays on a wide variety of seventeenth-century topics and author of book-length studies of Marlowe, Jonson, Isherwood, and Forster, his most recent books are *Gay Fictions: Wilde to Stonewall, E. M. Forster: A Guide to Research,* and *Homosexuality in Renaissance and Enlightenment England: Literary Representations in Historical Context.* His essays include studies of Marlowe, Shakespeare, Donne, Herbert, Herrick, Vaughan, Forster, Cather, Auden, Isherwood, and others.

MARY VILLEPONTEAUX is Assistant Professor of English at the University of Southern Mississippi. She has published on Spenser's *Amoretti* and is at work on a book about Spenser's treatment of feminine authority in *The Faerie Queene.*

RAYMOND B. WADDINGTON is Professor of English at the University of California, Davis. He has published widely on sixteenth- and seventeenth-century English literature, including *The Mind's Empire: Myth and Form in George Chapman's Narrative Poems.* He is coeditor of *The Age of Milton: Backgrounds to Seventeenth-Century Literature.*

Index

This index includes only primary works. Lengthy titles are abbreviated, and anonymous works are alphabetized by title.